THE WORLD OF WORDS

THE World OF Words

Vocabulary for College Students

THIRD EDITION

Margaret Ann Richek
Northeastern Illinois University

As part of Houghton Mifflin's ongoing commitment to the environment, this text has been printed on recycled paper.

HOUGHTON MIFFLIN COMPANY   Boston   Toronto
Dallas   Geneva, Illinois   Palo Alto   Princeton, New Jersey

Dedicated to Perry and Tolstoy

Sponsoring Editor: Mary Jo Southern
Development Editor: Robin Bushnell Hogan
Project Editor: Robin Bushnell Hogan
Design Coordinator: Martha Drury
Manufacturing Specialist: Holly Schuster
Marketing Manager: Diane Gifford

ISBN: 0-395-47313-6

EFGHIJ–D–9654

Contents

Chapter 7   Words Elements: Movement   *187*

Chapter 8   Word Elements: Together and Apart   *217*

Chapter 9   Word Elements: Numbers and Measures   *251*

To the Instructor

The World of Words, Third Edition, will help students master strategies for becoming independent learners of vocabulary, learn specific words that will be useful in their academic work, and develop a lifelong interest in words. Through a series of carefully paced lessons, students learn three vocabulary development strategies: using the dictionary, using context clues, and using Greek and Latin word elements.

This Third Edition of **The World of Words** continues to link students' general knowledge to vocabulary, covering such topics as popular music, sports, and the origins of names. I find that students enjoy these features and begin to see that learning vocabulary *is* relevant to their lives. While reinforcing these links, the text also seeks to supply information that will be useful in their academic work. Thus, as the book progresses, students read about science, the classics, and literature.

The word lists and the Greek and Latin word elements have been carefully selected on the basis of their appropriate level and usefulness in students' academic work. Word elements are presented so that students can easily recognize and use them in modern English words. Avoiding detailed discussions of infinitive, participial, and stem forms, the text provides the spellings of word elements most commonly found in English.

Feedback from students and instructors has enabled me to adapt this book to the needs of today's diverse student population. Instructors will find **The World of Words,** Third Edition, suitable for students of many cultural and linguistic backgrounds, including those for whom English is a second language.

Organization

Part 1 concentrates on dictionary skills and context clues; Part 2 stresses word elements (Greek and Latin prefixes, roots, and suffixes). A theme for each chapter (for instance, Words About People, Chapter 1) helps make vocabulary study more meaningful.

Each chapter of **The World of Words** contains these features:

- *Did You Know?* presents interesting word facts to help spark students' interest in vocabulary.

- *Learning Strategy* provides instruction to help students independently learn new words.
- *Words to Learn* presents twenty-four vocabulary words with pronunciations, definitions, and example sentences. Related Words help students see how one base word can be used in several different ways, and usage notes help students use their new vocabulary words correctly. The Words to Learn are divided into two parts containing twelve words each. Word facts, etymologies, and trivia quizzes provide a context for the words and help students remember the definitions.
- *Exercises* follow each set of Words to Learn; additional exercises are included at the end of each chapter. A wide variety of exercises, including Matching Definitions, Words in Context, Related Words, Companion Words, Writing with Your Words, and Practicing Strategies, provides thorough practice in both the Words to Learn and the Learning Strategy.
- The *Passages* uses many of the chapter words in context and gives students practice reading short essays. Each passage is followed by a brief exercise annd three discussion questions.

New to this Edition

Based on using this text for nine years at Northeastern Illinois University and reviewing constructive comments on the Second Edition from users across the country, I have been able to refine those features students found most useful and add the following new features to the Third Edition:

- Revision and updating of word lists, resulting in twenty-two new words
- Expanded treatment of prepositions in Chapter I
- A new exercise format, "Companion Words," to provide practice in using prepositions and other words that accompany the words to be learned
- New continuous discourse exercises for improving vocabulary and reading skills.
- Revision and updating of example sentences, exercises, and tests.

Support for Instructors

The *Instructor's Resource Guide* contains a complete testing program, answer keys to all exercises, chapter notes, additional exercises, and review exercises and tests. A set of enrichment words for each chapter, with exercises and tests, provides additional practice for more advanced students. The guide also contains blackline masters, a supplementary list of word elements, and a list of words in different academic fields that use the word elements taught in the text.

New computerized software vocabulary for students to practice skills is now available.

Acknowledgments

I wish to thank the many people who have contributed ideas, inspiration, and support for this book. The editorial staff of the Houghton Mifflin Company, especially Melody Davies, Robin Bushnell Hogan, Mary Jo Southern, and Kristen Estenberg, provided superb skills and a deep understanding of the purposes of this project. Also, John Beasley of The Wheetley Company gave invaluable assistance and support. The research library staff at Northeastern Illinois University responded creatively to hundreds of queries. M.J. Hilburger deserves special thanks in this regard. Thanks is also due to Perry Goldberg, Sandra Goldberg, Dorothy Genus, Stephen Richek, David Lang, Mara Lang, Elise Lang, Scott Stein, Mark Stein, Carolyn Stein, Harley London, Rick Santiago, James McDonald, Judy McDonald, and Neil Adelman. Special acknowledgment is due to José Luis Gamboa, whose writing exercise appears in the review section for Chapters 1-4. The following reviewers helped to formulate the shape and direction of the manuscript: Shirley A. Carpenter, Richard J. Daley College, IL; Jo-Ann D. Hamilton, The City University of New York; Milla L. McConnell-Tuite, College of San Mateo, CA; Debbie Simpson, Jamestown Community College, NY; and Merrit Stark, Henderson State University, AK.

THE WORLD OF WORDS

1

Dictionary Skills and Context Clues

Did you know that the size of your vocabulary predicts how well you will do in school? This book will improve your vocabulary so that you become a better reader, writer, listener, and speaker. As you master more words, you can improve your performance in all subjects—from astronomy to electronics to marketing to zoology. A larger vocabulary will also help you to make a good impression in a job interview. People judge others by the way they communicate, and vocabulary is a key to communication.

This book will help you to use words more precisely and vividly. Instead of describing a *friendly* gathering, you will be able to distinguish between a *convivial* party and an *amicable* meeting. Instead of saying that someone gave money to a charity, you may call that person a *philanthropist* or a *benefactor*. Learning these words will help you to express yourself in a more powerful manner.

As you work through this book, you will improve your vocabulary, first, by learning the words presented in each chapter and, second, by mastering learning strategies that will enable you to learn words on your own. Chapters 1 through 4 will teach you the strategies of using the dictionary and using context clues. In Chapters 5 through 12, you will learn the strategy of using word elements such as prefixes, roots, and suffixes.

Each chapter contains several sections:

Did You Know? highlights interesting facts about English words.
Learning Strategy presents methods that will enable you to learn words independently.

Words to Learn defines, and gives examples of, twenty-four words that appear frequently in college texts, magazines, and newspapers. Each Words to Learn section is divided into two parts, containing twelve words each.

The *Exercises* give you practice with the words and strategies. One set of exercises follows the first part of the Words to Learn section, another set follows the second part, and a final set appears at the end of the chapter.

The *Passage* presents a reading selection that includes several "Words to Learn" from the chapter. It is followed by an exercise that tests your understanding of words used in context and discussion questions that check your comprehension of the passage.

Parts of Speech

Parts of speech are essential to the definition and use of words. In order to master the vocabulary words in this book, you will need to know the part of speech for each word. In addition, if you understand how words can be changed to form different parts of speech, you can multiply your vocabulary by using one word in many different ways.

Nouns, adjectives, verbs, and adverbs are presented in this book.

A **noun** is a person, place, thing, or idea.

Paul is a *student.*
San Diego is a beautiful *city.*
Some *snow* clung to the *road.*
Liberty and *justice* are precious.

An **adjective** describes, or modifies, a noun.

The *happy* child played in the sun. (*Happy* modifies *child.*)
The evening was *cool.* (*Cool* modifies *evening.*)

A **verb** expresses an action or a state of being.

He *walked* to the store.
It *is* dark.

Verbs may be divided into two categories: transitive and intransitive. A **transitive verb** has an action that is directed toward someone or something. A transitive verb cannot stand alone in a sentence; it needs a direct object to make a sentence complete. In contrast, an **intransitive verb** does not need a direct object.

> Transitive verb: Delphine *bought* a computer. (*Computer* is the direct object.)
>
> Intransitive verb: The skunk *smelled*. (No direct object is needed.)

Verbs may express past, future, or present action. Past-tense verbs are usually formed by adding the ending *-ed* to form a past participle.

> Mary *rented* a house last year.

The future tense is often expressed through the use of the helping verb *will*.

> I *will shop* in the mall tomorrow.

When we use the present tense, we add an *s* to third-person singular verbs, that is, verbs that have any one person as the subject except "I" or "you." (Examples of subjects that require third-person singular verbs are "she," "Joe," or "the door.")

> The doctor *sees* patients each morning.
>
> Tucson *grows* rapidly each year.

We often express actions that started in the past and are still taking place by using a form of the helping verb *to be* and adding *-ing* to the end of the main verb. This is called the present progressive tense, and the *ing* form is called a present participle.

> I *am waiting* for the mail delivery.
>
> It *is raining*.

The *-ing* and *-ed* forms of verbs are also used to form other parts of speech. The *-ing* forms of verbs are called **gerunds** when they are used as nouns.

> *Smoking* is forbidden in the theater.
>
> It is a good day for *fishing*.

The *-ing* and *-ed* forms of verbs are called **participles** when they are used as adjectives.

> The *insulting* man made others feel bad. (In this sentence, the man insults other people.)
>
> The *insulted* man felt bad. (In this sentence, other people insult the man.)

An **adverb** modifies a verb, an adjective, or another adverb. Many adverbs end in *-ly*.

The man *slowly* climbed the stairs. (*Slowly* modifies *climbed*, a verb.)

We admired the *brightly* colored quilt. (*Brightly* modifies *colored*, an adjective.)

The disease spread *more rapidly* than we expected. (*More*, an adverb, modifies *rapidly*, another adverb. *Rapidly*, in turn, modifies *spread*, a verb.)

In addition to nouns, adjectives, verbs, and adverbs, parts of speech also include pronouns, prepositions, conjunctions, and interjections.

A **pronoun** replaces a noun.

Brenda locked the door when *she* left.

We will meet *him* at the airport.

A **conjunction** connects words, phrases, or clauses.

Barry ate peas *and* carrots.

Will Marie go to the movies *or* will she stay home?

An **interjection** is an exclamatory word that may appear by itself or in a sentence.

Wow!

Oh, look at that!

A **preposition** joins a noun or pronoun with another word in a sentence. Prepositions are found at the beginning of prepositional phrases, which usually function as adjectives and adverbs.

A fear *of* dogs made him nervous.

In this sentence, the preposition *of* joins the noun *dog* to another noun in the sentence, *fear*. *Of* is the first word in the prepositional phrase *of dogs*. The entire prepositional phrase functions as an adjective because it modifies the noun *fear*.

This sentence shows a prepositional phrase used as an adverb.

The child ran *over* the bridge.

Here, the preposition *over* connects the noun *bridge* to the verb *ran*. The prepositional phrase *over the bridge* functions as an adverb that modifies the verb *ran*.

Words and phrases commonly used as prepositions include: *about, above, according to, across, after, against, before, below, beside, by, during, for, from, in, inside, into, like, of, off, on, out, over, through, to, toward, up, under, until*, and *with*.

Since it is often difficult to predict which preposition should be used in a sentence, mastery of these small words can only come with practice. Therefore, one exercise in this book, "Companion Words," provides practice in using the correct preposition with the words you will learn in the book.

Word Endings and Parts of Speech

A single word can often be changed to form several different related words. These related words have similar meanings, but they usually function as different parts of speech. For example, as shown in the illustration on page 6, the word *nation* (a noun) can form *national* (an adjective), *nationally* (an adverb), *nationalize* (a verb), and *nationality* (another noun). Related words are formed by adding *suffixes*—groups of letters attached to the ends of words that change the part of speech. The following table gives a list of such suffixes and examples of words formed with them.

Suffix	Base word	Suffixed word
Suffixes that form nouns		
-ance, -ancy	insure, truant	insurance, truancy
-ence	differ	difference
-er	teach	teacher
-ion, -tion	confuse, compete	confusion, competition
-ism	real	realism
-ity	reliable	reliability
-ment	require	requirement
-ness	happy	happiness
-ure	fail	failure
Suffixes that form adjectives		
-able, -ible	wash, reverse	washable, reversible
-al	season	seasonal
-ful	watch	watchful
-ic	angel	angelic
-ous, -ious	fame, space	famous, spacious
-ive	react	reactive
-y	stick	sticky

Suffixes that form verbs

-ate	valid	validate
-ify	simple	simplify
-ize	idol	idolize

Suffix that forms adverbs

-ly	rapid	rapidly

When certain suffixes are added to words, they change the pronunciation of the new words that are formed. Some suffixes change the syllable of the word that we stress in speech. An accent mark (') is used to indicate which syllable of a word receives the main stress. A light accent mark (') shows that another syllable is also stressed, but not as strongly as the syllable with the dark accent mark. The following examples show the pronunciation changes in a word when these suffixes are added.

When *-ic* or *-tic* is added to a word, the stress moves to the syllable before the *-ic* or *-tic*.

cha' os	cha ot' ic
di' plo mat	di plo mat' ic

The stress remains on the syllable before the *-ic* or *-tic* even when another suffix is added.

cha' os	cha ot' ic	cha ot' i cal ly
di' plo mat	di plo mat' ic	di plo mat' i cal ly

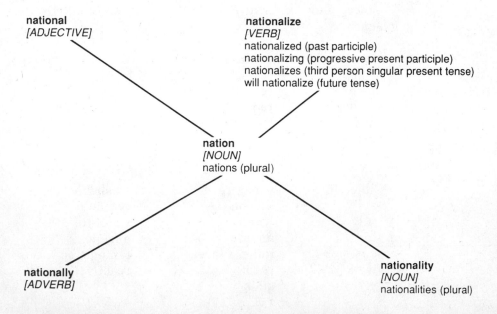

national
[ADJECTIVE]

nationalize
[VERB]
nationalized (past participle)
nationalizing (progressive present participle)
nationalizes (third person singular present tense)
will nationalize (future tense)

nation
[NOUN]
nations (plural)

nationally
[ADVERB]

nationality
[NOUN]
nationalities (plural)

When *-ion* or *-tion* is added to a word, the main stress falls on the syllable before the suffix. Sometimes an *a* is added before the *-ion* or *-tion*. Note the light and heavy stresses in these words.

pro hib′ it   pro′ hib i′ tion
con demn′   con′ dem na′ tion   (note the added *a*)

When *-ity* is added to a word, the main stress again falls on the syllable before the suffix.

gul′ li ble   gul′ li bil′ i ty
am′ i ca ble   am′ i ca bil′ i ty

As you can see, when you learn a new word, you will often be able to form a number of different, but related, words simply by adding a suffix. Related words formed in this way are listed with many of the words you will be studying. Since the changes in pronunciation caused by adding *-ic*, *-ion* (*-tion*), and *-ity* are explained here, these changes will not be repeated when related words are introduced in the text. As you work through the book, refer to the table of suffixes and the explanation of pronunciation changes whenever you meet words with the different endings, especially if you are unsure about how to pronounce them. To find out more about parts of speech and how related words can function in a sentence, you may want to consult a grammar book.

1

Words About People

Do you know a *frugal* shopper, a person *gullible* enough to believe anything, or an *insolent* teenager? The earth is home to over five billion people, and each of us has a different personality, different interests, and different friends. The words in this chapter will help you expand your ability to describe the people around you, and to think about yourself. You will find these words useful in school, on the job, and in your social life.

Chapter Strategy: Using the Dictionary

Chapter Words:

Part 1

adroit	capricious	fraternal
aficionado	competent	gullible
altruistic	disdain	hypocrite
ascetic	dominate	sinister

Part 2

affluent	dogmatic	insolent
alien	exuberant	novice
amicable	frugal	renegade
astute	gauche	worldly

Did You Know?

How Are First Names Changing?

Did you know that there are fashions in naming babies? In the mid-1950s, some of the most popular names for girls were Jane, Nancy, and Susan. Today these names are seldom given to babies. Instead, some recent popular names for girls are Megan, Kimberly, Kelly, and Leah. The meanings of these names give clues to the reasons why parents choose them.

Names that are no longer popular often suggest traditional feminine roles:

> Jane means "God's gift."
>
> Nancy means "full of grace, mercy, and prayer."
>
> Susan means "lily."

In contrast, today's popular names suggest new roles for women. Three are associated with the strength and warlike deeds that were once reserved for men.

> Megan means "the strong."
>
> Kimberly means "from the royal fortress meadow."
>
> Kelly means "warrior maiden."

A fourth name, Leah, may describe the modern-day, overloaded woman.

> Leah means "tired."

Perhaps the changing roles of women have inspired the change in naming trends.

The role of men in our society has remained more stable, and today's parents use the same names that were used for boys in the 1950s. The most popular male names and their meanings follow:

> John or Jose means "God's gracious gift."
>
> William or Guillermo means "protector."
>
> Charles or Carlos means "man."
>
> Joseph means "he shall add."
>
> Robert means "of bright, shining fame."
>
> Thomas means "the twin."
>
> Edward means "rich guardian."

Common names have many associations. The name *George,* for example, brings to mind a variety of people, places, things, and expressions.

1. *Saint George* is the patron saint of England. He probably lived around the year 300. According to legend, St. George slew a dragon that threatened to destroy a town with its poisonous breath. The town had managed to live with the dragon by fulfilling its demand for two sheep every day. When the dragon demanded a princess, though, George came to the rescue. In return for his services, he asked the townspeople to convert to Christianity. St. George is said to have baptized 15,000 people.

2. *By George!* is now a mild oath. It is a shortened form of *by Saint George,* which was once the battle cry of English soldiers. As they rode into battle, the English would swear "by Saint George" that they would conquer their foes.

3. England has had six kings named *George.* George I, who ruled from 1714 to 1727, came from Germany and could speak no English.

4. *Georgia,* a state in the United States, was named for the English king George II. It was founded as a colony where poor Englishmen who had been imprisoned for their debts could start a new life.

5. Did you think all Georges were male? *George Sand* was the pen name of Amandine Lucie Aurore Dudevant, a nineteenth-century French novelist. She took a man's name so that the public would accept her work. She also adopted the freedom of lifestyle generally reserved for males and is famous for her many love affairs.

Learning Strategy

Using the Dictionary

Learning strategies will teach you to figure out the meanings of unknown words on your own. This book presents about five hundred words that you will learn directly from the Words to Learn sections. By using techniques from the Learning Strategy sections, you will be able to multiply your vocabulary to include thousands of new words.

This chapter's learning strategy concentrates on the effective use of the dictionary. The dictionary is an important tool for improving your vocabulary, since it is the best source for finding the precise meaning of a word.

There are many different types of dictionaries. The smallest is the pocket or abridged dictionary, usually a paperback, which gives short definitions. The most complete kind is the unabridged dictionary. This includes many unusual words, extensive definitions, and full word histories. You may have seen an unabridged dictionary on a stand in the library. Between these two sizes is the college-level dictionary, which includes just enough detail for most college students.

Because a dictionary conveys much information in a small space, learning to use this important tool takes practice. A skillful dictionary user can find not only the meaning of a word but also its pronunciation, its history, and other words related to it.

Here is an entry from a college-level dictionary, the *American Heritage Dictionary, Second College Edition*. Each part is labeled.

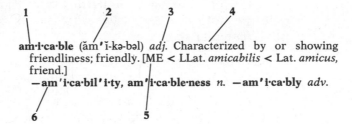

A standard dictionary entry contains the following parts.

1. The word. The entry word is printed in boldface type and divided into syllables.

2. The pronunciation. A key at the bottom of each page of a dictionary shows you how to interpret the pronunciation symbols. (You can also find a key to these symbols on the inside front cover of this textbook.) This key shows you how to pronounce each symbol by giving a common word that contains the sound represented by that symbol. For example, the symbol ă (which represents the first sound in *amicable*) should be spoken like the sound of *a* in the word *păt*.

   An accent mark (ʹ) follows the syllable that should be stressed when you pronounce a word. In *amicable* only the first syllable is stressed. If two syllables have accent marks, the syllable with the darker accent mark receives more stress.

3. The part of speech. The parts of speech you will most often encounter are commonly abbreviated as follows.

n. —noun	*v.* —verb
adj. —adjective	*tr. v.* —transitive verb
adv. —adverb	*intr. v.* —intransitive verb

These parts of speech and their functions were described in the Introduction to Part One.

4. The definition. Some words have more than one definition, and you must choose the one that best fits the sentence you are reading or writing.

  Dictionaries have different methods of ordering definitions. In the *American Heritage Dictionary, Second College Edition*, published by Houghton Mifflin Company, the most general definition of a word is given first, and the least general is given last. In *Webster's Ninth New Collegiate Dictionary*, published by Merriam-Webster, Inc., the oldest definition of a word appears first, and the newest definition last. In the *Random House College Dictionary, Revised Edition*, published by Random House, Inc., definitions are ordered from the most commonly used to the least commonly used.

  Dictionary definitions usually state only the precise, or *denotative*, meanings of words. But words also have implied, or *connotative*, meanings, which are suggested by the images, ideas, and emotions that we associate with them. For example, the words *skinny* and *slender* have the same denotative meaning, "thin," but they differ in connotative meaning. *Skinny* has negative associations, or connotations, and is an uncomplimentary word; *slender* has positive connotations and is a complimentary word. In the same way, *car* has a neutral connotation, *limousine* connotes an expensive, luxurious auto, and *wreck* connotes an auto that is worthless. Although dictionaries give some hints about connotative meanings, most information is learned simply by observing the ways people use words when they write and speak.

5. The etymology. In this section, the history of a word is traced to its origin. The word *amicable* comes to use in its present form from Middle English. Before this, the word appeared in Late Latin as *amicabilis*, which can be followed back still further to the Latin word *amicus*, meaning "friend." The dictionary includes a complete list of the abbreviations for languages used in etymologies. A few of the most common abbreviations follow.

ME—Middle English, spoken in England from A.D. 1100 to 1500
OE—Old English spoken in England before A.D. 1100
F—French, spoken in France today
OF—Old French, spoken in France from A.D. 800 to 1200
Lat.—Latin, spoken by the Romans in Italy about 2000 years ago
    (LLat., Late Latin, was spoken at a later time.)
Gk.—Ancient Greek, spoken in Greece about 2500 years ago

Etymologies are always enclosed in square brackets ([ ]) in a dictionary entry.

6. Related words. Sometimes several forms of a word are listed under one dictionary entry. Related words usually differ from the entry word because they contain *suffixes*, or word endings. Often these

suffixes make the related words into different parts of speech. For instance, under the main entry *amicable* (an adjective) two nouns (*amicability, amicableness*) and an adverb (*amicably*) are also listed. A discussion of suffixes and how they change the part of speech is found in the Introduction to Part One.

The dictionary entry for *amicable* is relatively simple; some entries are more complex. In the entry below, the word *rule* has many definitions. These are separated according to part of speech (underlined below).

rule (rool) *n.* **1. a.** Governing power or its possession or use; authority. **b.** The duration of such power. **2.** An authoritative direction for conduct, esp. one of the regulations governing procedure in a legislative body or a regulation observed by the players in a game, sport, or contest. **3.** A usual or customary course of action or behavior; *Violence is the rule in that area.* **4.** A statement that describes what is true in most or all cases. **5.** A standard method or procedure for solving a class of mathematical problems. **6.** *Law.* **a.** A court order limited in application to a specific case. **b.** A subordinate regulation governing a particular matter. **7.** A ruler (sense 2). **8.** *Printing.* A thin metal strip of various widths and designs, used to print borders or lines, as between columns. —*v.* **ruled, rul·ing, rules.** —*tr.* **1.** To exercise control over; govern. **2.** To dominate by powerful influence; hold sway over. **3.** To keep within proper limits; restrain. **4.** To decide or declare judicially; decree. **5. a.** To mark with straight parallel lines: *ruled note paper.* **b.** To mark (a straight line), as with a ruler. —*intr.* **1.** To exercise authority; be in control or command. **2.** To formulate and issue a decree or decision. **3.** To maintain a specified rate or level: *Prices ruled low.* —**phrasal verb. rule out.** To remove from consideration; exclude: *The snowstorm ruled out their weekly meeting.* —**idioms. as a rule.** In general; for the most part: *As a rule, we take the bus.* **rule of thumb.** A useful principle that has wide application but is not intended to be strictly accurate. [ME *reule* < OFr. < Lat. *regula* < *regere*, to rule.] —**rul'a·ble** *adj.*

This entry shows that *rule* can be used as either a noun or a verb. Notice, too, that it can be used as either an intransitive (*-intr.*) verb or a transitive (*-tr.*) verb. Sometimes a part of speech has several forms. In the entry above, *rule* has different forms when it is used as a verb. These are (1) *ruled* (2) *ruling* (3) *rules*, and they correspond to the (1) past participle, (2) the present participle, and (3) the third-person singular verb form.

If the entry had been for a verb of more than one syllable, these forms might have been listed without the first syllable. For example, the forms for the verb *answer* are listed in the dictionary as *-swered, -swering, -swers*, with the *an-* simply left out. Entries for nouns list the spelling of irregular plural forms; entries for adjectives list spellings for comparative forms, such as *prettier* and *prettiest*.

As you look at the definitions within each part-of-speech category of *rule*, you will notice three other features of the dictionary entry. First, two or more closely related definitions may be listed under one number. Definition 1 or *rule* as a noun has two parts, 1a and 1b. This is also true for definition 6 of *rule* as a noun, and for definition 5 of *rule* as a transitive verb.

Next you may notice that a word in italics (such as *Law* or *Printing*) is included in some definitions. This word (or abbreviation), which is called a label, indicates that this definition is used in a special manner. For example, the sixth definition of *rule* as a noun is labeled *Law* to show that this definition is used mainly in the area of law. Definition 8 is used in *Printing*.

Other labels give information about the style or use of a definition. For instance, the labels *Obs.* (for *obsolete*) and *Archaic* show that this meaning of a word is no longer commonly used. The label *Informal* shows that this use of the word is acceptable only in informal speech. *Nonstandard* indicates a usage that is not commonly accepted. A guide to these labels is found at the beginning of every dictionary.

A dictionary entry may also include examples of the word in phrases or sentences. These may be phrases in everyday usage, as are shown in definition 3 of *rule* as a noun and definition 3 of *rule* as an intransitive verb. At times, sentences written by well-known authors are quoted in dictionary entries. The names of these authors are given in parentheses after their quotes.

Finally, toward the end of the entry for *rule* you will see—*phrasal verb* and —*idioms*. These show how the word *rule* is used with other words. A phrasal verb is a phrase that functions as a verb. In the entry for *rule*, the phrasal verb "rule out" is defined. An idiom is a common phrase. In this entry, the idioms "as a rule" and "rule of thumb" are defined.

To check your knowledge of the dictionary, read the following definition and then answer the questions below.

> **lin·en** (lĭn′ən) *n.* **1. a.** Thread made from fibers of the flax plant. **b.** Cloth woven from this thread. **2.** Garments or articles made from linen or similar material. **3.** Paper made from flax fibers, or given a linenlike luster. —*adj.* **1.** Made of flax or linen. **2.** Resembling linen. [ME < *linen*, of cloth < OE *līnen* < Lat. *linum*, thread.]

1. What parts of speech does *linen* function as? _____

2. Which syllable of *linen* is stressed? _____

3. In which language did *linen* originate? _____

(*Answers:* 1. noun, adjective 2. the first syllable 3. Latin)

Words to Learn

Part 1

1. **adroit** (adjective) ə-droit′

   skillful; clever

   > The **adroit** politician avoided answering several embarrassing questions.

   > Joe Montana's **adroit** moves and passes make him one of the best quarterbacks in football.

   NOTE: The word *adroit* can refer to quickness of mind or of body.

   ▶ *Related Word*
   adroitness (noun) The mathematician's mental *adroitness* astonished us.

2. **aficionado** (noun) ə-fĭsh′ē-ə-nä′dō

   fan; admirer; follower

   > Many young girls are **aficionados** of the group "New Kids on the Block."

   > The football **aficionado** watched two games every Sunday.

   NOTE: An *aficionado* often connotes a fan with great knowledge.

3. **altruistic** (adjective) ăl′trōō-ĭs′tĭk

   unselfish; concerned for the good of others

   > The **altruistic** doctor willingly treated patients who could not afford to pay.

   > Although most people try to be **altruistic,** there is a bit of selfishness in each of us.

   ▶ *Related Word*
   altruism (noun) (ăl′trōō-ĭs′əm) The minister's *altruism* impressed people in his church.

4. **ascetic** (noun, adjective) ə-sĕt′ĭk

   a person who gives up pleasures and practices self-denial (noun)

   > The **ascetic** slept on a wooden board and ate only vegetables.

avoiding or giving up pleasures (adjective)

> Living alone in a single room and devoting himself to prayer, the man led an **ascetic** existence.

NOTES: 1. *Ascetics* are often religious men and women who feel that self-denial and social isolation will bring them closer to God. 2. Be careful! Do not confuse *ascetic* with *aesthetic*, which means beautiful or appealing to the senses. The two words sound almost the same.

Power is usually associated with luxury and wealth. But Mohandas Ghandi, one of the great leaders of this century, proved that an ascetic life can be a source of power too. Gandhi led the movement that brought India and Pakistan independence from Great Britain. Gandhi lived simply and even wove the cloth for his clothes. A vegetarian who sometimes fasted to make political statements, Gandhi refused to injure any living thing. Gandhi used nonviolent resistance against oppression. When he and his followers were attacked, they simply refused to fight back. In this way, they maintained personal dignity and showed the justice of their cause. Gandhi was assassinated in 1948, but his principles continue to inspire nonviolent change throughout the world.

---

5. **capricious** (adjective)   kə-prĭsh′əs

unpredictable; changeable; not based on reason or judgment; fickle

> Because of **capricious** enforcement of the law, many speeding drivers did not receive tickets.

> The teenager's **capricious** behavior was the first sign of her drug addiction.

▶ *Related Words*

caprice (noun) (kə-prēs′)   The unstable person's decisions were based on *caprice*.

capriciousness (noun)   The officer's *capriciousness* caused his men to distrust him.

The word *capricious* may originally have been associated with the sudden, unpredictable movements of the goat (*caper* in Latin). The goat also gives its name to *Capricorn*, one of the signs of the zodiac. People born under the influence of Capricorn, however, are not supposed to be capricious. They are said to exhibit another trait of the goat—stubborn determination in overcoming obstacles. If your birthday is between December 22 and January 19, you are a Capricorn.

---

6. **competent** (adjective)   kŏm′pĭ-tənt

capable; fit; having skills and qualifications

> A **competent** carpenter could easily build a bookcase.

> The judge ruled that the accused person was **competent** to stand trial. (In this case, competent means mentally sound, or sane.)

adequate, but not excellent

> Mario's essay was **competent,** but we were expecting a better job from such an outstanding student.

▶ *Related Word*
    competence (noun)   Because of her *competence* in speaking Russian and Polish, Raisa was chosen as an official interpreter.

7. **disdain** (verb, noun)   dĭs-dān′

to scorn; to treat as unworthy (verb)

> After Mr. Jones moved to a wealthy suburb, he **disdained** people from the poor section of the city.

> The politician **disdained** to respond to the insult.

scorn (noun)

> The criminal's actions showed **disdain** for the law.

▶ *Common Phrase*
    disdain to

▶ *Related Word*
    disdainful (adjective)   Maria was *disdainful* of her cousins.

8. **dominate** (verb)   dŏm′ə-nāt′

to rule; to hold power over

> Anna was **dominated** by her strong-willed husband.

> The desire to get into law school **dominates** the student's life.

▶ *Related Words*
    dominant (adjective)   The Ottoman Empire, centered in Istanbul, was a *dominant* world force from the 1400s to the 1900s.

    domination (noun)   The small boy resented the *domination* of his older brother.

9. **fraternal** (adjective)   frə-tūr′nəl

referring to brothers

> Juan and Jorge Perez enjoy a close **fraternal** relationship.

like a friend or comrade; brotherly

> Clarence had **fraternal** feelings for many of the members of his high school class.

▶ *Related Word*
fraternize (verb) (frăt′ər-nīz′) Our boss warned us not to *fraternize* on the job. (*Fraternize* means "to socialize.")

The word *fraternity* comes from *frater*, the Latin word for brother. These college organizations are meant to foster close relationships and usually consist only of men, called fraternity brothers. Some fraternities have recently become co-ed, however it is more common for women to join *sororities*. (*Soror* is the Latin word for sister.)

---

10. **gullible** (adjective)   gŭl′ə-bəl

easily deceived; easily cheated

> Martin was **gullible** enough to believe that standing on his head would cure warts.

> The crook tried to sell the Brooklyn Bridge to the **gullible** young man.

▶ *Related Word*
gullibility (noun) Marsha's *gullibility* made her an easy target for the dishonest salesperson.

11. **hypocrite** (noun)   hĭp′ə-krĭt′

a person who says one thing and does another

> The **hypocrite** spoke of the need for honesty, while taking bribes from local merchants.

▶ *Related Words*
hypocrisy (noun) (hĭ-pŏk′rə-sē) Their *hypocrisy* did not fool us.
hypocritical (adjective) When a stingy man tells us to give more money to charity, his advice is *hypocritical*.

NOTE: The word *hypocrite* comes from a Greek word meaning "actor."

12. **sinister** (adjective)   sĭn′ĭ-stər

threatening evil or trouble

The villain's **sinister** expression frightened the child.

Dracula is a sinister figure. Legend tells us that as a vampire, he rests in his grave during the day and at night rises and sucks the blood of the living—especially women. Dracula casts no shadow, and has no reflection in a mirror. He can be warded off by garlic or a crucifix (a religious cross) and killed by driving a stake through his heart.

Exercises

Part 1

■ Who's Who?

The sentences below begin by naming a type of person. For each example choose the letter of the word or phrase on the right that defines the type most accurately. Use each choice only once.

1. A sinister person _____ .

2. A gullible person _____ .

3. To disdain is to _____ .

4. Hypocrites will _____ .

5. A competent person _____ .

6. An altruistic person _____ .

7. Capricious people _____ .

8. Ascetics _____ .

9. People who dominate _____ .

10. An aficionado _____ .

a. is a fan

b. are brothers or close friends

c. give up pleasures

d. is unselfish

e. change their minds often

f. is angry

g. rule over others

h. is easily fooled

i. be scornful

j. say things they don't believe

k. threatens evil

l. is capable

©Copyright 1992 Houghton Mifflin Company

■ *Words in Context*

Complete each sentence with the word that fits best. Use each choice only once.

a. adroitness   e. capricious   i. fraternal
b. aficionado   f. competent   j. gullible
c. altruistic   g. disdain   k. hypocrite
d. ascetic   h. dominate   l. sinister

1. Cats show their _____ by walking easily on top of the narrow fences.

2. The _____ lived alone in the mountains and prayed most of the day.

3. We feared that the _____ man might harm us.

4. We hired the woman because we felt she would do a(n)

   _____ job.

5. Darius was a(n) _____ person who volunteered to tutor poor children in reading.

6. There was strong _____ feeling among the boys who had grown up in the same apartment building.

7. The music _____ traveled from Los Angeles to New York to see the Metropolitan Opera.

8. The _____ new immigrant believed that money grew on trees in the United States.

9. The _____ ten-year-old changed her friends every week.

10. The rich noble felt only _____ for the poor peasants on his land.

■ *Using Related Words*

Complete each sentence using a word from the pair of related words above it. You may need to capitalize a word when you put it into a sentence. Use each choice only once.

1. hypocritical, hypocrisy

    My husband's _____ attitudes annoy me. He tells
    our teenage son and daughter not to smoke, yet he smokes when
    he is away from home.

    I hope he stops this _____ and soon becomes a
    nonsmoker.

2. altruism, altruistic

    In many fraternities and sororities, being _____
    is as important as having fun. As part of his membership in Kappa
    Alpha Psi, Michael Long is working to help children suffering
    from cancer. Many black fraternities and sororities are leading

    a movement toward _____ .

3. dominated, domination

    Until recently, the central government of the Soviet Union has

    forcefully _____ its fifteen republics. However,

    recent events have lessened this _____ . Repub-
    lics such as Latvia, Lithuania, and Georgia should become more
    powerful now that the central Soviet influence has decreased.

4. fraternize, fraternal

    Soldiers from the U.S. 82nd Airborne Division developed

    _____ relationships when they served in the Per-
    sian Gulf War. Although they later scattered throughout the coun-

    try, they had a chance to _____ at yearly re-
    unions.

5. disdain, disdains

    Our state senator shows only _____ for the peo-
    ple in his district. He refuses to talk to them, and he rarely shows
    concern for the new roads, good schools, and safe parks that they

    need. Because he _____ people who could vote
    for him, we feel he will not be elected again.

■ *Which Should It Be?*

To complete the following sentences, choose the letter of the phrase that makes better sense.

1. A person likely to attend a large party would be _____ .
   a. one who was an ascetic   b. one who fraternized easily

2. You are likely to commit a crime if you are _____ .
   a. an altruistic person   b. a sinister person

3. A city mayor should be _____ .
   a. adroit in handling sensitive public issues
   b. dominated by a small group of citizens

4. A good lawyer would be _____ .
   a. gullible enough to believe every client
   b. competent in handling cases

5. A popular sportscaster would be _____ .
   a. disdainful of listeners   b. an aficionado of athletics

Words to Learn

Part 2

13. **affluent** (adjective)   ăf′lōō-ənt

    wealthy; prosperous

    > **Affluent** people can afford many vacations.
    > Enormous oil reserves have made Saudi Arabia an **affluent** country.

    ► *Related Word*
    affluence (noun) The immigrant rose from poverty to *affluence*.

14. **alien** (adjective, noun)   ā′lē-ən

    strange; foreign (adjective)

    > The custom of removing shoes before entering a room is **alien** to most Americans.
    > Cruelty was **alien** to his kind nature.

a foreigner; a person who is not a citizen (noun)

> The United States government requires **aliens** to register after their visas expire.

a being from outer space (noun); coming from outer space (adjective)

> The **alien** creature had seven eyes and three arms.

NOTE: All three meanings have the connotation (or hint) of being foreign or strange.

▶ *Related Words*

alienate (verb)   The man's cruelty *alienated* his friends. (Alienate means "to make hostile or unfriendly.")

alienation (noun)   His *alienation* from his family made him unhappy. (*Alienation* means "psychological isolation.")

15. **amicable** (adjective)   ăm′ĭ-kə-bəl

friendly; peaceful

> Although the two neighbors were not close friends, they had an **amicable** relationship.

> The United States maintains **amicable** relations with Iceland.

NOTE: Amicable indicates a friendly, but not very close, relationship.

▶ *Related Word*

amicability (noun)   The *amicability* of Mexico and the United States encourages trade between the two countries.

16. **astute** (adjective)   ə-stoot′

shrewd; having good judgment

> The **astute** worker knew that being well liked would help him to get a promotion.

NOTE: An *astute* person will know what is really important, rather than what people say is important.

▶ *Related Word*

astuteness (noun)   The politician's *astuteness* helped him to get on powerful city committees.

17. **dogmatic** (adjective)   dôg-măt′ĭk

arrogant in belief; opinionated

Workers found it hard to suggest new ideas to their **dogmatic** boss.

My **dogmatic** aunt insisted that writing with my left hand would ruin my schoolwork.

▶ *Related Word*
   dogmatism (noun)   (dôg'mə-tĭz'əm)   Because of the teacher's *dogmatism*, students feared to present their true opinions.

18. **exuberant** (adjective)   ĕg-zoo'bər-ənt

very enthusiastic; joyfully energetic

Exuberant at seeing his mother after a long absence, Trung grabbed her and held her tightly.

Fans applauded the **exuberant** cheerleaders.

▶ *Related Word*
   exuberance (noun)   The delighted child shouted with *exuberance*.

19. **frugal** (adjective)   froo'gəl

thrifty; economical; attempting to save money

The **frugal** homemaker carefully looked for sales when she shopped.

▶ *Related Word*
   frugality (noun)   Roxanne's *frugality* enabled her to put money into her savings account every month.

20. **gauche** (adjective)   gōsh

Awkward; lacking in social graces

The **gauche** woman described her uncle's surgery in front of her sick friend.

Our cousin was so **gauche** that he licked his fingers at a formal dinner.

In many languages, words that refer to the right side seem to be regarded positively and words that refer to the left side are seen as wrong or negative. Three words in this chapter have their roots in the concepts of "right" or "left." In French, *à droit* means "to the right," and in both French and English *adroit* is a positive word, meaning "skillful." *Sinister* means "on the left" and "unlucky" in Latin; in English it has the extended meaning of "threatening evil." *Gauche* means "left" in French, and means "awkward" or "clumsy" in English.

21. insolent (adjective) ĭn'sə-lənt

showing disrespect; rude

The teacher reported the boy's **insolent** remark to the principal.

▶ *Related Word*
insolence (noun)   The girl's *insolence* horrified her aunt.

Bart is the insolent family son in the T.V. cartoon series "The Simpsons." Always ready to insult parents or teachers, he will tell them "Don't have a cow, dude."

---

22. novice (noun) nŏv'ĭs

beginner; person in a new situation

The expert fisherman patiently instructed the **novice** in the art of fly casting.

Since the city council member was a political **novice,** he often said foolish things to the press.

23. renegade (noun) rĕn'ə-gād

traitor; deserter; outlaw

The army offered a reward for the capture of the **renegade.**

The Spanish empire ruled over much of Mexico, Central America, South America, and what became the southwestern United States for several centuries. As a result, most countries south of the United States are Spanish speaking. In addition, several million people within the United States speak Spanish. Not surprisingly, many Spanish words have entered American English.

Two such words are introduced in this chapter, *aficionado* and *renegade*. In Spanish, *aficionado* means "fan," in particular, a follower of the popular sport of bullfighting, and *renegado* means "deserter." Other examples of Spanish words are *corral, desperado, fiesta, patio,* and *rodeo*.

---

24. worldly (adjective) wûrld'lē

sophisticated; devoted to pleasures and interests of the world

My **worldly** uncle took us to the liveliest nightclub in the city.

When Thomas became a monk, he took a vow to give up **worldly** concerns.

NOTE: Worldly can be used as a negative word meaning *too* sophisticated.

Worldly men have often been portrayed romantically in movies. Clark Gable, as Rhett Butler, was the hard-drinking, insolent hero of the film *Gone with the Wind.* He fascinated women, including the famous Scarlett O'Hara. In *Casablanca,* Humphrey Bogart played the worldly, hard-bitten Rick Blaine, a man who had lost his ideals, but who sacrificed all for a woman he could not possess. More recently, Billy Dee Williams has played the worldly man that women love to hate in such movies as *Mahogany.*

Exercises

Part 2

■ Who's Who

The following sentences begin by naming a type of person. For each example choose the letter of the word or phrase on the right that defines the type most accurately.

1. An astute person is ___i___ .

2. A renegade is ___h___ .

3. A novice is ___e___ .

4. An exuberant person is ___a___ .

5. A frugal person is ___k___ .

6. An alien is ___d___ .

7. An amicable person is ___g___ .

8. An insolent person is ___c___

9. A worldly person is ___j___ .

10. An affluent person is _____ .

a. enthusiastic
b. wealthy
c. rude
d. a foreigner
e. a beginner
f. opinionated
g. friendly
h. a rebel
i. shrewd *clearly observant*
j. sophisticated
k. trying to save money
l. awkward, lacking social graces *= gauche*

■ *Words in Context*

Complete each sentence with the word that fits best. Use each choice only once.

a. affluent   e. dogmatic   i. insolent
b. alien   f. exuberant   j. novice
c. amicable   g. frugal   k. renegade
d. astute   h. gauche   l. worldly

1. As a freshman, I was a(n) _____ who knew nothing about college life.

2. My _____ father rarely feels he can afford new clothes.

3. The _____ dancer stepped on his partner's toes.

4. Although I am now a(n) _____, I soon hope to become a Canadian citizen.

5. The _____ deserted the army and joined the enemy.

6. The adoring crowd gave the marine a(n) _____ welcome home.

7. The insults of the _____ waiter upset the customer.

8. The unsophisticated young woman was fascinated by her _____ older sister's stories of Paris nightlife.

9. The divorcing man and woman tried to maintain a(n) _____ relationship for the sake of the children.

10. Nothing could change the opinion of the _____ man.

■ *Using Related Words*

Complete each sentence using a word from the pair of related words above it. You may need to capitalize a word when you put it into a sentence. Use each choice only once.

1. affluent, affluence

   Many citizens in the United States are _affluent_ people who can afford to buy cars and to take vacations. However, this _affluence_ does not extend to everyone. Over twenty percent of children in the U.S. are born into poverty.

2. astute, astuteness

   astute companies realize that they will have to show more sensitivity toward recycling. Recently, McDonald's and Arby's restaurants announced that they would use only recyclable paper wrappers for food. This decision shows much _astuteness_ in recognizing strong public feelings supporting recycling.

3. frugal, frugality

   The _frugality_ of the Japanese public contributes to the prosperity of Japan. While people in the U.S. tend to buy on credit, the _frugal_ Japanese generally pay cash for items and save more than Americans do.

4. dogmatic, dogmatism

   My aunt has _dogmatic_ opinions about the proper way to dress and behave. Despite current attitudes, she feels that women who leave the house should always wear dresses. She also expects that men will open doors for her and give her their seats on crowded buses. Her _dogmatism_ makes her unpopular with the younger members of the family.

5. amicable, amicability

   Morocco has a long history of _amicable_ relations with the United States. Morocco recognized the U.S. in 1777, only a year after the U.S. proclaimed its independence. To further show his _amicability_, Sultan Moulay Suliman presented a lion house to the U.S. consulate in 1821. Located in Morocco, it is now a U.S. National Historic Landmark.

■ *Which Should It Be?*

To complete the following sentences, choose the letter of the word or phrase that makes better sense.

1. A(n) _____*a*_____ person would be likely to spend money freely.
   a. affluent   b. frugal

2. People seek out others who are _____*b*_____.
   a. insolent   b. amicable

3. If your team won the state championship, you would feel _____*b*_____.
   a. dogmatic   b. exuberant

4. A(n) _____*a*_____ person is more likely to influence other people.
   a. astute   b. alien

5. A person who understands how things really are in life is _____*a*_____.
   a. worldly   b. gauche

Chapter Exercises

■ *Practicing Strategies: Using the Dictionary*

Read the definitions, and answer the questions that follow.

> **or·nate** (ôr-nāt′) *adj.*   **1.** Elaborately and heavily ornamented; excessively decorated.   **2.** Flashy, showy, or florid in style or manner; flowery. [ME < Lat. *ornatus*, p. part. of *ornare*, to embellish.]—**or·nate′ly** *adv.* —**or·nate′ness** *n.*

1. What part of speech does *ornate* function as?

   _____

2. Which syllable of *ornate* is stressed? _____

3. What noun is related to *ornate?* _____

4. In which language did *ornate* originate?

   _____

sen·tient (sĕn′shənt, -shē-ənt, -tē-ənt) *adj.*   **1.** Having sense perception; conscious: *"The living knew themselves just sentient puppets on God's stage"* (T.E. Lawrence).   **2.** Experiencing sensation or feeling. —*n.*   **1.** A sentient person or thing.   **2.** The mind. [Lat. *sentiens, sentient-,* pr. part. of *sentire,* to feel.] — **sen′ti·ent·ly** *adv.*

5. What two parts of speech does *sentient* function as?

_____

6. What part of speech does *sentiently* function as?

_____

7. In total, how many definitions does *sentient* have?

_____

max·i·mum (măk′sə-məm) *n., pl.* **-mums** or **-ma** (-mə).   **1. a.** The greatest possible quantity, degree, or number. **b.** The time or period during which the highest point or degree is attained.   **2.** An upper limit stipulated by law or other authority.   **3.** *Astron.* **a.** The moment when a variable star is most brilliant. **b.** The magnitude of the star at such a moment.   **4.** *Math.* **a.** The value of a function that is not exceeded by neighboring values. **b.** The greatest value assumed by a function within some subset of its domain of definition. **c.** The largest number in a set. —*adj.*   **1.** Having or being the greatest quantity or the highest degree that has been or can be attained: *maximum temperature.*   **2.** Of, pertaining to, or making up a maximum: *a maximum number in a series.* [< Lat., neuter of *maximus,* greatest. —see MAXIM.]

8. Write the full plural spellings of *maximum.* _____

9. What two parts of speech does *maximum* function as?

_____

10. Give the number and the part of speech of the definition of *maximum* most used in astronomy. _____

■ *Practicing Strategies: Using a Dictionary Pronunciation Key*

It takes practice to use a pronunciation key efficiently. For each of the following words, use the key that is located on the inside of the front cover of this book to figure out the pronunciation. Try saying each word out loud several times.

1. accolade   ăk′ə-lād
2. pseudonym   sōō′də-nĭm′
3. cuisine   kwĭ-zēn′
4. epitome   ĭ-pĭt′ə-mē
5. psyche   sī′kē

■ Practicing Strategies: Using the Dictionary Independently

Use a dictionary to research independently the answers to the following questions. Be sure to consult a recently published college-level or unabridged dictionary.

1. In what language was the word *sheriff* first recorded? _____

   _____

2. What is *myrrh?* _____

   _____

3. Which syllable of the word *plasmagene* receives most stress? ____

   _____

4. If you felt *myasthenic,* how would you feel? _____

   _____

5. What is a *mallemuck?* _____

   _____

■ Companion Words

Complete each sentence with the word that fits best. Choose your answers from the words below. You may use words more than once.

Choices: for, by, to, with

1. The Bulls game was dominated _____ Michael Jordan.

2. The custom of bowing is alien _____ me.

3. Jose has amicable relationships _____ his neighbors.

4. The renegade had disdain _____ the government.

5. I have fraternal feelings _____ my brother.

■ *Writing with Your Words*

This exercise will give you practice in using the vocabulary words in your own writing. Each sentence is started for you. Complete it with an interesting phrase that also indicates the meaning of the italicized word.

1. One custom *alien* to me is _____

_____ .

2. When I am *affluent,* I will _____

_____ .

3. A *novice* at driving might _____

_____ .

4. A *capricious* ruler might _____

_____ .

5. A *competent* student _____

_____ .

6. Only a *gullible* person would believe that _____

_____ .

7. If you *dominate* a conversation _____

_____ .

8. A person might show *disdain* by _____

_____ .

9. My *gauche* friend _____

_____ .

10. *Exuberant* people might express themselves by _____

_____ .

Passage

The 1960s: Decade of Changing Youth

Long hair, protest, folk music, and "dropping out"—these are symbols of **(1)** the sixties, an era **dominated** by youth. Society seemed to explode with the **exuberance** of the young. The issues of the sixties—peace, love, informality, civil rights, and helping others—are still with us today.

The year 1961 began with the new presidency of John F. Kennedy, the youngest leader ever to govern the U.S. **(2)** His opening address called for a spirit of **altruism,** as he said: "Ask not what your country can do for you; ask what you can do for your country." Soon afterward, Kennedy formed the Peace Corps program, in which thousands of young Americans volunteered to help people in Samoa, Nigeria, and other underdeveloped countries. Volunteers faced difficulties trying to live in **alien** cultures. **(3)** Many young Americans were **novices** who knew little about the language and customs of the people they served. The volunteers lived, for the first time, **ascetically,** without the modern conveniences of running water and electricity.

Meanwhile, changes were brewing at home, as citizens forged the Civil Rights movement that would bring new rights to African Americans. At "sit-ins," young blacks at "whites only" restaurants waited in vain for lunch counter service, **(4)** while bravely facing **insolent** crowds. When the Rev. Martin Luther King, Jr., was imprisoned for his protests, John Kennedy called to offer his support. **(5)** Thus Kennedy **adroitly** aided the Civil Rights cause. Despite many setbacks, the Civil Rights movement gradually triumphed.

The nation was shocked when, in 1963, an assassin's bullet murdered President Kennedy. Many young people felt they had lost their special leader.

At first the new president, Lyndon Johnson, seemed **astute** at judging political realities, as he successfully guided a Civil Rights bill through Congress. However, he soon encountered difficulty. **(6)** For despite mounting evidence that the war in Vietnam was in trouble, Johnson **dogmatically** refused to withdraw his support.

Faced with the prospect of fighting this unpopular war, the youth movement exploded. Across college campuses, protests raged. Students became **aficionados** of folk singers Bob Dylan and Joan Baez, who **advocated** peace. Meanwhile the Beatles popularized songs of **alienation,** such as "Nowhere Man."

Young people translated the messages of these songs into action. **(7) Renegades** refused to register for the U.S. draft, and burned their draft cards or crossed the border to Canada to avoid military service.

Many older people looked on in disapproval, feeling that these young people were **gullible** to believe that the world could live in peace. **(8)** Students, in turn, openly questioned the **competence** of their elders to govern.

A new freedom burst forth in all areas of college living. In 1960, many colleges had dress codes that required skirts and stockings for women. Men were expected to have short hair. Curfews were set at 10:30 P.M., and ten "late minutes" were enough to imprison women in their dorms for several nights. By 1969, both sexes were wearing jeans and long hair. Women and men were living together in co-ed dorms; fraternities were admitting women. Signs shouted "Make love, not war," and students appeared to be following this advice quite openly. **(9)** New styles seemed totally **capricious.** As youth grew more hair, they seemed to wear fewer clothes. In fact, the popular musical *Hair* featured a brief scene with nude actors.

The 1960s was a time of new dress, action, and thought for young people.

Some students decided to "drop out" completely. Many families who had saved **frugally** for their children's education discovered that John or Mary was living as a "flower child" in San Francisco's Haight-Ashbury district. Dressed in rags and wandering aimlessly, flower children looked desperately poor. **(10)** In fact, many were the children of the **affluent.** In the summer of 1969, the sixties ended as 400,000 young people gathered at a farm near Woodstock, New York, to listen to music and to "groove" at the most famous of all rock concerts.

More than twenty years later, we look back at the youngsters who so **exuberantly** embraced the message of love. They helped create a new freedom of dress, of action, and of thought for those who now follow them in the 1990s.

■ *Exercise*

1. The sixties were an era _____ by youth.
   a. seen   b. ruled   c. told   d. started

2. His address called for a spirit of _____ .
   a. leadership   b. courage   c. life   d. unselfishness

3. Many young Americans were _____ .
   a. beginners   b. helpless   c. comfortable   d. experts

4. Blacks bravely faced _____ crowds.
   a. large   b. violent   c. insulting   d. hopeless

5. John Kennedy _____ aided the Civil Rights cause.
   a. quickly   b. bravely   c. wisely   d. skillfully

6. Johnson _____ refused to withdraw his support.
   a. unexpectedly   b. now   c. really   d. stubbornly

7. _____ refused to register for the draft.
   a. Rebels   b. Cowards   c. Students   d. Males

8. Students openly questioned the _____ of their elders
   a. decisions   b. intentions   c. goodness   d. capability

9. New styles seemed totally _____ .
   a. ugly   b. unpredictable   c. bad   d. planned

10. They were the children of the _____ .
    a. educated   b. leaders   c. wealthy   d. divorced

■ Discussion Questions

1. How did Lyndon Johnson's popularity change?

2. Name three ways in which life became more free in the 1960s.

3. Name two changes of the 1960s that have lasted into the 1990s; defend your choices.

CHAPTER

Words in the News

Even on a remote mountain top, we are never more than a few seconds away from the news. A touch of a radio button brings us the latest reports of international events, accidents, sports scores, and gossip about our favorite stars. Television transports images from thousands of miles away into our living rooms; we learn about the weather throughout the world, and in our own backyards. Daily newspapers give us in-depth political analysis, advice columns, and tips on daily living. This chapter presents many words that will help you to understand the news better.

Chapter Strategy: Context Clues of Substitution

Chapter Words:

Part 1

accord	consumer	intervene
attrition	diplomacy	media
bureaucracy	entrepreneur	subjugate
catastrophe	indulge	Third World

Part 2

apprehend	epitome	radical
capitulate	ludicrous	liberal
chaos	supplant	conservative
defer	thrive	reactionary

©Copyright 1992 Houghton Mifflin Company

Did You Know?

How Many Ways Can a Team Win or Lose?

If you read the sports pages of the newspapers, you know what clever writing they contain. Sportswriters are masters of the English language. They express game results in exciting ways that make fans read on eagerly. Every day football, basketball, baseball, or hockey games are reported in newspapers; day after day, sportswriters make their reports sound fresh and enthusiastic.

How do they do it? After all, most of the events are basically the same:

1. The game is played.

2. One team or player wins.

3. The other team or player loses.

Because sportswriters have had to report wins and losses over and over again, they have developed clever synonyms (words that mean the same thing) for the words *win* and *lose*.

Let's look at some of the many ways to say *win* with examples taken from newspaper sports pages.

> A's *beat* Yankees.
>
> Bears *top* Vikings.

And here are some examples of ways to say *lose.*

> Ohio State *is canned* by Michigan.
>
> Nuggets *falter* in overtime.

Sportswriters vary their expressions depending on the amount of winning (or losing) points. For example, these headlines show that the winners won by a big score, really "killing" their opponents.

> Purdue *crushes* winless Northwestern.
>
> Giants *stun* Expos.
>
> Falcons *smash* Oilers.

On the other hand, these headlines show that the winners barely got by.

> Nebraska *struggles past* Baylor.
>
> Reds *edge* Astros.

Sometimes the name of a team is used in an imaginative way. The headlines that follow are *metaphors,* or figurative uses of names.

Flyers *soar past* Islanders. (Something that flies can soar.)

Hawks' win over Jets is a *real trip*. (Trips are taken in jets.)

Pirates *slice up* Cubs. (The pirates take their swords and "slice up" the cubs.)

49ers *shear* Rams. (A ram is a sheep; sheep get sheared.)

At other times, rhyme is used.

Bears *sack the Pack*.

Astros *shake, bake* Bulls. (The food product "Shake and Bake" has seasoned crumbs for coating chicken and pork.)

Sometimes a short headline tells much about a game. What do you think happened in these games?

1. Bruins' rally on ice from 2 down stuns Rangers 4—3.

2. Iowa State surprises Minnesota in overtime.

3. Bulls surprise Bucks, end road slump.

(*Answers:*   1. The Bruins were losing 3—1, but, to the Rangers' surprise, the Bruins ended up winning the ice hockey game 4—3.   2. Minnesota, not Iowa State, was expected to win. The game was tied at the end, so it went into overtime. Iowa State won.   3. The Bulls had been playing away from their home town and had been losing games. Surprisingly, they won this game, which was also away from home.)

Learning Strategy

Context Clues of Substitution

Using *context clues* is a powerful strategy that can help you to figure out the meaning of unknown words. *Context* refers to the group of words or paragraphs surrounding a word. When you use context clues, you use the words that you do know in a sentence to make an intelligent guess about the meaning of an unknown word.

You may think that it is not a good strategy to guess at words. After all, it is better to know the answer on a test than just to guess. However, intelligent guessing is a very important strategy to use when you are reading. English has so many words that even the best readers cannot know them all. Good readers often use context clues, or intelligent guesses, when they meet unfamiliar words.

Context clues have two important advantages for you.

1. You do not have to interrupt your reading to go to the dictionary.

2. Using context clues allows you to rely on your own common sense. Common sense is your own best learning tool.

You probably use context clues already. Context clues, for example, are the only way to choose the correct meaning for words that have more than one meaning, such as *cold*. You must use context clues to figure out what the word *cold* means in the following sentences.

a. He took an aspirin because he was getting a *cold*.

b. She greeted him in a *cold* manner.

c. Because she hadn't worn warm clothing, she felt *cold*.

In which sentence does *cold* mean

1. low in body temperature?

2. a type of illness?

3. unfriendly?

(*Answers:* 1. c   2. a   3. b)

Let's turn to a more difficult word. What are the meanings of the word *concession* in these sentences?

a. He bought some food at the hot-dog *concession*.

b. Because the country wanted peace, the leaders made a *concession* of land to the enemy.

In which sentence does *concession* mean

1. something that is surrendered or given up?

2. a business that sells things?

(*Answers:* 1. b   2. a)

Context clues and the dictionary are natural partners in helping you to determine the meaning of unknown words. Context clues usually give you an approximate meaning for a word and allow you to continue your reading without interruption. After you have finished reading, you can look up the word in your dictionary. Why not simply use the dictionary? People usually remember words they figured out for themselves far better than those they simply looked up in the dictionary.

You may be wondering exactly how to figure out unknown words that you find in your reading. Many people find the following steps helpful.

1. As you are reading, try to pinpoint words you do not know. This advice sounds almost silly, but it isn't. Many people lose the opportunity to learn words simply because they let unknown words slip by. Don't let this happen to you. Try to capture your unknown words!

2. Use context clues to make an intelligent guess about an unknown word's meaning. The strategies you will learn here and in the following chapters will help you to do this. Remember that context clues will often give you an approximate—not an exact—meaning.

3. Write down the word and later check it with the dictionary. This step will tell you whether you guessed correctly and will give you a more exact definition of the word.

How does a person learn to make the "intelligent guesses" referred to above? In this book, we will present three different methods: substitution in context (in this chapter), context clues of definition (in Chapter 3), and context clues of opposition (in Chapter 4).

Substitution in context is perhaps the most useful way to determine a word's meaning. To use this strategy, simply substitute a word or phrase that makes sense in place of an unknown word. The word you substitute will usually be an approximate definition for the unknown word. Here are some examples.

> Ron's two brothers were hitting each other, but he would not join the *fray*. (Since people often hit each other in a fight, the word *fight* is a good substitution and provides an approximate meaning.)

> The *indigent* student could not afford books or school supplies. (A person who cannot afford things necessary for school is poor, and the word *poor* may substitute for *indigent*.)

Of course, context clues of substitution cannot be used all the time. Some sentences simply do not provide enough context clues. For example, in the sentence "Jane saw the *conger*," it would be impossible to find a good substitution for *conger*. (A *conger* is a type of eel.) However, since most sentences do provide context clues, substitution in context will help you much of the time.

Two additional examples are given below. Try using context clues of substitution to make intelligent guesses about the meanings of the italicized words. To do this, take out the unknown word and substitute a word you know that seems to make sense in the sentence.

1. Your smiling *countenance* suggests that you are happy.
2. A broken traffic light is a *vexation* to a driver.

(*Answers:* 1. face 2. annoyance)

You can now try using the substitution strategy to make intelligent guesses about the meanings of some words to be studied in this chapter.

Each of the following sentences contains a word that will be presented in the Words to Learn section. Read the sentence and use a context clue of substitution to make an intelligent guess at the meaning of the italicized word.

1. The rise in prices made us *defer* our purchase until the next year.

   Defer means _____ .

2. The outdated computer manual was *supplanted* by a new edition.

   Supplanted means _____ .

3. The two countries reached a final *accord* that enabled them to stop fighting.

   Accord means _____ .

(*Answers:* 1. delay 2. replaced 3. agreement)

Words to Learn

Part 1

1. **accord** (noun, verb) ə-kôrd′

   agreement; harmony (noun)

   > The news reported that Mideast countries had reached an arms **accord**.

   > We are in complete **accord** with your views.

   to give or grant (verb)

   > The judge **accorded** Mrs. Mozzi $500.00 in damages.

   ▶ *Common Phrases*
   in accord with
   reach an accord

2. **attrition** (noun) ə-trĭsh′ən

   slowly wearing down; wearing away

Water changes stone to sand by a process of **attrition.**

The two countries gradually weakened each other in the war of **attrition.**

3. **bureaucracy** (noun)   byŏŏ-rŏk′rə-sē

government by appointed officials

The newly elected mayor found she had to deal with an inefficient **bureaucracy.**

My check from the university was delayed because it had to be approved by several levels of **bureaucracy.**

NOTE: Bureaucracy is usually a negative word that refers to a government involving too many officials and too much delay. The members of a bureaucracy are appointed, rather than elected, and they often are more concerned with following rules than with getting things done.

▶ *Related Words*

bureaucratic (adjective)   The *bureaucratic* forms annoyed us.

bureaucrat (noun)   For twenty years, the *bureaucrat* made four copies of every letter he received.

Bureaucracy is often associated with the term "red tape" in sentences such as "There is too much bureaucratic red tape." In the 1700s, red tape was actually used to bind piles of English government documents. Since the government was bureaucratic and inefficient, "red tape" came to refer to excessive and silly official routines.

---

4. **catastrophe** (noun)   kə-tăs′trə-fē

a great disaster

The 1988 earthquake in Soviet Armenia was a **catastrophe** that killed over 55,000 people.

The closing of the factory was a **catastrophe** for the people in the town.

▶ *Related Word*

catastrophic (adjective)   kăt′ə-strŏf′-ĭk)   The Exxon *Valdez* oil spill had *catastrophic* effects on Alaskan wildlife.

5. **consumer** (noun)   kən-sōō′mər

a buyer

Shop owners try to please **consumers.**

▶ *Related Words*

> **consume** (verb)   The child *consumed* half of a cake.
>
> **consumption** (noun)   (kən-sŭmp′shən)   Jadwila's *consumption* of food was light.
>
> Conspicuous *consumption* means making unneeded purchases in order to impress other people.

NOTE: As you can see, *consumption* and *consume* relate to eating as well as to buying.

Society owes much to the consumer advocacy movement, which has investigated products and campaigned for laws to protect the consumer. Ralph Nader, one widely known consumer advocate, investigated automobile safety and published his findings in the 1965 book *Unsafe at Any Speed.* The problems he uncovered ranged from gas tanks that exploded at the slightest impact to seats that easily came loose and caused injuries to passengers. Public concern over Nader's findings led to the design of safer cars and more government regulation of automobile manufacture.

---

6. **diplomacy** (noun)   dĭ-plō′mə-sē

official relationships among nations

> **Diplomacy** failed to settle the dispute between Viet Nam and Cambodia.

tact; politeness

> Jantima's great **diplomacy** enabled her to criticize others without hurting their feelings.

▶ *Related Words*

> **diplomat** (noun, person)   John R. Hubbard is the *diplomat* who represents the United States in India.
>
> **diplomatic** (adjective)   Harold entered the *diplomatic* service.

7. **entrepreneur** (noun)   ŏn′trə-prə-nûr′

A person who organizes and runs a business

> The Chinese-American **entrepreneur,** An Wang, built Wang Laboratories into one of the largest computer firms in the United States.

► *Related Word*

entrepreneurial (adjective)   My *entrepreneurial* brother-in-law started with one fruit stand and now runs a nationwide business.

In the twentieth century, entrepreneurs have emerged from many backgrounds. Black entrepreneur John H. Johnson founded the enormous Johnson Publishing Company in 1942. Berry Gordy developed Motown Record Corporation (now Motown Industries), the Detroit-based company that revolutionized rock music with such Detroit-based singers as the Supremes and Marvin Gaye. Cuban-born Roberto C. Goizueta is the C.E.O. of Coca Cola. Many women have also become successful entrepreneurs. Estee Lauder and Mary Kay Ash have both founded major firms in the cosmetics industry, and Debbi Fields is the force behind Mrs. Fields' cookies.

---

8. **indulge** (verb)   ĭn-dŭlj′

to pamper; to yield to desires

Grandparents often **indulge** their grandchildren.

The magazine reported that the movie star **indulged** herself by buying a ten-carat diamond ring.

If you **indulge** in too many chocolates, you will gain weight.

► *Common Phrases*
indulge in

indulge oneself (*Indulge* often uses a reflexive pronoun, such as *myself, yourself,* or *herself.*)

► *Related Words*
indulgence (noun) *Indulgence* can weaken moral fiber.

indulgent (adjective) The *indulgent* godfather granted the three-year-old's every wish.

9. **intervene** (verb)   ĭn′tər-vēn′

to act in a matter involving others; to interfere

The U.S. government **intervened** to stop illegal hunting of rare animals.

Mother **intervened** to settle the fight between Mary and Joe.

► *Related Word*
intervention (noun) Allied *intervention* ended the Iraq's occupation of Kuwait.

NOTE: To *intervene* can also mean to come between points of time, as in "Two years intervened between the skating competitions."

10. **media** (plural noun, adjective)   mē′dē-ə

means of communication, especially TV, radio, and newspapers (plural noun)

> Many politicians believe that the **media** play a decisive role in electing the president of the United States.

referring to the media (adjective)

> In these times, a candidate must have good **media** coverage to win an election.

NOTE: Medium is the singular form of the plural noun *media.*

11. **subjugate** (verb)   sŭb′jə-gāt′

to conquer and rule; to enslave

> Hitler invaded the country of Poland in 1939 and **subjugated** its people.

NOTE: Subjugate usually suggests very harsh or cruel conquest.

▶ *Related Word*
   subjugation (noun) Slaves lived in a state of *subjugation.*

The ancient Romans had an empire that extended across much of the Middle East and Europe. It was said that when the Romans conquered new territory, they made the inhabitants walk under an arch built of spears to symbolize subjugation.

---

12. **Third World** (noun, adjective)   thûrd wûrld

economically underdeveloped countries of Asia, Africa, and Latin America (noun)

> The **Third World** is a powerful voting force in the United Nations.

referring to countries of the Third World (adjective)

> Many **Third-World** countries have high infant death rates.

Exercises

Part 1

■ Matching Words and Definitions

Check your understanding of words in the news by matching each word with the letter of its definition. Use each choice only once.

1. bureaucracy _____   a. person who runs a business

2. consumer _____   b. disaster

                                c. wearing away
3. indulge _____
                                d. official relationships among nations
4. attrition _____
                                e. means of communication
5. subjugate _____
                                f. buyer

6. diplomacy _____   g. to enslave

7. intervene _____   h. agreement

                                i. government by appointed officials
8. media _____
                                j. underdeveloped countries
9. accord _____
                                k. to act in a matter involving others.
10. Third World _____
                                l. to yield to desires

■ Words in Context

Complete each sentence with the word that fits best. Use each choice only once.

a. accord   e. consumer   i. intervene
b. attrition   f. diplomacy   j. media
c. bureaucracy   g. entrepreneur   k. subjugate
d. catastrophe   h. indulge   l. Third World

1. The police had to _____ to stop the fight.

2. The _____ owned several restaurants.

3. The _____ gave much coverage to the suffering of the Kurdish people.

4. People who use _____ when they deal with others are usually well liked.

5. People in the _____ often took several days to approve forms.

6. Over the years, the college lost a number of teachers by a process

of _____ .

7. The five-hundred-point drop in the stock market average was a(n)

_____ for investors.

8. The economies of many _____ countries are beginning to develop.

9. Since we are in _____ with each other, there will be no arguments.

10. I would like to _____ myself by buying an expensive car.

■ *Using Related Words*

Complete each sentence using a word from the group of related words above it. You may need to capitalize a word when you put it into a sentence. Use each choice only once.

1. consumption, consumer

   In the past several years, _____ of liquor has decreased. Campaigns by groups such as MADD (Mothers Against

   Drunk Driving) have convinced the _____ that if people drank less, there would be fewer automobile accidents.

2. entrepreneurial, entrepreneurs

   An _____ spirit has helped to build the economies of many countries. Clothes worn throughout the world have

   been manufactured by firms in South Korea. _____ have helped the Korean economy to grow.

3. intervened, intervention

As many animal species are in danger of becoming extinct, zoos

have _____ to save them. Animals that have been

helped by the _____ of zoo preservation pro-
grams include the Madagascar tortoise, the okapis (a relative of
the giraffe), and a rare type of Asian leopard.

4. indulge, indulgence

When traveling, professional basketball player B. J. Armstrong

likes to _____ himself with a good book. Any

time he wants to relax and treat himself with _____,
he reads.

5. subjugate, subjugation

After World War II, the U.S.S.R. was able to _____
many Eastern European countries. Countries such as Hungary

and Czechlosvokia lived under the _____ of the
U.S.S.R. for over forty years.

■ *Reading the Headlines*

This exercise presents five headlines that might have been taken from
newspapers. Read each headline and then answer the questions that follow. (Remember that small words, such as *a* and *the*, are often left out
of newspaper headlines.)

TRANSPORTATION SYSTEM RUN BY BUREAUCRACY IS A CATASTROPHE

1. Is transportation run by elected officials? _____

2. Is the transportation system working well? _____

TWO COUNTRIES REACH ACCORD NOT TO INTERVENE IN WAR OF ATTRITION

3. Will the countries interfere? _____

4. Will the war be over quickly? _____

DIPLOMATIC ENTREPRENEUR TAKES CONTROL OF MEDIA COMPANY

5. Is the entrepreneur rude? _____

6. Is the company involved in communication? _____

CONSUMERS INDULGE IN LUXURY ITEMS

7. Are people interested in shopping? _____

8. Are the people satisfying their desires? _____

THIRD WORLD COUNTRY SUBJUGATED BY REBEL FORCES

9. Is the country economically developed? _____

10. Did the people of the country elect their rulers? _____

Words to Learn

Part 2

13. **apprehend** (verb)   ăp′rĭ-hĕnd′

    to arrest or take a criminal into custody

    > The police **apprehended** the escaped convicts.

    to understand mentally; to grasp

    > I only vaguely **apprehend** the principles of calculus.

    ▶ *Related Words*
    apprehension (noun) The *apprehension* of the criminal meant our worries were over. I had *apprehensions* about the test. (In the first sentence, *apprehension* means "arrest"; in the second sentence, it means "fear.")

    apprehensive (adjective) I am *apprehensive* about the test.

    NOTE: The related word *apprehension* can mean "an arrest," "a mental understanding," or "fear." *Apprehensive* always means "fearful."

14. **capitulate** (verb)   kə-pĭch′-ə-lāt′

    To surrender; to give in

The cornered criminals **capitulated** to the police.

The city-state of Athens, defeated by Sparta in 404 B.C., had to **capitulate** to demands for land.

▶ *Related Word*
capitulation (noun)   World War II ended in 1945 with the *capitulation* of Germany and Japan.

15. **chaos** (noun)   kā'ŏs'

a state of total disorder or confusion

A power failure left the city in **chaos.**

In a single day, the five active children reduced the orderly room to **chaos.**

▶ *Related Word*
chaotic (adjective)   The quickly-called meeting was *chaotic.*

16. **defer** (verb)   dĭ-fûr'

to delay

Because of an earthquake in San Francisco, the 1989 World Series had to be **deferred** for a few weeks.

to show respect; to submit to the wishes of another

When boarding a bus, you should **defer** to elderly people by letting them on first.

I **deferred** to my father's wishes and attended college.

▶ *Common Phrase*
defer to

▶ *Related Words*
deference (noun)   (dĕf'ər-əns)   He showed his *deference* by bowing to the king. (*Deference* means "respect.")

deferential (adjective)   The lawyer was *deferential* to the judge.

17. **epitome** (noun)   ĭ-pĭt'ə-mē

the best example; the defining example; a symbol

Because of her unselfish work with poor people, Mother Teresa is considered the **epitome** of a modern-day saint.

▶ *Related Word*
epitomize (verb)   Rising 630 feet into the air, the graceful Gateway Arch has come to *epitomize* the city of St. Louis.

NOTE: The final *e* of *epitome* is pronounced.

An epitome can be fictional or real. The fictional comic book character Superman is the epitome of a superhero. Superman is able to fly, to bend steel with his bare hands, and to see through solid objects. He uses these abilities to battle criminals and to fight for truth and justice. However, if he is exposed to the fictional element Kryptonite, he loses his powers.

Real-life heros can also epitomize ideals. In South Africa, Nelson Mandela, who was imprisoned for over 30 years, epitomizes the struggle of blacks against apartheid. Anatole Sharansky, persecuted for his religious beliefs, is the epitome of the Jewish people's struggle to worship in the U.S.S.R.

18. **ludicrous** (adjective)   loo'dĭ-krəs

absurd; ridiculous; outrageous

It is **ludicrous** to suggest that a dog could fly.

The ten-year-old child looked **ludicrous** dressed up in her mother's clothing and wearing heavy make-up.

▶ *Related Word*

ludicrousness (noun)   The *ludicrousness* of the report that every American owned a Cadillac made us laugh.

19. **supplant** (verb) sə-plănt′

    to replace

    > In developed countries, the automobile has **supplanted** the horse as the most common means of transportation.

    > No other pet could ever **supplant** the girl's first puppy in her affections.

20. **thrive** (verb) thrīv

    to grow vigorously; to prosper

    > The hard work of its citizens has enabled Thailand's economy to **thrive**.

    > Our plants **thrived** when we gave them more sunlight.

    > Many athletes **thrive** on competition.

    The next four words—radical, liberal, conservative, and reactionary—refer to political opinions that range from left to right.

    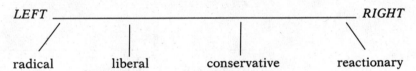

    LEFT _____ *RIGHT*

    radical   liberal   conservative   reactionary

    Radical and liberal politicians are called *left-wing* because they sat on the left side (or wing) of the semicircular seating of the French National Assembly of 1789. Other European assemblies have continued this custom. Radical politicians want swift reforms that will benefit poor people, minorities, and those without political power. Liberal politicians favor the extension of rights and privileges through gradual reform.

    Conservatives and reactionaries are spoken of as *right-wing* because they sat on the right wing of the French National Assembly. Conservative politicians favor tradition and oppose change. They want to protect business interests, religious rights, and the traditional family. Reactionary politicians oppose change so strongly that they often want to return to the way things used to be.

    Each of these words also has a nonpolitical meaning.

21. **radical** (adjective) răd′ĭ-kəl

    favoring great change; extreme

    > **Radical** opinion favors massive income redistribution.

    > China went through a **radical** social revolution during the 1950s and 1960s.

Robin tore down most of the walls in her house during the **radical** remodeling.

▶ *Related Word*
radical (noun)   The *radical* favored revolution. (*Radical* means a person holding radical beliefs.)

22. **liberal** (adjective)   lĭb′ər-əl

favoring gradual progress and reform

Liberal opinion favors providing unemployment support for those who have lost their jobs.

having liberty; free; not restrained

My parents' rules for curfew were **liberal,** and I could stay out later than my friends.

We ate **liberal** quantities of the delicious white chocolate.

▶ *Related Words*
liberal (noun)   The *liberal* voted for increased legal aid for the poor. (*Liberal* means a person holding liberal beliefs.)

liberalize (verb)   Students wanted to *liberalize* college rules to allow greater freedom on campus.

23. **conservative** (adjective)   kən-sûr′və-tĭv

favoring traditional beliefs and actions; traditional

The **conservative** senator favored prayer in schools.

Coming from a **conservative** background, the student had a hard time adjusting to the idea of women and men living together in dorms.

George's gold earring was a strange contrast to his **conservative** business suit.

cautious or moderate

Emanuel made the **conservative** choice of working as a bank teller rather than joining a rock group.

We gave a **conservative** estimate that there were twenty thousand people at the rally; there may have been more.

▶ *Related Words*
conservative (noun)   Senator Ruggles, a *conservative*, voted for policies that favored business owners rather than workers. (*Conservative* means a person holding conservative beliefs.)

conserve (verb)   It is important to *conserve* trees by recycling newspapers. (*Conserve* means "to save.")

24. **reactionary** (adjective)   rē-ăk′shə-nĕr′ē

opposing progress in an extreme way

> The **reactionary** politician wanted to separate boys from girls in all schools.

▶ *Related Word*
reactionary (noun) The *reactionary* wanted to take away the vote from eighteen-year-olds. (*Reactionary* means a person holding reactionary beliefs.)

NOTE: Reactionary usually has a negative connotation.

Exercises

Part 2

■ Matching Words and Definitions

Check your understanding of words in the news by matching each word with the letter of its definition. Use each choice only once.

1. thrive _____

2. capitulate _____

3. liberal _____

4. conservative _____

5. defer _____

6. reactionary _____

7. epitome _____

8. apprehend _____

9. supplant _____

10. radical _____

a. favoring gradual progress and reform

b. ridiculous

c. to replace

d. confusion

e. to grow

f. best example

g. favoring great change

h. to surrender

i. to understand

j. favoring traditional beliefs

k. to delay

l. opposing progress in an extreme way

■ Words in Context

Complete each sentence with the word that fits best. Use each choice only once.

a. apprehend   e. epitome   i. radical
b. capitulate   f. ludicrous j. liberal
c. chaos   g. supplant   k. conservative
d. defer   h. thrive   l. reactionary

1. The _____ person wanted to maintain a traditional family structure.

2. Joe Louis was the _____ of a great boxer.

3. The _____ was opposed to all progress.

4. It is _____ to believe that an ant could lift up an elephant.

5. There was _____ on the main street when all the traffic lights broke down.

6. This _____ proposal will change everything in our political system.

7. The defeated soldiers had to _____ to the victors.

8. Because snow blocked the road, we had to _____ our meeting until the next week.

9. Children usually _____ in a warm, loving home.

10. Compact disc players will soon _____ record players.

■ *Using Related Words*

Complete each sentence using a word from the group of related words above it. You may need to capitalize a word when you put it into a sentence. Use each choice only once.

1. apprehend, apprehended, apprehensive

Soon after he robbed a house, the man was _____

by the police. He was _____ about the possibility of going to jail for his crime. So, during his trial, he tried to

_____ all of the complex rules of the legal system.

2. deference, deferred, deferential

I filled out the wrong forms, and the university _____ my financial aid until the next semester. When I asked the dean

for help, I tried to treat her with _____ . My

_____ behavior made her happier to assist me.

3. liberalize, liberals

Many _____ feel that there is too much censorship of books in the United States. They would like to

_____ government policies to permit more freedom of expression.

4. conserve, conservatives

Political _____ often feel that it is important to provide opportunities for business. They state that while it is

important to _____ forest land and the wilderness, it is also economically important for the oil and forestry industries to develop.

■ *Reading the Headlines*

This exercise presents five headlines that might have been taken from newspapers. Read each headline and then answer the questions that follow. (Remember that small words such as *a* and *the* are often left out of newspaper headlines.)

LUDICROUS MOVIE IS THE EPITOME OF BAD TASTE

1. Is the movie silly? _____

2. Is the movie an example of good taste? _____

CHAOS RESULTS WHEN POLICE TRY TO APPREHEND CRIMINAL

3. Is the situation calm? _____

4. Are the police trying to catch the criminal? _____

REACTIONARIES CAPITULATE AND ALLOW VOTING REFORM

5. Do reactionaries favor progress and reform? _____

6. Have the reactionaries won? _____

LIBERALS SUPPLANT RADICALS IN PARLIAMENT

7. Are liberals taking the places of radicals? _____

8. Do radicals want fewer changes than liberals? _____

LAWS PUT FORWARD BY CONSERVATIVES THRIVE IN SENATE

9. Do the people putting forward the laws want great changes

in the structure of society? _____

10. In general, are senators voting to pass the laws? _____

Chapter Exercises

■ *Practicing Strategies: Context Clues of Substitution*

In each of the following sentences one difficult word is italicized. Using context clues of substitution, make an intelligent guess at the meaning of the word as it is used in this sentence. Your instructor may ask you to look up these words in your dictionary after you've finished the exercise.

1. The crowd regarded the hero with *veneration*.

   Veneration means _____ .

2. There is much wisdom in the *apothegm* "Lost time is never found again."

   Apothegm means _____ .

3. The town hall was a large and beautiful *edifice*.

   Edifice means _____ .

4. Injuries to their two best players had a *deleterious* effect on the football team.

   Deleterious means _____ .

5. The road was *truncated* when several miles were closed down.

   Truncated means _____ .

6. The *parsimonious* millionaire bought a cheap used car.

   Parsimonious means _____ .

7. Antonio made a *grievous* error on the exam, which lowered his grade from an A to a D.

   Grievous means _____ .

8. Eating fruits and vegetables, visiting the doctor regularly, and exercising have a *salubrious* effect.

   Salubrious means _____ .

9. The desert is a *desiccated* place where few plants and animals can obtain water.

   Desiccated means _____ .

10. The painting glowed with soft *hues* of blue and green.

    Hues mean _____ .

■ *Practicing Strategies: New Uses of Familiar Words in Context*

Context clues can often help you determine the meaning of words used in unusual ways. Make an intelligent guess at the meaning of the italicized word or phrase in each of the following sentences.

1. Neslihan wanted to *air* her opinions in public.

   Air means _____ .

2. He couldn't vote since he was a few months *shy of* eighteen.

   Shy of means _____ .

3. After spending the day at the library, they *repaired* to the restaurant.

   Repaired means _____ .

4. President Jackson was alone *save* for a few friends.

   Save means _____ .

5. In her anger, she *stormed* out of the room.

   Stormed means _____ .

■ Companion Words

Complete each sentence with the word that fits best. Choose your answers from the words below. You may use each word more than once.

Choices: to, with, on, of, in, myself, by

1. Wars _____ attrition are difficult to fight.

2. We hope never to be subjugated _____ our enemy.

3. Nobody dared to intervene _____ the fistfight.

4. Occasionally, I like to indulge _____ an expensive meal.

5. I like to indulge _____ by taking bubble baths.

6. I defer _____ my superiors.

7. The defeated rebels capitulated _____ the army.

8. I am in accord _____ your views.

9. Monica thrived _____ healthy food.

10. Chi Chi Rodriguez is the epitome _____ a fine golfer.

■ Writing with Your Words

This exercise will give you practice in writing effective sentences using the vocabulary words. Each sentence is started for you. Complete it with an interesting phrase that also indicates the meaning of the italicized word.

1. A *bureaucracy* _____

   _____ .

2. *Chaos* would erupt if _____

_____ .

3. A person might *intervene* in _____

_____ .

4. An example of a *ludicrous* statement is _____

_____ .

5. I would favor a *radical* change in _____

_____ .

6. People in a *subjugated* country _____

_____ .

7. I am in *accord* with the government on _____

_____ .

8. I cannot *apprehend* how _____

_____ .

9. People often *indulge* themselves by _____

_____ .

10. Two things a *conservative* might favor are _____

_____ .

Passage

How Advertising Persuades Us

Advertising, the art of persuading **consumers** to buy products, has become a multibillion-dollar business in America. Every day the **media** carry thousands of advertisements.

One of the most important goals of advertising is the development of brand loyalty. Advertisers try to make consumers loyal to one type of soap, cigarettes, or other product, despite the fact that the advertised brand may be no different from another brand. **(1)** Advertisers also try to persuade consumers not to allow any other product to **supplant** their favorite brand. If the local store runs out of "Silly Soap" or "Chummy Cigarettes," advertisers hope that people will actually **defer** making a purchase.

Cigarettes are an excellent example of how brand loyalty is developed. Advertisers try to give each brand of cigarettes a different personality. **(2)** For instance, the Virginia Slims cigarette advertisement has come to **epitomize** one popular, if simplified, view of a liberated woman. A corner of the advertisement shows a woman of the early 1900s being **subjugated** by a group of **reactionary** men. **(3) Chaos** has erupted, for they have **apprehended** her in the act of daring to smoke! In the center of the page, a confident modern woman is displayed with a Virginia Slims cigarette in her hand. The caption reads: "You've come a long way, baby!"

In contrast, Marlboro cigarettes have a male image, appealing to men who would never be seen with a Virginia Slims. The "Marlboro Man" scorns an easy lifestyle, preferring to put on his boots and cowboy hat and ride his horse into the wilderness. The only luxury he **indulges** in is, of course, a pack of Marlboro cigarettes.

A foreign-sounding name can add glamour to a product. Häagen Dazs ice cream, which sounds as if it comes from Sweden, was actually first manufactured in New York City.

Sometimes advertisers try to change the image of an entire product rather than a specific brand. An example of this is the prune. Sales in the prune industry had been declining for many years before producers sought the help of market researchers. **(4)** A survey revealed that people's image of the prune was a marketing **catastrophe.** Some people associated it with boarding-house food, others with medicine. Still others reported that the black color of the prune reminded them of witchcraft. **(5)** Advertisers needed to change this image **radically. (6)** Suddenly ads appeared showing the prune as a healthy, delicious, candy-like dessert, best eaten in **liberal** quantities. Beautiful women and athletic youngsters sang the virtues of the pretty prune. Slogans cried out: "Prunes help bring a glow to your face." In recent years the raisin industry has improved its product's image by featuring animated raisins that dance to the popular tune "I Heard It Through the Grapevine."

Sports figures can be used to advertise products. Bo Jackson, professional baseball and football player, advertises Nike sneakers; football player Joe Montana appears in L.A. Gear commercials. In Right Guard deodorant commercials, **(7)** famous figures appear in humorous, "high-class" situations using language that sounds **ludicrously** formal in the sports world. Wrestler Hulk Hogan, for example, paints a picture on a seashore while declaring "It is inappropriate to be odoriferous" (It is not good to smell). In another Right Guard commercial, an athlete is attended by a butler. Sometimes a sports figure's name is used to sell a product. **(8)** McDonalds hopes that the name McJordan (for basketball player Michael Jordan) will help sandwich sales to **thrive**. **(9)** To appeal to a more **conservative,** family-oriented audience, mothers of athletes can now be seen in commercials.

(10) A recent **entrepreneurial** trend is the placement of products in movies. Businesses pay thousands of dollars to have their products appear, hoping that the public will want to purchase what they see the actors using. Product placement apparently works well. It is reported that, after the creature-hero in *E.T.* enjoyed the candy Reese's Pieces on screen, sales increased more than sixty percent in real life. Similarly, when Tom Cruise wore Wayfarer sunglasses in *Risky Business* and the Aviator model in *Top Gun,* sales soared. Product placement continues in movies of the 1990s. In *Teenage Mutant Ninja Turtles,* the four turtle heros ordered a Domino's Pizza—and got, true to policy, a discount when it was delivered late!

■ *Exercise*

Each numbered sentence below corresponds to a sentence in the Passage. Fill in the letter of the choice that makes the sentence mean the same thing as its corresponding sentence in the Passage.

1. Advertisers try to persuade consumers not to allow any other prod-

    uct to _____ their favorite brand.
    a. cheapen   b. outsell   c. replace   d. harm

2. The Virginia Slims cigarette advertisement has come to _____ one popular, if simplified, view of a liberated woman.
    a. help   b. replace   c. fight   d. symbolize

3. _____ has erupted.
    a. Horror   b. Truth   c. Warfare   d. Disorder

4. The image of the prune was a(n) _____.
    a. help   b. lesson   c. reality   d. disaster

5. Advertisers needed to change this image _____ .
    a. in a slight way
    b. in a positive way
    c. in an extreme way
    d. in a healthy way

6. Ads showed the prune as a healthy dessert, best eaten in _____ quantities.
   a. large   b. small   c. medium   d. limited

7. Famous figures use language that sounds _____ formal.
   a. wonderfully   b. very   c. ridiculously   d. stupidly

8. McDonalds hopes the name McJordan will help sales to _____ .
   a. begin   b. grow   c. fall   d. stop

9. To appeal to a _____ audience, mothers of athletes can be seen in commercials.
   a. friendly   b. traditional   c. intelligent   d. changing

10. A more recent _____ trend is the placement of advertisements in movies.
    a. healthy   b. business   c. illegal   d. research

■ Discussion Questions

1. What image are advertisers trying to give to the prune?

2. Do you think the cigarette ads described contain stereotypes of males and females? Defend your answer.

3. Describe a current advertisement, including in your description the emotions it appeals to.

3

Words for Feeling, Expression, and Action

Have you ever *cogitated* over a difficult decision, heard the roars of a *boisterous* crowd, or seen a person *goad* a rival into a fight? English has many vivid words we can use to describe how we feel, how we express ourselves, and how we act. This chapter will present words that you can use to describe your own behavior and the thoughts and actions of others.

Chapter Strategy: Context Clues of Definition

Chapter Words:

Part 1

bland	confrontation	enigma
boisterous	contend	goad
clarify	elated	skeptical
concise	emphatic	thwart

Part 2

appall	cogitate	flaunt
articulate	condemn	harass
belligerent	counsel	prohibit
chagrin	elicit	undermine

Did You Know?

How Do Cars Get Their Names?

The process of naming cars shows how expression, feeling, and action can relate to each other. A car's name is an important part of its image. Every year, in Detroit and other centers of car production, auto makers spend millions of dollars researching car names that will appeal to the customer. By using words that express speed, power, or glamour, manufacturers hope to give you positive feelings about their cars. These feelings translate into actions when you decide to buy one. Larger cars get names that suggest powerful images:

Grand Prix refers to a series of international sports car competitions held in several European countries.

El Dorado is Spanish for "the Land of Gold." European explorers searched in the Americas for El Dorado, a city said to be so rich that its ruler coated his body with gold.

Thunderbird was, according to Native American legend, a birdlike god of storm that caused thunder by flapping its wings and lightning by blinking its eyes.

Royalty and titles are also suggested.

Dodge *Dynasty*—a set of kings from one family.

Mercury *Grand Marquis* and Chrysler *Le Baron*—"marquis" and "baron" are French titles of nobility.

Ford *Crown Victoria*—named after Victoria, the famous queen of Great Britain (England) in the 1800s.

Expensive cars named for animals often suggest speed or fierceness.

Jaguar
Mercury *Cougar*

However, less expensive, smaller cars suggest smaller or younger animals.

Plymouth *Colt*
Volkswagen *Fox*

Astrological signs have also made an appearance.

Ford *Taurus*—the sign of the bull.
Dodge *Aries*—the sign of the ram.

Names of famous and romantic places are often used for cars.

Chrysler *New Yorker*
Dodge *Monaco*—a small European country famous for gambling.
Mercury *Capri*—an island in the south of Italy.

Other names gives images of combat.

Buick *LeSabre*—French for "the sword."
Dodge *Cutlass*—the curved sword used by pirates.
Dodge and Plymouth *Conquest*—to overcome by force.

As small cars have become more popular, their names have also come to suggest speed and excitement.

Chevrolet *Sprint*—a short, fast run.
Isuzu *Impulse*—something done "on impulse" is done quickly.

Recently, more car names suggest harmony and friendship.

Honda *Accord*—agreement.
Isuzu *Amigo*—Spanish for friend.
Ford *Escort*
Suzuki *Sidekick*

Perhaps reflecting the age of high-technology, many new luxury cars have letters and numbers in their names.

Mitsibushi 3000GTS
Accura NSX
Audi 5000 Turbo Quattro
Nissan 300 ZX

Car manufacturers think long and hard before they assign a name to a new product. Most names are designed to create an image—and thus to increase car sales.

Learning Strategy

Context Clues of Definition

The learning strategy in this chapter will focus on *context clues of definition*. Often words that you don't know will actually be defined for you as they are used in sentences. Sometimes a sentence provides a *syno-*

nym (a word that means nearly the same thing) for the unknown word. For example, look at the word *effervescent* as it is used in a sentence.

Coca-Cola is an *effervescent,* or bubbly, beverage.

The word *effervescent* means? . . . bubbly. Thus, *bubbly* is a synonym for effervescent.

Clues of definition are quite easy to use if you can recognize them. These clues include

1. Words set off by commas, dashes, or parentheses:

    The man's altruistic, *unselfish,* motives caused him to donate money to charity.

    The man's altruistic — *unselfish* — motives caused him to donate money to charity.

    The man's altruistic *(unselfish)* motives caused him to donate money to charity.

2. Direct definition:

    She thought his motives were altruistic, *which means unselfish.*

    She thought his motives were altruistic, *that is to say, unselfish.*

3. Indirect definition:

    He was an altruistic person *who often acted out of unselfish motives.*

4. The use of *or* and *and:*

    The man's altruistic, *or unselfish,* motives pleased his family. (The use of commas with *or* is an extra hint signaling that a context clue of definition is being used.)

    The man's altruistic *and unselfish* motives pleased his family. (Sometimes words joined by *and* and *or* do not mean the same thing. Examples are: "The man was lazy and dishonest." and "People shouldn't be lazy or dishonest.")

5. Words signaling agreement, such as *therefore, likewise, in the same way, as well as,* and *similarly:*

    The man was altruistic; *therefore he donated money to charity and did volunteer work with children.*

As you can see, the word *altruistic,* which you learned in Chapter 1, has been defined in each sentence. Many sentences gave the synonym *unselfish.* Others gave a longer definition through examples, such as *donated money to charity and did volunteer work with children.*

Three more examples of context clues of definition are given on the following page. Can you make an intelligent guess about the meaning of each italicized word?

1. The margin of the leaf was *sinuated*, and indented curves ran along the edge. (An *and* clue is used.)

2. We used *tricot*, a heavy knitted cloth, to make a jacket. (A phrase is set off in commas.)

3. Women were granted *suffrage* rights in 1920. Similarly, voting privileges were extended to eighteen-, nineteen-, and twenty-year-olds in 1975. (A work signaling agreement is used.)

(*Answers:*   1. having indented curves 2. a heavy knitted cloth 3. voting)

Now try using context clues to figure out the meanings of some words you will be learning in this chapter.

1. The French philosopher Pascal was a *skeptical* thinker who doubted many accepted beliefs. (An indirect definition clue is used.)

Skeptical means _____ .

2. Because we couldn't understand the concept, we asked the professor to *clarify* it, or make it easier to understand. (An *or* clue is used.)

Clarify means _____ .

3. The great actor *elicited* laughter from the audience, as well as bringing forth tears. (Words signaling agreement are used.)

Elicit means _____ .

(*Answers:*   1. doubting 2. to make clear 3. to bring forth)

Words to Learn

Part 1

1. **bland** (adjective)   blănd

nonirritating

> The governor's **bland** responses calmed the angry crowd.
>
> Doctors may recommend a **bland** diet for a person with an ulcer.

dull

> The speech was so **bland** that I fell asleep.

2. **boisterous** (adjective)   boi'stər-əs

noisy; rowdy; rough

> The party became so **boisterous** that the neighbors called the police.

► *Related Word*
   boisterousness (noun)   Because of the audience's *boisterousness*, it was difficult to hear the music.

3. **clarify** (verb)   klăr'ə-fī'

to make clear or sensible

> We asked the teacher to **clarify** her expectations for the paper.

► *Related Word*
   clarification (noun) Reporters asked for *clarification* of the prime minister's statement.

4. **concise** (adjective)   kən-sīs'

short; clear but using few words

> Most students prefer a **concise** definition of a word to a more lengthy one.

The history of the word *concise* shows how action words can come to describe expressions. *Concise* comes from the Latin verb *considere*, which means "to cut up." When a cloth or ribbon is cut, it is made shorter. In the same way, the action of cutting was used as a figure of speech to describe the shortening of speech or writing.

---

5. **confrontation** (noun)   kŏn'frŭn-tā'shən

hostile meeting; direct fight

> Although he knew his mother did not approve of his lifestyle, he tried to avoid a direct **confrontation** on the subject.

> Many teenagers were injured in the **confrontation** of the two gangs.

► *Related Word*
   confront (verb) (kə-frŭnt') A strong person is able to *confront* obstacles. (*Confront* means "to meet.")

6. **contend** (verb)   kən-těnd**'**

to fight; to compete

> Greeks from Sparta, Athens, and many other cities **contended** in the ancient Olympic games.

to put forth a point of view

> When Lucy **contended** that women were more intelligent than men, her boyfriend became angry.

▶ *Related Words*
  contender (noun, person)   The athlete was a *contender* in the race.
  contention (noun)   Jason's *contention* was that men were smarter than women.
  contentious (adjective)   A *contentious* person often starts fights.

NOTE: The phrase *contend with* means "to cope with." Effie had to *contend with* a class of naughty children.

7. **elated** (adjective)   ĭ-lāt**'**əd

thrilled; very happy

> Michael was **elated** when he won the twenty-million dollar lottery.

8. **emphatic** (adjective)   ĕm-făt**'**ĭk

strong; definite; done with emphasis

> My father was so **emphatic** in his refusal that I didn't dare to ask again.

> The Los Angeles Dodgers scored an **emphatic** victory over the Chicago Cubs.

▶ *Related Word*
  emphasis (noun)   The employer placed great *emphasis* on promptness.

9. **enigma** (noun)   ĭ-nĭg**'**mə

something unexplainable or puzzling

> For centuries, scientists have been trying to solve the **enigma** of the universe's origin.

> Leroy was an **enigma** to us. He claimed that he wanted a job, but he was always turning down good opportunities.

▶ *Related Word*
enigmatic (adjective)   We couldn't explain Alma's *enigmatic* behavior.

According to Greek myth, the Sphinx was a winged monster with a human head and the body of a lion. It stopped travelers and asked them to solve riddles. Those unfortunates who could not answer correctly were killed. People who guard their secrets as carefully as the Sphinx kept the answers to its enigmas are often said to be *sphinx-like*. A stone statue of the Sphinx can be seen beside the Egyptian pyramids.

---

10. **goad** (verb)   gōd

to urge strongly; to excite

The gang members **goaded** their rivals into starting a fight.

The cheerleader **goaded** her team on by shouting, "Win, win, win!"

▶ *Common Phrases*
to goad into
to goad on

11. **skeptical** (adjective)   skĕp′tĭ-kəl

doubting; tending to disbelieve

The jury members were **skeptical** of the witness's truthfulness.

Skeptical people make good scientists because they demand proof for everything.

▶ *Common Phrase*
skeptical of

▶ *Related Words*
skeptic (noun)   The *skeptic* asked for proof of each statement.
skepticism (noun)   Dimitri's *skepticism* made him doubtful.

12. **thwart** (verb)   thwôrt

to prevent from happening

The guards **thwarted** the prisoner's plans to escape.

Mickey's efforts to score in the basketball game were **thwarted** by an alert guard.

Poverty can **thwart** a student's wish to finish college.

Exercises

Part 1

■ Definitions

The following sentences deal with feelings, thoughts, and expressions. Complete each statement by choosing the letter of a word or phrase from the right-hand column. Use each choice only once.

1. A confrontation is a _____ .

2. A bland story is _____ .

3. A concise expression is

   _____ .

4. Elated is _____ .

5. To thwart is to _____ .

6. An enigma is a _____ .

7. To goad is to _____ .

8. An emphatic statement is

   _____ .

9. To contend is to _____ .

10. If we feel skeptical, we are

    _____ .

a. dull

b. hostile meeting

c. doubtful

d. compete; put forth a point of view

e. puzzle

f. noisy

g. make clear

h. thrilled; very happy

i. prevent from happening

j. short

k. excite

l. definite; strong

■ Words in Context

Complete each sentence with the word that fits best. Use each choice only once.

a. bland   e. confrontation   i. enigma
b. boisterous   f. contend   j. goad
c. clarify   g. elated   k. skeptical
d. concise   h. emphatic   l. thwart

1. The _____ report she gave took only three minutes.

2. If you tell my mother about the party, you will _____ our plans to surprise her.

3. Perry's directions to the house were confusing, so we asked him to

   _____ them.

4. I was _____ to find that I was named employee of the year.

5. I am _____ of her claims that she can see through walls.

6. The _____ soccer fans shouted loudly at the players when they lost the game.

7. The coach tried to _____ the boy into running faster by shouting "Get a move on!"

8. The _____ of the two enemies resulted in a fist fight.

9. Ishmael had a _____ manner and never became excited.

10. The cause of the many mysterious disappearances that have taken

    place in the Bermuda Triangle remains a(n) _____ .

■ Using Related Words

Complete each sentence using a word from the group of related words above it. You may need to capitalize a word when you put it into a sentence. Use each choice only once.

1. contended, contender, contention, contentious

   Jesse Owens, the great black athlete, _____ in the Olympic Games of 1936. These games, held in Germany, were attended by the racist leader, Adolph Hitler. It was Hitler's

   _____ that the white "Aryan" race was superior

   to all others, and that no black _____ could win. However, Owens took two gold medals in the 50-yard dash. Hitler was so _____ that he refused to attend the award ceremonies. Owens, who died in 1978, remains a symbol of the black athlete's struggle for equality.

2. enigma, enigmatic

In 1591, Englishmen returning to the new colony of Roanoke, Virginia, found that everyone had vanished. Their disappearance was

an _____. The initials "CRO" carved into a door-

post was the only clue to their _____ disappearance. Were they killed? Did they wander away? To this day, no one knows.

3. clarify, clarification
The student asked for _____ of the math problem. Realizing that it was unclear to many of people in his class,

the professor was happy to _____ it.

4. emphatic, emphatically

Baseball umpires' calls must be _____ so that the public can understand them. Calls that are not

_____ made may not be clear to a large crowd. Therefore, umpires make gestures to indicate their calls.

■ *True or False?*

Each of the following statements uses at least one word from this section. Read each statement and then indicate whether you think it is probably true or probably false.

_____   1. Boisterous laughter is soft.

_____   2. It is wise to goad your friends into insulting policemen.

_____   3. Emphatic views are stated in a weak manner.

_____   4. A confrontation is usually pleasant.

_____   5. Chili peppers are a bland tasting food.

_____   6. Shouting and crying helps to clarify our thinking.

_____   7. A concise statement is short.

_____   8. An enigma puzzles people.

_____   9. You would be elated if your plans for a vacation were thwarted.

_____   10. We would be skeptical of the contention that the earth is flat.

Words to Learn

Part 2

13. **appall** (verb)   ə-pôl′

    to fill with horror, dismay, or shock

    > The prospect of nuclear war **appalls** me.
    > The writer was **appalled** by his niece's bad grammar.

    ▶ *Related Word*
    appalling (adjective) The starvation in Ethiopia is *appalling*.

    NOTE: Appall can refer to very serious matters, like murder or starvation, or simply annoying things, like manners.

    The word *appall*, which is now used to describe feelings, is derived from an action word. In Latin the word *pallere* means "to become pale." It was thought that an appalled person grew pale as shock or horror decreased the blood supply to the face.

    ---

14. **articulate** (adjective)   är-tĭk′yə-lĭt; (verb)   är-tĭk′-yə-lāt′

    skilled in using language; clearly and well expressed (adjective)

    > An **articulate** person often has a well-developed vocabulary.
    > The candidate's **articulate** speech persuaded us to vote for her.

    to express clearly and distinctly (verb)

    > Jose **articulated** his reasons for a raise so well that his boss gave him one immediately.
    > The singer **articulated** the words so that we could understand each one.

▶ *Related Word*
   articulation (noun)   Francoby proposed marriage after he gave *articulation* to his feelings of love.

15. **belligerent** (adjective)   bə-lĭj′ər-ənt

hostile; engaged in warfare

> The two **belligerent** countries bombed each other's territory.
>
> The **belligerent** students marched into the office of the university president and demanded lower tuition.

▶ *Related Word*
   belligerence (noun) The gangster's *belligerence* frightened the people in the neighborhood.

Belligerent comes from the Latin words *bellum*, "war" and *gerere*, "to carry on." *Bellum* is also the root of the word *rebellion*, a war waged against a ruling power. The United States gained its independence in a rebellion against Great Britain that lasted from 1775 to 1783.

---

16. **chagrin** (noun)   shə-grĭn′

embarrassment or humiliation caused by failure or disappointment

> I was **chagrined** when the professor called my carefully done assignment "a sloppy job."
>
> To my **chagrin,** my children spilled tomato juice on a neighbor's carpet.
>
> To Jodi's **chagrin,** at her sixteenth birthday party, her mother showed everyone her baby pictures.

17. **cogitate** (verb)   kŏj′ə-tāt′

to think deeply about; to ponder

> Shakespeare's hero, Hamlet, **cogitated** for too long before taking action.
>
> The philosopher **cogitated** over the meaning of life.

▶ *Related Words*
   cogitation (noun) Rodin's statue *The Thinker* shows a man deep in *cogitation*.

   cogitative (adjective) Hamlet's *cogitative* nature caused him to delay action.

18. **condemn** (verb) kən-dĕm′

to express strong disapproval of

> The candidate **condemned** his opponent for not supporting the rights of the people in his district.
>
> Pit bull terriers have been **condemned** for their viciousness.

to give a punishment; to find guilty

> The judge **condemned** the dishonest stockbroker to five years in prison.

▶ *Common Phrase*
condemn to

▶ *Related Word*
condemnation (noun) The lawyer issued a *condemnation* of the decision to return the child to abusive parents.

19. **counsel** (noun, verb) koun′səl

advice; guidance (noun)

> She sought the **counsel** of her advisor when she planned her school program.

to advise (verb)

> When you are in school, people **counsel** you to study hard.

NOTE: Do not confuse *counsel* (advice) with *council* (a group of officials).

▶ *Related Word*
counselor (noun) The marriage *counselor* helped the couple.

20. **elicit** (verb) ĭ-lĭs′ĭt

to draw forth (a response)

> The hilarious acts on "In Living Color" **elicited** laughter from the TV audience.
>
> Mouth-to-mouth resuscitation finally **elicited** a response from the child who had stopped breathing.

▶ *Related Word*
elicitation (noun) The *elicitation* of laughter requires skill.

21. **flaunt** (verb) flônt

to display obviously or showily

The heiress **flaunted** her wealth by wearing expensive jewelry and employing a driver.

NOTE: Be careful not to confuse *flaunt* (to display) with *flout* (to disregard or ignore).

22. **harass** (verb)   hə-răs'

to annoy or attack repeatedly

The class bully **harassed** the guys he knew wouldn't fight back.

▶ *Related Word*
harassment (noun) The police stopped the gang's *harassment* of elderly citizens.

Harass comes from the Old French *"Hare!"*—a command telling a dog to "Get it!" This cry was used in hunting, a traditional sport of nobles and rich landowners. Hunters set out on horseback with their dogs, who followed the scent (smell) of foxes. When the nobles finally saw the fox, they ordered "Hare!" and the dogs chased the fox.

---

23. **prohibit** (verb)   prō-hĭb'ĭt

to forbid

Cars are **prohibited** on sidewalks.

My mother **prohibited** my sister from dating until she reached eighteen.

▶ *Common Phase*
prohibit (someone) from

▶ *Related Word*
prohibition (noun) The city issued a *prohibition* against smoking in elevators.

You may have read about the Prohibition Era in the United States. In 1919, a constitutional amendment prohibited people from making, selling, or drinking alcoholic beverages. Prohibition did not succeed in its aims. In fact, drinking became more fashionable than ever. As shown in the photo, people found many ways to hide liquor. Realizing that the law was a failure, Congress repealed Prohibition in 1933.

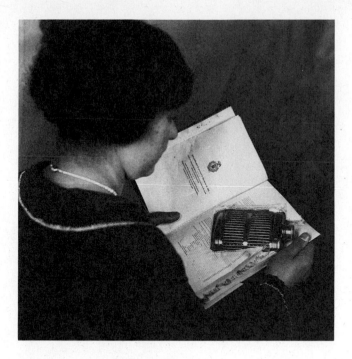

24. **undermine** (verb) un'dər-mīn'

to weaken or injure slowly

> Smoking tends to **undermine** a person's health.
>
> Our competitor **undermined** our reputation by spreading vicious rumors.

NOTE: Often *undermine* refers to a secret or hidden activity: The spy *undermined* the security of his nation by selling scientific information to the enemy.

Exercises

Part 2

■ *Definitions*

The following sentences deal with feelings, thoughts, and expressions. Complete each statement by choosing the letter of a word or phrase from the right-hand column. Use each choice only once.

1. To feel chagrin is to feel _____ .

2. To prohibit is to _____ .

3. When we elicit a response, we

   _____ .

4. To harass is to _____ .

5. Articulate people are _____ .

6. To cogitate is to _____ .

7. To appall is to _____ .

8. A belligerent person is _____ .

9. To condemn is to _____ .

10. Counsel is _____ .

a. weaken

b. hostile

c. annoy repeatedly

d. think

e. advice

f. fill with shock

g. draw it forth

h. express disapproval

i. forbid

j. skilled in using language

k. display obviously

l. embarrassment

■ Words in Context

Complete each sentence with the word that fits best. Use each choice only once.

a. appall   e. cogitate   i. flaunt
b. articulate   f. condemn   j. harass
c. belligerent   g. counsel   k. prohibit
d. chagrin   h. elicit   l. undermine

1. Because Maria was so _____, she was often asked to give speeches.

2. To my _____, I spilled coffee on my boyfriend's mother.

3. Do not _____ people until you are sure that they have acted wrongly.

4. Laws _____ drivers from drinking too much liquor.

5. The _____ teenagers threatened to start a fight.

6. Dogs often _____ cats by chasing and barking at them.

7. The tennis player tried to _____ his opponent's confidence by insulting him during the game.

8. The other students became jealous when the girl began to

_____ her good grades.

9. Many people seek the _____ of their relatives and friends before making an important decision.

10. A tragic play may _____ an audience's tears.

■ *Using Related Words*

Complete each sentence using a word from the group of related words above it. You may need to capitalize a word when you put it into a sentence. Use each choice only once.

1. elicit, elicitation

Telethons try to _____ donations for worthy causes, such as research to cure disease. Recently, many telethons have raised money to fight Acquired Immune Deficiency Syn-

drome (AIDS). The _____ of funds is often made easier when people suffering from AIDS appear on the telethons to talk about their pain and distress.

2. cogitate, cogitation

Students often _____ for a long time before planning their education after high school. Options include a college, business school, or technical institute. Only after much

_____ can students make choices with which they will be comfortable.

3. condemned, condemnation

The U.S. Senate _____ one senator for taking bribes. After a thorough investigation, the Senate issued a formal

_____ .

4. prohibition, prohibit

The durian, an unusual fruit, is popular in Thailand. Although its taste is wonderful, its terrible smell reminds people of garbage. Because of the odor, some hotels and airlines

_____ the fruit. However, this _____ has not affected the popularity of the delicious, but strange-smelling food.

5. undermining, undermine

Pollution from car exhaust is _____ air quality and causing smog in places like Los Angeles and Mexico City. Because these two cities are located in valleys, car emissions become trapped. Since poor air quality can seriously

_____ health, efforts are being made to build more public transportation in Los Angeles and to limit car use in Mexico City.

■ *True or False?*

Each of the following sentences uses at least one word from this section. Read each statement and then indicate whether you think it is probably true or probably false.

____ 1. A disabled child usually elicits sympathy from adults.

____ 2. People enjoy being harassed.

____ 3. You usually make a quick decision when you cogitate.

____ 4. People would be likely to condemn you for stealing from your mother.

____ 5. You would be chagrined if your little brother told all of your family secrets to the neighbors.

____ 6. If you flaunt a diamond ring, people will not notice it.

____ 7. The sale of dangerous medicines should be prohibited.

____ 8. A belligerent person would be likely to start a fight.

____ 9. We would be appalled by an articulate person expressing himself badly.

____ 10. When you give good counsel, you undermine those who ask for your opinion.

Chapter Exercises

■ *Practicing Strategies: Context Clues of Definition*

In each of the following sentences a difficult word is italicized. Using context clues of definition, make an intelligent guess at the meaning of the word as it is used in this sentence. Your instructor may ask you to look up these words in your dictionary after you have finished the exercise.

1. The child's *dyslexia*—serious reading disorder—was being investigated by a team of psychologists and teachers.

   Dyslexia means _____ .

2. The plans were *clandestine*, and almost no one knew about them.

   Clandestine means _____ .

3. The two close friends held a *tête-à-tête*, that is to say, a private conversation.

   Tête-à-tête means _____ .

4. Ira was a *buffoon* in class, as well as being a person who was always trying to amuse people at home.

   Buffoon means _____ .

5. Carlos was *cognizant* of the responsibilities he was accepting, for he had been made aware of them beforehand.

   Cognizant means _____ .

6. President Calvin Coolidge was a *taciturn* person who seldom talked to others.

   Taciturn means _____ .

7. The judge showed *clemency* to criminals and treated them with mercy.

   Clemency means _____ .

8. The *vestige*, or small remaining part, of the fossil revealed the impression of a bird's wing.

   Vestige means _____ .

9. He *prevaricated*, which, put more plainly, means he lied.

   Prevaricated means _____ .

10. They feared they might get *embroiled*, or involved, in another country's politics.

   Embroiled means _____ .

■ *Practicing Strategies: Using the Dictionary*

Read the following definition. Then answer the questions below it.

> **faint** (fānt) *adj.* **-er, -est.** **1.** Lacking strength or vigor; feeble. **2.** Lacking conviction, boldness, or courage; timid. **3.** Lacking clarity and brightness; dim; *a faint recollection.* **4.** Likely to fall into a faint; dizzy and weak: *felt faint.* —*n.* An abrupt, usually brief loss of consciousness, generally associated with failure of normal blood circulation. —*intr. v.* **faint-ed, faint-ing, faints.** **1.** To fall into a faint. **2.** *Archaic.* To weaken in purpose or spirit; languish. (ME < OFr., p. part. of *faindre,* to feign. —see FEIGN.) —**faint′er** *n.* —**faint′ly** *adv.*

1. What three parts of speech does *faint* function as?

   _____

2. In what language was *faint* first recorded? _____

3. Give the number and the part of speech of the definition that is no

   longer in use. _____

4. Give the number and the part of speech that best fits in this sentence:

   The bulb cast a faint light. _____

5. Give the number and the part of speech which best fits in this sentence: I fainted after I received the shocking news.

   _____

■ Companion Words

Complete each sentence with the word that fits best. Choose your answers from the words below. You may use each word more than once.

Choices: to, of, by, into, over, from

1. The public was appalled _____ the negative campaign ads.

2. We cogitated _____ that decision for a long time.

3. People are prohibited _____ eating in the theater.

4. I am skeptical _____ the wisdom of your decision.

5. He undermined his health _____ eating junk food.

6. You don't need to goad me _____ working harder.

7. Our plans for the picnic were thwarted _____ rain.

8. We asked for clarification _____ the assignment.

9. Many great artists were condemned _____ lives of poverty.

■ Writing with Your Words

This exercise will give you practice in writing effective sentences using the vocabulary words. Each sentence is started for you. Complete it with an interesting phrase that also indicates the meaning of the italicized word.

1. An *articulate* person _____

_____.

2. I would be *elated* if _____

_____.

3. My plans for getting a good job would be *thwarted* if _____

_____.

4. If someone *harassed* me, I would _____

_____.

5. It is *appalling* that _____

_____ .

6. I would feel *chagrin* if _____

_____ .

7. Most people would *condemn* a person who _____

_____ .

8. I am *skeptical* that _____

_____ .

9. I would *counsel* a fourteen-year-old to _____

_____ .

10. One way to *elicit* laughter is _____

_____ .

Passage

Jackie Robinson, Baseball Hero

Forty years ago, a quiet man became a pioneer of baseball history. In 1947, Jackie Robinson was the first black ever to play major league baseball. He bravely faced **appalling** persecution **(1)** and helped to **undermine** racial prejudice in America. Jackie Robinson "broke the color line."

Before Robinson signed with the Brooklyn Dodgers, blacks had been **prohibited** from playing in major-league baseball. Although many black players were as good as, or better than, white major league players, blacks were **condemned** to receive no national attention.

(2) When the Dodgers' management decided to sign Robinson, they issued a purposely **bland** announcement: "The Brooklyn Dodgers today purchased the contract of Jackie Roosevelt Robinson from the Montreal Royals." The baseball world reacted strongly. Some applauded the move to end discrimination. Others predicted disaster. How could a black succeed in white baseball? Some critics **contended** that Robinson would never be able to live peacefully with white teammates. Others felt that insulting fans would **goad** him into starting fights. **(3)** Still others were **skeptical** of Robinson's ability as a baseball player.

All the doubters were wrong.

(4) The Dodgers' manager, Branch Rickey, had **cogitated** over the problem before making his choice. **(5)** Rickey ensured Robinson's success in the major leagues by **counseling** him in responding to **harassment.** "Hey," he would say, impersonating a hotel clerk. "You can't eat here." He imitated a prejudiced white ballplayer and charged into Robinson saying, "Next time get out of my way, you bastard." Robinson was puzzled: "Are you looking for a Negro who is afraid to fight back?" Replied Rickey, "I'm looking for a ballplayer with guts enough not to fight back. Those **boisterous** crowds will insult you, **harass** you, do anything to **goad** you into starting a fight. And if you fight back, they'll say, 'Blacks don't belong in baseball.' "

Of all the struggles Jackie was to have, the hardest one would be to keep calm in the face of insults. Nobody would be able to **elicit** an outburst of temper from Jackie Robinson. This fiercely competitive man, who had refused to sit in the back of an army bus, found the ultimate courage—the courage to be quiet.

In the 1947 season, Robinson was to face **harassment** that would have defeated a lesser man. **(6)** Roars of "Go home!" and "Kill him!" were heard from **belligerent** crowd members. Robinson was hit in the head by more "beanballing" pitchers than any other player in the major leagues. Sometimes it became too much for his friends. Robinson's teammate, Pee Wee Reese, once challenged some **harassers** by telling them to "take on somebody who could fight back." **(7)** But Robinson himself avoided **confrontations** and he never **articulated** his grievances publicly.

Robinson is remembered for his daring base stealing.

Robinson claimed revenge in another way. To the amazement of his critics, he succeeded brilliantly in the major leagues. **(8)** Although he never **flaunted** his skill, it was apparent that he was a marvelous ball-player. In his first year in the majors he had a batting average of .297, the team high, and was named Rookie of the Year. In his ten years in baseball, his superior playing helped his team to win the pennant six times. He must have been **elated** when he was elected the first black member of the Baseball Hall of Fame.

Robinson is perhaps best remembered for his daring base stealing. Sleepy pitchers had to beware, for Robinson could steal a base at a moment's notice. As he ran from base to base, he confused defense players into making mistakes and losing control of the ball. **(9)** A fellow player gave a **concise** description of Robinson as "a hard out." He stole home base eleven times! This feat has never been equaled.

In his later years Robinson became ill with diabetes. Although he left baseball, he never stopped fighting for a just society. He championed civil rights and made investments to help build good housing in slum areas.

Jackie Robinson's name lives on in history. We all owe a debt to a brave man who bore the troubles of a prejudiced society. **(10)** No one could **thwart** the ambitions of this great baseball player and great man.

■ Exercise

Each numbered sentence below corresponds to a sentence in the Passage. Fill in the letter of the choice that makes this sentence mean the same thing as the corresponding sentence in the Passage.

1. He helped to _____ racial prejudice in America.
   a. delay b. increase c. weaken d. strengthen

2. The Dodgers' management issued a purposely _____ announcement.
   a. exciting b. short c. long d. dull

3. Still others were _____ of Robinson's ability as a baseball player.
   a. confident b. doubtful c. hopeful d. talking

4. The Dodgers' manager, Branch Rickey, had _____ over the problem before making his choice.
   a. planned b. thought c. met d. argued

5. Rickey ensured Robinson's success in the major leagues by

   _____ him.
   a. insulting b. avoiding c. advising d. complimenting

6. Roars were heard from _____ crowd members.
   a. adoring b. ridiculous c. excited d. hostile

7. But Robinson himself avoided _____ .
   a. attention b. fights c. competitions d. praise

8. Although he never _____ his skill, it was apparent that he was a marvelous ballplayer.
   a. showed off b. fully understood
   c. wondered about d. succeeded with

9. A fellow player gave a(n) _____ description of Robinson as "a hard out."
   a. short b. silly c. excellent d. emotional

10. No one could _____ the ambitions of this great man.
    a. aid b. prevent c. know d. accomplish

■ *Discussion Questions*

1. What was Robinson's greatest skill as a baseball player?

2. Why do you think Robinson's refusal to lose his temper was important?

3. In 1955, Rosa Parks refused to obey a law that required blacks to sit in the back of a bus. How is Robinson's struggle similar to her act, and how is it different?

Other Useful English Words

In this chapter you will find a variety of words that college students have identified as useful to know. These words were collected from textbooks, newspapers, magazines, and similar materials. Students reported seeing the words many times, and they felt they were important to learn. You, too, should find them valuable additions to your vocabulary.

Chapter Strategy: Context Clues of Opposition

Chapter Words:

Part 1

abominable	cosmopolitan	obsolete
accolade	dynamic	pinnacle
augment	mandatory	procrastinate
complacent	meticulous	territoriality

Part 2

accelerate	cultivate	mitigating
adulation	euphemism	perpetual
chronological	extraterrestrial	successive
copious	mammoth	withstand

Did You Know?

How Does English Get New Words?

What language is the second most widely spoken in the world? What language is used for international communication in business and science? What language has the most words? The answer to all three questions is English!

English is not the most widely spoken native language in the world. (Mandarin Chinese holds that position.) However, when we add people who speak English as a first language to people who speak it as a second language, it emerges as the world's most popular language. About 775 million people spoke English in 1985, and the number is constantly growing. English is now the international language of science, technology, and business. Japanese and German businesses, for instance, train many employees in English. People doing research often find that international scientific journals are published in English.

In keeping with the large number of people who speak English, many experts estimate that English has more words than any other spoken language. The complete *Oxford English Dictionary, Second Edition,* consists of twenty volumes, and it is available on compact disc for use on a computer screen.

The vocabulary of English grows continually as new inventions, discoveries, and customs emerge. New words introduced in the last few years include *zap, software, boom box, couch potato, audiophile, laser, fax, carcoon,* and *chunnel.*

Where do new words come from? Some are from comic strips. The creators of the Buck Rogers comic strip first used *zap* to describe the sound of a fictional "paralysis gun." Today the word means to kill, defeat, or destroy. Tad Dourgan (1877–1929), a cartoonist, introduced such words as *hot dog* and *dumbbell.*

Computer science has given English such terms as *software* (or computer program), *modem* (long-distance communication system), *microprocessor* (small computer), and *user friendly.*

Radio and television have inspired many new words. A large handheld radio is called a *boom box* because of its booming sound. Do you often like to just relax and watch television? If you do this several hours a day, you might be called a *couch potato.*

Ancient Greek and Latin word parts are also used to create new words. A person who is interested in the latest forms of stereo equipment is an *audiophile.* This word is formed from the Latin verb *audire* (to hear) and the ancient Greek noun *philos* (love).

Other English words are made from acronyms, which abbreviate a series of words by using the first letters. For example, *laser* stands for *L*ight *A*mplification by *S*imulated *E*mission of *R*adiation. *Radar* comes from *Ra*dio *De*tection *a*nd *R*anging.

New words can also be created through shortening. *Fax* has come from the word *facsimile,* and refers to a copy of a document that can be sent across the world in seconds using telephone lines. In the sentence "Fax it to me immediately," *fax* functions as a verb.

One new word can also be formed from two old ones. Since traffic is often heavy in the Los Angeles area, people spend several hours a day in cars. Some treat their cars as miniature homes by having great stereos, facilities for dressing, and telephones. The new word *carcoon* has been coined to describe this. *Carcoon* is composed of *car* and *cocoon.* Similarly, a newly built *tunnel* joins France and England by going beneath the English *channel.* Thus, it is called the *chunnel.*

English has also borrowed words from other languages. *Cotton* comes from Arabic; *pajamas* from Urdu, a language of India and Pakistan; and *tea* from Chinese. *Chocolate* and *tomato* came from languages spoken by the Aztecs, who lived in Mexico. The Algonquin Indians, of the northeastern United States, gave us *raccoon.* *Potato* came from the Taino, native inhabitants of the West Indies. *Banana* came from Africa. *Piano* is from Italian, *boss* from Dutch, *ranch* from Spanish, and *hamburger* from Germany. (In fact, the hamburger was named for the German city of Hamburg.) A word for a video game entered English within the last ten years. The game, named for a 100-year-old company in Kyoto, Japan is called *Nintendo.*

The word *scud,* first recorded in the 1500s, meant "to run hurriedly." Today, however, this meaning is rarely used. As millions learned by watching media coverage of the Persian Gulf War, *scud* is now used to refer to a Soviet-made missile. *Scud* is an easy word to remember because it suggests such negative words as *scum.*

Finally, English speakers expand the language by using old words in new ways. Many English words have gradually changed their meanings over the centuries. *Husband* once meant "master of the house." *Lady* meant "kneader of bread." The common word *nice,* which has been in English since 1100, has gone through several changes of meaning. In its long career it has meant foolish or stupid, sexy, strange, lazy, and shy. None of these meanings is in common use today.

Learning Strategy

Context Clues of Opposition

This chapter's learning strategy presents *context clues of opposition.* These clues give the opposite definition or sense of the word you are trying to understand. A simple opposition clue is *not.* Take the following example.

> The food was *not* hot, but *cold.*

Hot is, of course, the opposite of *cold.* Clues of opposition can be used for more difficult words.

> Since it was something not usual or normal in nature, it was considered an *anomaly.* (An anomaly is something not usual or normal, a "freak.")

Often a clue of opposition will provide an *antonym,* or a word opposite in meaning. In the first example, *hot* is an antonym of *cold.* Clues of opposition are easy to use if you become familiar with opposing structures in sentences. Some of the common structures are as follows.

1. The use of *not* and *no.*

> Peggy was *not happy,* but despondent.

2. Words signaling opposition. These include *but, nevertheless, despite, rather than, regardless of the fact, unless, if not, although.*

> Peggy was despondent *despite* the fact that her sister was *happy.*

3. Words with negative senses. Certain words have a negative meaning, such as *merely, mere, barely, only, rarely, never, hardly.*

> Peggy was despondent and *rarely* felt happy.

4. Words containing negative prefixes, such as *anti-, un-, dis-, non-,* and *in-.* For example, when the prefix *un-* is added to *happy,* it forms *unhappy,* which means the opposite of happy.

> Peggy was despondent and felt *unhappy.*

From these examples, it is clear that *despondent* means "sad" or "depressed." In the examples, the antonym of *despondent (happy)* is given as a context clue.

Three examples of context clues of opposition are given below. Can you guess at the meaning of the italicized words? Remember that context clues of opposition, like all context clues, may give only the general sense of a word.

1. He was not shy and was, in fact, an *extrovert.* (A *not* clue is used.)

2. There was so much *enmity* between James and Harold that they refused to speak to each other. (A word with a negative sense is used.)

3. Although Kristin thought the candidate was *despicable,* her friend thought he was wonderful. (A word signaling opposition is used.)

(*Answers:* 1. a person who enjoys the company of others 2. hatred 3. worthless, bad)

Some words that you will study in this chapter are used in the following sentences, which contain clues of opposition. Try to make an intelligent guess at the meaning of each italicized word.

1. The *meticulous* person rarely made a careless error. (A word with a negative sense is used.)

   Meticulous means _____ .

2. Everyone disliked the *abominable* person. (A negative prefix is used.)

   Abominable means _____ .

3. Corn was scarce and not at all in *copious* supply. (A *not* clue is used.)

   Copious means _____ .

(*Answers:* 1. careful   2. hateful   3. plentiful)

Words to Learn

Part 1

1. **abominable** (adjective)   ə-bŏm′ə-nə-bəl

   worthy of hatred; very unpleasant

   > Amnesty International reported the **abominable** practice of torturing children.

   > Because of his **abominable** table manners, Aurelio was never invited out to dinner.

   ▶ *Related Words*
   abominate (verb)   I *abominate* violence.
   abomination (noun)   The murder was an *abomination*.

   NOTE: Although *abominable* is usually a very strong word, we can also apply it to everyday situations.

   > He has *abominable* taste in ties.

   You may know about the legend of the abominable snowman of the Himalaya Mountains. Although some travelers claim to have seen footprints or even to have caught sight of him, no one has been able to prove his existence.

   ---

2. **accolade** (noun)   ăk′ə-lād′

praise, honor, award

> The concert received **accolades** from the press.
>
> At the honorary dinner, the man received many **accolades** for his charitable work.
>
> In 1984, Archbishop Desmond Tutu of South Africa received the **accolade** of the Nobel Peace Prize.

NOTE: Although an *accolade* is usually praise or approval, it can also refer to an official prize.

3. **augment** (verb)   ôg-měnt′

to increase

> Jesse took a second job to **augment** his income.

▶ *Related Word*
augmentation (noun)   The *augmentation* of Tim's income helped him to pay his bills.

4. **complacent** (adjective)   kəm-plā′sənt

overly self-satisfied

> After achieving straight A's, Rick became **complacent** and stopped studying.

NOTE: Complacent is a somewhat negative word.

▶ *Related Word*
complacency (noun)   The *complacency* of the company enabled its competitors to succeed.

5. **cosmopolitan** (adjective)   kŏz′mə-pŏl′ə-tən

from several parts of the world; international

> Los Angeles has a **cosmopolitan** population.

free from local bias; having a world view

> Residence in many countries had given Renée a **cosmopolitan** world view.

▶ *Related Word*
cosmos (noun)   (kŏz′məs)   The nature of the *cosmos* is still a mystery. (*Cosmos* means "universe.")

The ancient Greek word *cosmos* means "world." It is said that the Greek philosopher Diogenes was asked to name the city-state of which he was a citizen. He replied, "I am a citizen *(polites)* of the world *(cosmos)*." The word *cosmopolitan* was coined from his reply.

6. **dynamic** (adjective)   dī-năm'ĭk

energetic; forceful; fast-moving

> Pee Wee Herman's **dynamic** movements capture children's attention.
>
> Oprah Winfrey's **dynamic** personality has made her a national star.
>
> The **dynamic** force of falling water provides electric power for much of the southwestern United States.

NOTE: Dynamic can refer to both physical force and force of personality.

▶ *Related Word*
  dynamism (noun)   (dī'nə-mĭz'əm)   The *dynamism* of the chief executive officer astonished us.

7. **mandatory** (adjective)   măn'də-tôr'ē

required; commanded

> English 101 was **mandatory** for college graduation.
>
> It is **mandatory** for all residents of the United States to register births and marriages.

▶ *Related Words*
  mandate (noun)   (măn'dāt')   The government issued a *mandate* returning land to the Cherokee nation. (*Mandate* means "command," especially one involving land.)
  mandate (verb)   The government *mandates* taxes.

NOTE: Mandate can also refer to the unspoken wishes of the people who have elected an official, as in "The governor felt he had a clear *mandate* to veto the law."

8. **meticulous** (adjective)   mə-tĭk'yə-ləs

extremely careful; concerned with details

The **meticulous** care Diane took of her car increased its resale value.

A computer programmer must be **meticulous,** for even a small mistake will ruin a program.

▶ *Related Word*
meticulousness (noun)   Accountants value *meticulousness* in keeping business records.

9. **obsolete** (adjective)   ŏb′sə-lēt′

no longer in use; outmoded; old-fashioned

Computers rapidly become **obsolete** as new models are developed.

The word *thou* is an **obsolete** way of saying "you."

▶ *Related Words*
obsolescent (adjective)   (ŏb′sə-lĕs′ənt)   Few people wanted to buy the *obsolescent* computer. (*Obsolescent* means "becoming obsolete.")

obsoleteness (noun)   No one questions the *obsoleteness* of the quill pen.

10. **pinnacle** (noun)   pĭn′ə-kəl

top; highest point

Edmund Hillary and Tenzing Norgay were the first people to reach the **pinnacle** of Mount Everest.

The Keck telescope, the largest in the world, is located at the **pinnacle** of Mauna Kea in Hawaii.

At the **pinnacle** of his career, the TV anchor earned more than a million dollars per year.

11. **procrastinate** (verb)   prō-krăs′tə-nāt′

to delay; to put off

I always manage to **procrastinate** when it is time to study.

My brother **procrastinates** when he should make an appointment with the dentist.

▶ *Related Words*
procrastinator (noun)   *Procrastinators* accomplish little.

procrastination (noun)   *Procrastination* is a common human habit.

12. **territoriality** (noun)   tĕr′ə-tôr-ē-ăl′ə-tē

feeling of ownership toward land or place

Wolves have a strong sense of **territoriality** about the land surrounding their homes.

▶ *Related Word*
territorial (adjective)   (tĕr′ə-tôr′ē-al)   Foreign fishing boats are not allowed into a nation's *territorial* waters.

Territoriality is an example of a long word formed from a shorter word, *territory*. Often, looking for short, base words will help you to decode a long word. Can you find the base words in these long words?

1. disheartening

2. irreducible

3. renationalized

4. industrialization

(*Answers:*   1. heart   2. reduce   3. nation   4. industry)

Exercises

Part 1

■ Matching Words and Definitions

Check your understanding of useful words by matching each word in the left-hand column with a definition from the right-hand column. Use each choice only once.

1. augment _____

2. cosmopolitan _____

a. to delay

b. award

c. overly self-satisfied

3. complacent _____   d. very careful

4. pinnacle _____   e. no longer used

                             f. worthy of hatred

5. procrastinate _____   g. energetic

6. territoriality _____   h. required

7. obsolete _____   i. feeling of ownership toward land

                             j. to increase

8. accolade _____   k. highest point

9. meticulous _____   l. from several parts of the world

10. dynamic _____

■ *Words in Context*

Complete each sentence with the word that fits best. Use each choice only once.

a. abominable	e. cosmopolitan	i. obsolete
b. accolade	f. dynamic	j. pinnacle
c. augment	g. mandatory	k. procrastinate
d. complacent	h. meticulous	l. territoriality

1. The _____ man stole money from his relatives.

2. It is _____ for drivers to have a valid license.

3. Coal burning stoves are _____ and have been replaced with gas or electric stoves.

4. My father showed his _____ by keeping the door to his workshop room locked.

5. The champion boxer was defeated because he became

   _____ and did not train for the fight.

6. The farm workers tried to be _____ about separating the good strawberries from the spoiled ones.

7. From the _____ of the highest pyramid at Teotihuacán we could see miles of the Mexican countryside.

8. Mary Kay's _____ personality has made her a forceful leader in the cosmetics business.

9. People from many nations were represented in the

_____ crowd.

10. U.S. General Colin Powell, now Chairman of the Joint Chiefs of Staff,

received the _____ of the Purple Heart for his performance in combat.

■ *Using Related Words*

Complete each sentence using a word from the group of related words above it. You may need to capitalize a word when you put it into a sentence. Use each choice only once.

1. obsolescent, obsolete

The invention of the transistor in the 1950s enabled scientists to miniaturize many appliances and tools. Radios built with tubes

became completely _____ . Smaller and more powerful radios replaced them. Twenty-five years ago, room-sized computers built with tubes were in use, but were already

_____ . Today, a computer with more memory than the earlier version can fit on a desktop.

2. mandatory, mandate

The new mayor interpreted his large victory as a

_____ for conservation. Within a year, recycling

was _____ for all residents.

3. abominable, abominate

The weather outside is _____ . Freezing rain is falling over the piled snow, making the roads into sheets of ice.

The temperature has dropped below zero. I _____ this weather. Next year, perhaps I'll move to San Diego.

4. augment, augmentation

With careful investment, even beginners can _____
their assets. People need to decide whether to invest in commercial paper, stocks, treasury notes or other products. The

_____ of assets is an important goal.

5. dynamic, dynamism

Born in China and raised in Hong Kong, the _____
Yue-Sai Kan has been a pioneer in television programming. Ar-
riving in New York in 1972, she studied English intensively. That
year, she and a friend started a cable network show for Chinese-

speaking people in New York. Her _____ led her
in many other directions. She produced programs about China
for American television. Her series, "One World," was done for
China Central Television.

■ *True or False?*

Each of the following statements contains at least one word from this
section. Read each statement and then indicate whether you think it is
probably true or probably false.

____   1. Abominable spelling is easy to read.

____   2. You need not pay a mandatory tax.

____   3. A meticulous housekeeper would dust everything.

____   4. A bellman would be happy if he received the accolade of
"Employee of the Year."

____   5. An obsolete invention is widely used.

____   6. Procrastinators do things immediately.

____   7. If you had feelings of territoriality you would be unhappy
if someone else settled on your land.

____   8. A cosmopolitan person is usually acquainted with the
world situation.

_____   9. Dynamic people are generally complacent.

_____   10. People generally augment their income between the beginning and the pinnacle of their careers.

Words to Learn

Part 2

13. **accelerate** (verb)   ăk-sĕl′ə-rāt′

to speed up; to go faster

> The racing driver **accelerated** to 60 miles per hour in 3.7 seconds.

> The discovery of large oil deposits **accelerated** Mexico's economic development

▶ *Related Words*
   acceleration (noun)   The use of the computer has caused *acceleration* in the pace of business record keeping.

   accelerator (noun) The racer pressed the *accelerator* to the floor.

14. **adulation** (noun)   ăj′o͝o-lā′shən

extreme admiration or flattery

> The bride looked at her groom with **adulation** as she said "I do."

> The heroine received the **adulation** of the citizens.

> The professor did not allow the student's **adulation** to affect grading policies.

▶ *Related Words*
   adulate (verb)   Many teenagers *adulate* rock stars.

   adulatory (adjective)   (ăj′o͝o-lə-tôr′ē)   Tony's *adulatory* comments flattered his boss.

Many music stars have been objects of adulation. In the 1950s and 1960s, teenagers would go to any lengths to get tickets to an Elvis Presley concert. Once there, they would shriek so loudly that they couldn't hear him! Elvis's old clothes were sold at auctions, and anything he had even touched was considered sacred by his fans. In the 1960s and 1970s the four Beatles replaced Elvis in the hearts of teenagers. The 1980s and 1990s have seen the adulation of the talented Madonna, Bon Jovi, and Janet Jackson.

15. **chronological** (adjective)   krŏn'ə-lŏj'ĭ-kəl

arranged in order of time

> The secretary arranged the files in **chronological** order, placing the most recent ones in the front of the cabinet and the oldest in the back.

> The textbook outlined the events of Chinese history in **chronological** order.

▶ *Related Word*

chronology (noun) (krə-nŏl'ə-jē) The students memorized the *chronology* of the Civil War.

16. **copious** (adjective)   kō'pē-əs

plentiful; abundant

> The student's **copious** lecture notes filled ten pages.

NOTE: Copious usually refers to amount, number, or quantity. It does *not* refer to separate things. We would say "a copious amount of sand," but not "a copious piece of cake."

17. **cultivate** (verb)   kŭl'tə-vāt'

to grow deliberately

> The gardener **cultivated** a rose that shaded from white to deep red.

to seek out

> The poor student **cultivated** his rich aunt, who he hoped might help him pay tuition.

▶ *Related Words*

cultivated (adjective) John was a *cultivated* person who knew much about music and books. (*Cultivated* often describes people who are cultured and have interests in art, classical music, books, etc.)

cultivation (noun) John's musical *cultivation* impressed us.

18. **euphemism** (noun) yōō′fə-mĭz′əm

substitution of a positive word or phrase for a negative word

The salesman used the **euphemism** "previously owned" to describe the used car.

▶ *Related Word*

euphemistic (adjective) "Discomfort" is a *euphemistic* word for pain.

Euphemisms are used frequently. A bank recently announced that it was "rightsizing" itself by "lowering payroll costs through reducing head count." In other words, it was firing people.

Do you know what these common euphemisms stand for?

1. She *stretched the truth a bit.*

2. He was *taken into custody.*

3. I'm a little *under the weather* today.

(*Answers:* 1. lied 2. arrested 3. sick)

---

19. **extraterrestrial** (adjective) ĕk′strə-tə-rĕs′trē-əl

from outer space; from beyond the earth

Extraterrestrial fragments of moon rocks are on display at the Smithsonian Museum in Washington, D.C.

The 1982 movie *E.T.* has an **extraterrestrial** being as its central figure.

The word element *terra*, meaning "earth" in Latin, is used in many English words, such as *territoriality*, *terrace*, *terrier* (a dog that digs in the earth), and *inter* (to bury in the earth). The word for "earth" appears in Spanish as *tierra*.

20. **mammoth** (adjective)   măm′əth

huge; very large

> The **mammoth** high-rise made all other buildings in the city seem small.

> Effective handling of garbage has become a **mammoth** problem.

The word *mammoth* originated as a Russian word for a type of extinct elephant that was once found in cold climates. Like *mammoth*, other animal words and phrases have come into general use in English. To *parrot* means to repeat. To *lionize* means to worship or adore. A *chicken* refers to a person without courage. A *catty* person likes to talk negatively about others.

Do you know what these words and phrases mean?

1. on a high horse

2. mulish

3. a snake in the grass

Answers: 1. snobbish; disdainful   2. stubborn   3. sneaky, untrustworthy person

---

21. **mitigating** (adjective)   mĭt′ə-gāt′ĭng

making less severe or intense; moderating

> The boy's warmheartedness had a **mitigating** effect on his teacher's stern attitude.

> Tony admitted he was late, but offered the **mitigating** circumstance that his car had a flat tire on the way.

▶ *Related Word*
   mitigate (verb)   Grandmother *mitigated* her harsh words with a wink.

22. **perpetual** (adjective)   pər-pĕch′ōō-əl

lasting forever; eternal

> Religion teaches that God is **perpetual**.

continuous

> Her severe financial problems kept the welfare mother in a **perpetual** state of anxiety.

► *Related Words*

perpetually (adverb)   The mother was *perpetually* worried.

perpetuate (verb)   (pər-pĕch'ōō-āt')   Poor education *perpetuates* poverty.

23. **successive** (adjective)   sək-sĕs'ĭv

following one after another without interruption

> After Rupert was late for six **successive** days, his boss fired him.

► *Related Word*

succession (noun)   I had a *succession* of classes from nine to three.

The prince's *succession* to the throne was greeted with much celebration. (*Succession* can mean the inheritance of a crown or title.)

24. **withstand** (verb)   wĭth-stănd'   (past tense: **withstood**)

not to surrender; to bear (the force of)

> People differ in their ability to **withstand** cold weather.

> Unable to **withstand** the force of the hurricane, the tree broke in half.

> The fortress **withstood** many attacks without falling to the enemy.

Gitobu Imanyara, editor of Narobi Law Monthly, has withstood much persecution as publisher of a magazine that speaks freely about Kenyan politics. At times, the magazine has been banned. Mr. Imanyara was physically attacked and has served time in prison. For his bravery, Mr. Imanyara was chosen International Editor of the Year 1990 by *World Press Review*.

Exercises

Part 2

■ Matching Words and Definitions

Check your understanding of useful words by matching each word in the left-hand column with a definition from the right-hand column. Use each choice only once.

1. euphemism _____
2. cultivate _____
3. mitigating _____
4. adulation _____
5. mammoth _____
6. perpetual _____
7. chronological _____
8. accelerate _____
9. successive _____
10. extraterrestrial _____

a. very large
b. lasting forever
c. not to surrender
d. plentiful
e. extreme admiration
f. making less severe
g. in order of time
h. use of a positive word
i. to grow deliberately
j. from outer space
k. to speed up
l. following one after another

■ *Words in Context*

Complete each sentence with the word that fits best. Use each choice only once.

a. accelerate   e. cultivate   i. mitigating
b. adulation   f. euphemism   j. perpetual
c. chronological   g. extraterrestrial k. successive
d. copious   h. mammoth   l. withstand

1. The _____ company was the largest in Canada.

2. A cool breeze has a(n) _____ effect on hot weather.

3. The _____ slime invaded the earth.

4. Seattle has had light rain for four _____ days.

5. The great opera singer received the _____ of the crowd.

6. The earth is in _____ motion as it rotates on its axis.

7. Food was in _____ supply at the picnic, and we ate well.

8. The man wished to _____ the friendship of the famous artist.

9. The English teacher used the _____ "not quite acceptable" to describe a failing paper.

10. Unable to _____ the great tension, the man lost his temper.

■ *Using Related Words*

Complete each sentence using a word from the group of related words above it. You may need to capitalize a word when you put it into a sentence. Use each choice only once.

1. acceleration, accelerated

   In high school, I took an _____ math class. In this ninth-grade class, I learned trigonometry. The

   _____ of the curriculum enabled me to master calculus by the time I entered college.

2. chronology, chronological

   At my grandparents' fiftieth wedding anniversary party, an expert from the town's historical society narrated the family his-

   tory in _____ order. The _____ revealed that my grandmother's family had come to Canada during the Irish Potato Famine of the mid 1800s.

3. adulation, adulatory

   In 1927, Charles Lindberg made the first solo flight across the

   Atlantic Ocean. He received the _____ of thou-

   sands of people. Their _____ comments praised his courage and skill. His plane, *The Spirit of St. Louis*, is now on display at the Lambert-St. Louis Airport.

4. cultivate, cultivation, cultivated, cultivating

   Many people are now _____ rare flowers and fruits as a hobby. One of my friends is a member of a society dedicated to the _____ of rare apples, such as the Melrose and the Cornish Gilliflower. In this society, people

can _____ each other's acquaintance, and share

a common interest. My friend is also a _____ person who enjoys listening to classical music, visiting museums, and reading.

■ *Which Should It Be?*

Complete the following sentences by choosing the phrase that makes better sense.

1. Most people would rather _____ .

   a. arrange a file in chronological order
   b. receive the adulation of a crowd

2. In front of four-year-old children, we would probably use _____ .

   a. a euphemism to describe bad behavior
   b. a mammoth word to tell them what to do

3. People in northern Canada hope for _____ .

   a. many successive months of cold weather
   b. cold weather mitigated by some warmth

4. If you were on a highway, you would rather _____ .

   a. accelerate your car
   b. see a copious amount of snow on the road

5. It would be a more unusual experience to _____ .

   a. encounter an extraterrestrial being
   b. cultivate an interest in art

Chapter Exercises

■ *Practicing Strategies: Context Clues of Opposition*

In each of the following sentences a difficult word is italicized. Using context clues of opposition, make an intelligent guess at the meaning of the word as it is used in this sentence. Your instructor may ask you to look up each word in your dictionary after you have finished the exercise.

1. The *dauntless* speaker was not at all frightened by the hostile crowd.

    Dauntless means _____ .

2. The ancient priest's *cryptic* message could not be understood.

    Cryptic means _____ .

3. She thought she would be *recompensed*, but she was never paid.

    Recompensed means _____ .

4. He *feigned* ignorance, although he knew about all of their plans.

    Feigned means _____ .

5. Since we were at an equal point on the pay scale, there was no *disparity* between my salary and hers.

    Disparity means _____ .

6. Suddenly called upon to talk publicly, Jesse Jackson gave a brilliant *extempore* speech.

    Extempore means _____ .

7. The editor's efforts were usually *disparaged*, but she was given occasional praise.

    Disparaged means _____ .

8. Barbara is *reticent* about revealing her background despite the fact that she talks freely about other things.

    Reticent means _____ .

9. This *diminutive* type of hummingbird hardly ever grows over three inches long.

    Diminutive means _____ .

10. Melody displayed *fortitude* in climbing the mountain, although the climb was tiring and many other people had to quit.

    Fortitude means _____ .

▪ *Writing with Your Words*

This exercise will give you practice in writing effective sentences using the vocabulary words. Each sentence is started for you. Complete it with an interesting phrase that also indicates the meaning of the italicized word.

1. When I *procrastinate* _____

   _____ .

2. It is *mandatory* to _____

   _____ .

3. When I reach the *pinnacle* of success, I will _____

   _____ .

4. A *cosmopolitan* person _____

   _____ .

5. Something that I find *abominable* is _____

   _____ .

6. There is a *copious* supply of _____

   _____ .

7. A *dynamic* leader would _____

   _____ .

8. To *mitigate* the punishment, my mother _____

   _____ .

9. A *cultivated* person _____

   _____ .

10. It is difficult for me to *withstand* _____

   _____ .

Passage

Australia: From Prison to Paradise

When we think of Australia today, we think of a sunny, prosperous country visited yearly by thousands of tourists. But for generations, the very name Australia brought fear to the hearts of the English people, because Australia was founded to serve as a prison for England.

In the late 1700s, England was a country of contrasts. Gentlemen lived on rich estates with beautiful gardens. Yet in the city of London, poor families crowded together into single rooms near the dark, evil-smelling factories where they worked. In the early days of industrialization, children as young as six held jobs. **(1)** Young girls ruined their eyes doing **meticulous** sewing in dim light. Boys grew up with backs bent from years of carrying coal.

Yet those who worked were relatively fortunate, for thousands had no jobs. Without government help, the unemployed were simply left to starve. **(2)** Crime **augmented,** as poor families were forced to steal to stay alive.

The rich of England knew little about the fate of the poor. **(3) Complacent** in their own situations, and unaware of the depth of this poverty, many simply believed that there was a "criminal class." To try to control it, the government passed laws of extreme harshness. Hanging was made **mandatory** for stealing property worth 40 shillings, burning a pile of straw, or cutting down an ornamental bush. Public executions were considered "educational." Still, desperate poverty caused the crime rate to **accelerate.**

Finally, sickening of the sight of death for small offenses, **(4)** the government began to **mitigate** the harsh punishments. It was decided that if "royal mercy" were granted, the death sentence could be replaced by sending prisoners out of the country to do forced labor. However, no one could decide where to send criminals, so, within a few years, prisons became stuffed with convicts awaiting transportation. **(5)** Government officials could **procrastinate** no longer; they had to send the prisoners somewhere.

The **mammoth** island of Australia seemed a wise choice. The British Empire had claimed rights to it, and needed to support their **territoriality** with settlement. Prisoners could do the hard labor needed to establish farms, and those who wished to escape would simply drown. Best of all, the "criminal element" would be 8,000 miles from England.

Who were the "criminals" transported to Australia in 1787? They included Thomas Chaddick, who ate twelve cucumber plants, and William Francis, who stole a book. Eleven-year-old James Grace took ribbons and a pair of stockings; Elizabeth Beckford, seventy years old, stole cheese.

For these crimes, each was sentenced to years of hard labor in an unknown land. **(6)** Many prisoners believed that exile would be **perpetual,** and they would never see England again. Parting from their families was difficult to **withstand.** One man wrote to his wife, "I don't mind where I go nor what I suffer, if I have your company to cheer my almost broken heart." Yet he sailed off alone, in chains.

Many of the prisoners died in Australia's first years. **(7)** The land proved difficult to **cultivate.** For three **successive** years, supply ships from England failed to come, forcing the population into near starvation. One Australian remembered living on a diet of boiled seaweed and whale blubber.

Nature, too, was unwelcoming and unfamiliar. **(8)** People tried to build ships from Australia's **copious** supply of pines, but the trees had brittle, useless bark. Winter and summer were reversed in the southern hemisphere. Unfamiliar kangaroos and parakeets replaced cows and horses. The ground had aloe plants, but grew no grass.

Convicts were forced to work for bosses who might refuse them food or sentence them to whippings. **(9)** Humane governors received criticism, rather than **accolades,** from the English government. Doctors who treated the poor might earn the **adulation** of convicts, but they received little pay.

Yet, convicts built the country. One freed convict, Samuel Terry, became the largest landowner in Australia. Simeon Lord became an im-

Australia is now a prosperous country with a low crime rate.

portant manufacturer; James Underwood's firm constructed ships. Mary Haydock, transported at age thirteen, built a chain of warehouses and boats. **(10)** As the "criminal class" became a **dynamic** force in Australia's success, it became more respectable. Soon the **euphemism** "government man" was substituted for "convict." Later the term became "empire builder." Amazingly, the children of transported convicts committed almost no crimes.

Today, Australia, a prosperous country with a **cosmopolitan** population, continues to have one of the world's lowest crime rates. For these blessings, Australia must thank the 160,000 "criminals" who were sentenced to years of hard labor in a strange land for crimes as small as shoplifting.

■ *Exercise*

Each numbered sentence below corresponds to a sentence in the Passage. Fill in the letter of the choice that makes this sentence mean the same thing as the corresponding sentence in the Passage.

1. Young girls had their eyes ruined from years of _____ sewing.
   a. difficult b. dark c. horrible d. careful

2. Crime _____ .
   a. hurt b. grew c. stopped d. paid

3. _____ in their own situations, they assumed there was a criminal class.
   a. ignorant b. helpful c. placed d. satisfied

4. The government began to _____ the harsh punishment.
   a. soften b. change c. increase d. consider

5. The government could _____ no longer.
   a. help b. stay c. finish d. delay

6. Many believed that exile would be _____ .
   a. difficult b. permanent c. poor d. ridiculous

7. The land proved difficult to _____ .
   a. farm b. hold c. build d. buy

8. People tried to build ships from Australia's _____ supply of pine trees.
   a. helpful b. plentiful c. healthy d. increasing

9. Humane governors received criticism, rather than _____ .
   a. praise   b. money   c. help   d. employment

10. The "criminal class" became a(n) _____ force in Australia's success.
    a. effective   b. energetic   c. wonderful   d. tremendous

■ *Discussion Questions*

1. How did "royal mercy" change a punishment?

2. From the evidence in this passage, does crime appear to stem from evil people or from economic conditions? Defend your answer.

3. Do you find parallels between the treatment of criminals as described in the passage and in today's word? Why or why not?

REVIEW

Chapters 1–4

■ Reviewing Words in Context

Complete each sentence with the word that fits best.

a. adulation   g. elicit   l. mandatory
b. ascetic   h. gauche   m. obsolete
c. boisterous   i. goad   n. procrastinate
d. contend   j. hypocrite   o. prohibit
e. defer   k. intervene   p. subjugate
f. dogmatic

1. It is wise to _____ to the wishes of your boss.

2. It is usually _____ that people crossing national boundaries have a passport.

3. The national Canadian government will _____ to settle the dispute between the two provinces.

4. Students who _____ often hand in papers late.

5. Jack tried to _____ Carl into fighting, but Carl refused to respond.

6. The sad looks of a puppy will _____ sympathy in most people.

7. As a popular first lady, Jackie Kennedy was the object of many

   people's _____ .

8. In 1990 Saddam Hussein invaded Kuwait and tried to

   _____ its people.

9. The vacuum tubes once used in televisions and radios are now

   _____ .

10. Strict laws _____ drunk people from driving.

11. The two swimmers will _____ in the championship race.

12. My clumsy attempts to impress were so _____ that I decided to just be myself.

13. The crowd became _____ and started shouting insults at the players.

14. His _____ beliefs are never changed by contrary evidence.

15. The _____ denied himself all luxuries.

■ *Passage for Word Review*

Complete each blank in the Passage with the word that makes the best sense. The choices include words from the vocabulary lists and related words. Use each choice only once.

a. adroitly   e. conservative   i. indulge
b. affluent   f. copious   j. meticulous
c. appalled   g. defer   k. mitigated
d. astute   h. elated   l. pinnacle

A Family Christmas

(This essay was written by college student José Luis Gamboa.)

Christmas is the most special time of the year to me, for my family and friends gather together in a huge celebration. My mother and

aunts cook (1) _____ amounts of traditional foods: tamales, enchiladas, frijoles, and rellenos for main courses, plus chópes,

gorditas de dulce, and buñuelos for dessert. I (2) _____ myself by eating all my favorites. We sing, dance, and watch fights on

television. This year, my joy will be (3) _____ with some sadness, for my two eldest sisters now live in San Jose, California, and will not be with us.

Watching my nephews on Christmas Eve reminds me of my own childhood. Boy, could I get into trouble! One year, a few days before Christmas, my parents went shopping, leaving my brother and me alone.

Unable to (4) _____ our wish to know what our presents would be, we decided to open just one. We chose the largest and

most beautiful package, which had been wrapped with (5) _____ care. We saved the paper so that the gift could be wrapped up again.

We were **(6)** _____ to find that it was the toy gas

station that we had wished for all year. We **(7)** _____
put the pieces together and spent some time admiring our work.

   But, when we went to put it back, we could not take it apart. We

were **(8)** _____! When my parents found out, something
awful would happen. Quickly, we stuffed the toy into a closet.

   When my parents returned, they saw that a package was missing.
From our strange behavior, they soon guessed what had happened. They

were **(9)** _____ enough to realize that we meant no
harm, and instead of punishing us, they merely laughed and kissed us.

   This Christmas I wish for world peace. Until the problem of pov-

erty is solved, I hope that **(10)** _____ people will give
charitably to the poor. Most of all, I remember the gift of my parents'
forgiveness. Sometimes an opened present can be more meaningful than
a wrapped one.

■ *Reviewing Learning Strategies*

Dictionary Skills   Complete each sentence with the answer that fits
best.

1. An etymology gives the _____ of a word.
   a. pronunciation   b. meaning   c. history

2. The most complete dictionary is called a(n) _____
   dictionary.
   a. unabridged   b. college   c. pocket

Context clues   Using context clues, make an intelligent guess at the
meaning of the italicized word in each sentence.

3. There was *bedlam*, or total confusion, after the riot.

   Bedlam means _____ .

4. Since the dodo bird died out centuries ago, it is no longer *extant*.

   Extant means _____ .

5. The *noxious* gas caused sickness and death.

   Noxious means _____ .

6. The *fervor* of his plea was emphasized by his wild gestures.

   Fervor means _____ .

7. He had a *propensity* to be lazy; in other words, he tended to avoid work.

   Propensity means _____ .

8. In school, the unfortunate child could not master even the *rudiments* of arithmetic.

   Rudiments means _____ .

9. The *refractory* mule refused to move from the spot, despite our urging.

   Refractory means _____ .

10. You are *niggling* again, and I'd be grateful if you would not argue about small points and discuss the issues instead.

    Niggling means _____ .

P A R T

2

Word Elements

Part Two of this book focuses on word elements, the parts of words that have separate meanings. For example, the parts *re* (meaning "back") and *tract* (meaning "pull") are the two elements in the word *retract* (meaning "to pull back"). If you break up an unknown word into its separate elements, you can often figure out the meaning. If you then combine context clues, which you learned about in Part One of this book, with the word element clues you will learn in Part Two, you will have two powerful ways to understand new words. Context clues provide hints in the sentence surrounding a word; word elements give hints within the word itself.

Prefixes, Roots, and Suffixes

There are three kinds of word elements: prefixes, roots, and suffixes. A **prefix** is a group of letters that attaches to the beginning of a word root. A **root** is the central, or main, portion of a word. A **suffix** is a group of letters that attaches to the end of a word root. An example of a word that contains all three elements is *impolitely: im-* is the prefix; *polite* is the root; and *-ly* is the suffix. Now let us look at each element separately.

Prefixes. A prefix, such as *im-*, joins on to the beginning of a word root and changes its meaning. The hyphen at the end shows that it is a prefix. In the example above, the prefix *im-* means "not." When *im-* is joined to the root word *polite*, the new word formed by the root and prefix means "not polite." Next, we can see what happens when the prefix *co-*, which means "together," is joined to two familiar word roots.

co- (together) + *exist* = *coexist* (to exist together)
co- (together) + *operate* = *cooperate* (to work or operate together)

In both of these examples, the prefix *co-* changes the meaning of the root word.

Roots.   A root is the central portion of a word, and it carries the basic dictionary meaning. There are two types of roots: base words and combining roots. A **base word** is simply an English word that can stand alone, such as *polite* or *operate*, which may be joined to a prefix or a suffix. **Combining roots** cannot stand alone as English words; they are derived from words in other languages. For example, the combining root *ject* is derived from the Latin word *jacēre*, which means "to throw." Although the root *ject* is not an English word by itself, it can combine with many prefixes to form words. Two examples are *reject* and *eject*.

e- (a prefix meaning "out") + *ject* (a root meaning "throw") = *eject*
re- (a prefix meaning "back") + *ject* (a root meaning "throw") = *reject*

How do a prefix and a root create a word with a new meaning? Sometimes the new word's meaning is simply the sum of its root and its prefix. Thus, *eject* means "to throw out." At other times the meaning of a word may be different from the combined prefix and root. *Reject* does not mean "to throw back," but rather "not to accept." These two meanings are related, since we could imagine that someone who did not accept something might throw it back. In fact, "to throw back" gives an imaginative mental picture of *reject*. Prefixes and roots often give an image of a word, rather than a precise definition. This image may help you to remember the meaning of a word. The formation of several words from *ject* is illustrated on page 125.

Suffixes.   A suffix, such as *-ly*, is added to the end of a root. The hyphen at the beginning shows that it is a suffix. Most suffixes change a word from one part of speech to another (see the table on pages 5 and 6). For example, *-able* changes a verb *(reach)* to an adjective *(reachable)*. Suffixes may also indicate a plural or a past tense, as in boy*s* and reach*ed*. A few suffixes extend the basic meaning of a word root. The word element used as a combining root, *psych* (mind), and the suffix *-logy* (study of) are joined to form *psychology* (the study of the mind). Many common words contain word elements. Each of the following words consists of a prefix, a root, and a suffix: *reaction, unlikely, exchanges, reviewing,* and *invisibly*. Can you identify each element?

Using Word Elements

Word elements provide valuable clues to the meanings of unknown words, but they must be used carefully.

Some word elements have more than one spelling. For example, the root *ject* is occasionally spelled *jac*. The prefix *anti-* is also spelled *ant-* (as in *antacid* and *antagonist*). Some spelling differences make words easier to pronounce. Others reflect the history of a word element. Fortunately, spellings usually vary by only one or two letters. Once you learn to look for the common letters, you should easily be able to identify word elements.

Some word elements have more than one meaning. For example, the combining root *gen* can mean both "birth" and "type." This book gives all the common meanings of roots, prefixes, and suffixes, and some hints about when to use them. When you encounter word elements that have more than one meaning, remember to use the context clues you learned in Part One of this book. If you combine your knowledge of word elements with context clues, you can usually determine the most appropriate meaning.

Finally, when you see a certain combination of letters in a word, those letters may not always form a word element. For instance, the appearance of the letters *a-n-t-i* in a word does not mean that they always form the prefix *anti-*. To find out whether or not they do, you must combine context clues with the use of word elements. To illustrate this,

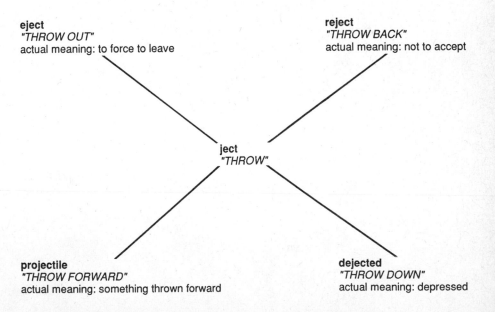

eject
"THROW OUT"
actual meaning: to force to leave

reject
"THROW BACK"
actual meaning: not to accept

ject
"THROW"

projectile
"THROW FORWARD"
actual meaning: something thrown forward

dejected
"THROW DOWN"
actual meaning: depressed

a-n-t-i is used in two sentences below. Which sentence contains the prefix *anti-* (meaning "opposite" or "against")?

1. The *antihero* was a villain.

2. We *anticipate* you will come.

The answer is the first sentence; *antihero* (or villain) is the opposite of *hero*.

Despite these cautions, the use of word elements is an excellent way of increasing your vocabulary. Prefixes, roots, and suffixes can help you unlock the meanings of thousands of difficult words. The chapters in Part Two of this book present many different word elements. Each one is illustrated by several new words that will be valuable to you in college. As you work through the word elements in Part Two, keep in mind the context clues that you learned in Part One. Together, word elements and context clues will give you very powerful strategies for learning new words independently.

Word Elements: Prefixes

The rich cultural heritage that the ancient Greeks and Romans left to us includes many word elements that are still used in English. This chapter introduces some prefixes from both ancient Greek and Latin, the language of the ancient Romans. Learning these prefixes will help you to figure out the meanings of many difficult words.

Chapter Strategy: Word Elements: Prefixes

Chapter Words:

Part 1

anti-	antagonism	re-	recession
	antidote		revelation
	antithesis		revert
equi-	equilibrium	sub-	subconscious
	equitable		submissive
	equivocal		subordinate

Part 2

auto-	autobiography	im-, in-	impartial
	automaton		ingenious
	autonomous		interminable
ex-	eccentric		invariably
	exorbitant		invoke
	exploit		
	extricate		

Did You Know?

Where Does English Come From?

The origins of language are lost in the mists of time. Archaeologists discover examples of ancient jewelry, weapons, and art, but no one knows how or why people first spoke. We do know that most of the languages of Europe, the Middle East, and India are descended from a common source. Linguists trace these languages back to a possible parent language called *Indo-European*, which would have been spoken at least five thousand years ago. The Indo-European root *mater* (mother) shows up in many different languages.

Languages No Longer Spoken		*Modern Languages*	
Ancient Greek	mētēr	English	mother
Latin	mater	German	mutter
Old English	modor	Italian	madre
		Spanish	madre
		French	mère
		Polish	matka

English vocabulary descends from Indo-European through several other languages that are no longer spoken. In modern English, much of our difficult vocabulary comes from ancient Greek and Latin. (These are often called the *classical languages*.) A knowledge of the Greek and Latin word elements used in English will help you to master thousands of modern English words.

Who were these Greeks and Romans from whom so much language flows? The civilization of the ancient Greeks flourished between 750 and 250 B.C. Greece was a land of small, separate city-states, which created the first democracies and the first concept of citizenship. Sparta and Athens were two important city-states. The citizens of Sparta were accomplished athletes and excelled in warfare, whereas Athens was a center of art and learning. Athenians produced the first lifelike sculpture, wrote the first tragedies and comedies, and learned philosophy from Socrates and Plato. Unfortunately, the vigorous Greek civilization also had its dark side. The economic system was based on slavery, and only a small percentage of the population—free men—were full citizens. Women had few political rights. Greek history was also marred by tragic wars between city-states.

In contrast to the divided Greek city-states, the city of Rome steadily took over first the whole of Italy, then more and more countries, to rule a vast empire. From around 200 B.C. to 450 A.D., the Roman empire, which stretched from Israel to Britain, gradually brought peace to much of the known world. Roman officials introduced a highway system, a postal service, water supplies, public baths, and border patrols to many uncivilized areas, and Latin was the official language of the empire. But like Greece, Rome had its troubles. After the first emperor, Augustus, died, plots and murders became common in the Roman court. Several Roman emperors were poisoned or smothered with pillows. Meanwhile, officials and the army continued to rule the empire efficiently.

If you have studied the ancient Greeks and Romans, you may be able to answer these questions.

1. The epic poem the *Iliad* tells of a Greek war that started when Helen, the daughter of Zeus, was stolen from her husband. Helen is often

   called "Helen of _____ ."
   a. Athens b. Sparta c. Troy d. Crete

2. _____ was a famous Roman leader who said, "I came, I saw, I conquered."
   a. Augustus b. Brutus c. Cato d. Caesar

3. Cleopatra, queen of Egypt, did *not* have a romance with _____ .
   a. Augustus b. Caesar c. Anthony

(Answers: 1. c 2. d 3. a)

Learning Strategy

Word Elements: Prefixes

Our heritage from the Greeks and Romans includes many word elements that are still used in English. The learning strategy in this chapter concentrates on *prefixes*, word elements added to the beginning of word roots. The seven prefixes presented in this chapter (see the following table) are very common, and learning them will help you build a large vocabulary. One dictionary lists over four hundred words that use *ex-* and more than six hundred formed from *in-* or *im-*.

Element	Meaning	Origin	Chapter Words
		Part 1	
anti-, ant-	against; opposite	Greek	antagonism, antidote, antithesis
equi-, equa-	equal	Latin	equilibrium, equitable, equivocal
re-	back; again	Latin	recession, revelation, revert
sub-	below; under; part of	Latin	subconscious, submissive, subordinate

Part 2

auto-	self	Greek	autobiography, automaton, autonomous
ex-, e-, ec-	out of; former	Latin	eccentric, exorbitant, exploit, extricate
im-, in-	not; in	Latin	impartial, ingenious, interminable, invariably, invoke

Prefixes give clues to word meaning when they join with word roots. Let us look first at how prefixes can combine with roots that are base words.

anti- (against) + *poverty* makes *antipoverty*, meaning "against poverty."
   Food stamps were part of the *antipoverty* program.
sub- (below) + *normal* makes *subnormal*, meaning "below normal."
   Subnormal temperatures are colder than usual.
auto- (self) + *suggestion* makes *autosuggestion*, meaning "a suggestion made to yourself."
   Some people use *autosuggestion* when they try to diet.

See if you can use prefixes to determine the meaning of the following words. Write in the word and its meaning.

equi- (equal) + *distant* makes _____, meaning

_____ .

re- (again) + *appear* makes _____, meaning

_____ .

in- (not) + *direct* makes _____, meaning

_____ .

Now let's look at how prefixes join with combining roots (roots that cannot stand alone as English words). The Latin root *scrib* or *script* (write) combines with some prefixes in our list to make English words, whose meanings are the combined meanings of the prefix and root.

in- (in) + *scrib* makes *inscribe*, "to write in."
   People often *inscribe* their names in books.
sub- (under) + *script* makes *subscript*, "written under."
   A *subscript* is a tiny number or letter written beneath a line, such as the 2 in H_2O, the chemical symbol for water. Subscripts are used mainly in math and science.

At other times, the meaning of a word is rather different from the combined meanings of a prefix and combining root. Still, word elements will give you valuable clues to the meaning of the word. The Latin root *vert* (to turn) combines with three prefixes that you will study in this chapter to make three different English words, but the idea of "turn" appears in all of them.

re- (back) + *vert* (turn) makes *revert*, or "turn back."
   When people *revert* they take up an old habit again. Perhaps you know someone who *reverted* to smoking cigarettes after having quit.
in- (in) + *vert* (turn) makes *invert*, or "turn in."
   Invert means to turn inside out, upside down, or to change in order. If you *invert* a pocket, you turn it inside out.
sub- (under) + *vert* (turn) makes *subvert*, or "turn under."
   Subvert means to make something worse by corrupting it or trying to overthrow it. Traitors seek to *subvert* the governments of their countries.

As you can see, using prefixes sometimes requires a little imagination. Prefixes and roots may not give the *entire* meaning of an unknown word, but they do provide excellent hints. If you combine the use of context clues with the use of word elements, you can often figure out the precise meaning of a difficult word.
   Two words formed from a prefix and a root are presented below. The meanings of the roots and prefixes are given, followed by a sentence using the word. Write in the meaning of each word.

equilateral, from *equi-* (equal) and *latera* (sides)
   An *equilateral* triangle has all three sides of equal length.

   Equilateral means   _____ .

incredulous, from *in-* (not) and *cred* (to believe)
   She was *incredulous* when she heard the fantastic story.

   Incredulous means   _____ .

Prefixes

Part 1

Four prefixes are presented in Part 1 of this chapter. Each prefix is described below.

anti-, ant- (against; opposite)

The two meanings of *anti-* are related and therefore easy to remember. *Antifreeze* protects a car radiator from freezing, and an *antiallergic* medicine helps to relieve allergies. New English words continue to be formed with *anti-*, especially as people find new things to protest "against," as in the *antinuclear* war movement.

equi-, equa- (equal)

Equi- is used in many English words. Two homes that are *equidistant* from a school are the same distance from the school. Two equally powerful forces may be called *equipotent*.

re- (back; again)

Re- has two distinct meanings. It usually means "again" when it is attached to other English words (or base words). For example, when *re-* is added to the base words *wind* and *do* it forms *rewind* (wind again) and *redo* (do again). However, when *re-* is added to combining roots that cannot stand alone, it often means "back." *Recede*, for instance, means "to go back" and comes from *re-* (back) and *cēdere* (to go).

sub- (below; under; part of)

In the word *substandard*, *sub-* means "below the standard." *Sub-* can also refer to a classification that is "part of" something else, as a *subdivision* is part of a division. In biology, animals from one species may be classified into several *subspecies*, which are part of, or classified under, the category of the species.

Words to Learn

Part 1

anti-

1. **antagonism** (noun)   ăn-tăg′ə-nĭz′əm

   From Greek: *anti-* (against) + *agon* (contest)

   hatred; hostility

   > There was **antagonism** between the divorcing man and woman.

   rivalry; opposition

   > The **antagonism** between the city's two baseball teams made the season exciting.

   ▶ *Related Words*
   antagonist (noun, person)   Jennifer Capriati defeated her *antagonist* in the championship tennis match. (*Antagonist* means "rival.")

antagonistic (adjective) The *antagonistic* feelings between the two sisters made family parties uncomfortable.

antagonize (verb) The mayor's plan to increase taxes *antagonized* many citizens.

2. **antidote** (noun) ăn'tĭ-dōt'

From Greek *anti-* (against) + *didonai* (to give) (to give a remedy against something harmful)

A substance that acts against a poison

The doctor gave Maria an **antidote** to fight the effects of the rattlesnake bite.

Something that acts against a harmful effect

A lively party can be an **antidote** to depression.

The prefix "anti-" is widely used in medicine. Health care professionals prescribe *antibiotics* such as penicillin and ampycillin to kill the organisms that can cause disease. The word *antibiotic* comes from *anti-* and *bio*, meaning "life." We take an *antihistamine* to stop the sneezing and runny nose of a cold or an allergy. *Antihistamine* comes from *anti-* plus *histi*, the ancient Greek word element meaning "tissue" or body substance. Immunizations against smallpox, measles, polio, and tuberculosis allow us to form *antibodies* that prevent these diseases. Currently, medical researchers are trying to locate substances that will form antibodies against the deadly AIDS virus.

---

3. **antithesis** (noun) ăn-tĭth'ə-sĭs

From Greek: *anti-* (against) + *tithenai* (to put)

contrast; opposite

John's rude behavior was the very **antithesis** of good manners.

▶ *Related Word*
antithetical (adjective) (ăn'tə-thĕt'ĭ-kəl) War is *antithetical* to peace.

equi-

4. **equilibrium** (noun) ē'kwə-lĭb'rē-əm

From Latin: *equi-* (equal) + *libra* (balance)

balance between forces; stability

The reaction was in **equilibrium,** as an equal number of molecules were changing from ice to water as from water to ice.

The tightrope walker almost lost his **equilibrium.**

His **equilibrium** vanished when he became angry.

▶ *Common Phrase*
in equilibrium

NOTE: The concept of balance can be used in several ways, including evenness of temperament.

The astrological sign of Libra comes directly from the Latin root *libra,* meaning "balance." Libras are born between September 23 and October 23. They are said to have calm, even natures and a sense of justice. The symbol for Libra is a balanced scale, which also relates to the meaning of *equilibrium.*

---

5. **equitable** (adjective)   ĕk′wə-tə-bəl

From Latin: *equi* (equal)

fair; just

The **equitable** professor graded all students by the same standard.

Grandmother felt it was most **equitable** to leave the same amount of money to all of her grandchildren.

NOTE: In *equitable,* the *equi* word element is used as a root.

6. **equivocal** (adjective)   ĭ-kwĭv′ə-kəl

From Latin: *equi-* (equal) + *vox* (voice) (When something is equivocal, it seems as if two equally strong voices are giving off different messages.)

having two or more meanings or interpretations

The treasurer's statement that "the company is doing better" was **equivocal** because it didn't tell whether the company was now out of debt.

doubtful

Although people pay high prices for her paintings, her position as a great artist is **equivocal.**

NOTE: Equivocal statements are often meant to mislead and deceive people.

► *Related Words*

equivocate (verb) (ĭ-kwĭv'ə-kāt') Don't *equivocate;* answer directly.

equivocation (noun)   The politician's *equivocation* annoyed the reporters.

re-

7. **recession** (noun)   rĭ-sĕsh'ən

From Latin: *re-* (back) + *cēdere* (to go) (In a recession, the economy "goes backward.")

a modest decline in the economy

> The government feared that a **recession** would end the period of prosperity.

withdrawing

> The graduates began their **recession** from the hall when the music started playing.

► *Related Word*
recede (verb) (rĭ-sēd') The tide will soon *recede.*

8. **revelation** (noun)   rĕv'ə-lā'shən

From Latin: *re-* (back) + *vēlāre* (to veil) This makes *revēlāre,* "to draw back the veil." (When a veil is drawn back, something shocking may be discovered.)

dramatic disclosure; shocking news

> The newspaper's **revelation** of corruption among public officials caused a scandal.

NOTE: Revelation can have a positive religious meaning. The prophet Mohammed, founder of the Islamic religion, made many *revelations* to his followers.

► *Related Word*
reveal (verb) (rĭ-vēl') The newspaper reporter *revealed* the truth.

9. **revert** (verb)   rĭ-vûrt'

From Latin: *re-* (back) + *vert* (turn)

to return to a former practice or condition

> Unfortunately, the man **reverted** to using drugs soon after he left the treatment program.

After 100 years of British rule, the city of Hong Kong will **re-vert** to Chinese control in 1997.

▶ *Common Phrase*
revert to

sub-

10. **subconscious** (adjective, noun)   sŭb'kŏn'shəs

From Latin: *sub-* (under) + *conscius* (aware of)

not aware (or conscious) in the mind (adjective)

Colors can have **subconscious** meanings; red often suggests excitement and blue suggests peace.

Advertisers try to appeal to our **subconscious** desires.

the part of the mind that is beneath awareness (noun)

When the psychiatrist Sigmund Freud explored the **subconscious,** he found that some dreams were disguised wishes.

NOTE: The *unconscious* (not-conscious) is that part of the mind which can *never* become conscious. The word *unconscious* also describes a sleeping person or someone in a coma. The *subconscious* can be made conscious, but only with great effort.

11. **submissive** (adjective)   səb-mĭs'ĭv

From Latin: *sub-* (under) + *mittere* (to send, throw) This makes *sub-mittere*, "to place under."

surrendering to the will or power of another

The corporal was **submissive** to the general.

The **submissive** puppy obeyed the child's every command.

▶ *Common Phrase*
submissive to

▶ *Related Words*
submission (noun)   *Submission* to his mother's wishes brought peace to the family.

submit (verb)   Because he set off the metal detector at the airport, Gregory had to *submit* to a body search.

NOTE: Submit also means "to offer or suggest for approval." The architect *submitted* plans to the town council.

12. **subordinate** (adjective, noun)   sə-bôr'də-nĭt;
(verb)   sə-bôr'də-nāt

From Latin: *sub-* (under) + *ōrdīnāre* (to arrange in order)

less important; of lower rank (adjective)

> Regina holds a **subordinate** position to the president of the company.

a person of lower rank or importance (noun)

> The vice president is a **subordinate** of the president.

to place in a lower or less important position (verb)

> I try to **subordinate** my personal wishes to the needs of the rest of my family.

▶ *Common Phrases*
subordinate to (adjective)
a subordinate of (noun)

NOTE: The pronunciation of these words tells us whether a speaker is using the adjective and noun or the verb.

Exercises

Part 1

■ Definitions

Match each word in the left-hand column with a definition from the right-hand column. Use each choice only once.

1. revert _____
2. antagonism _____
3. equitable _____
4. revelation _____
5. antidote _____
6. submissive _____
7. antithesis _____
8. equilibrium _____

a. doubtful
b. less important in rank
c. shocking news
d. beneath awareness
e. surrendering to the power of another
f. opposite
g. something that acts against harm
h. hatred
i. return to a former practice
j. fair

9. subconscious _____   k. balance

10. recession _____   l. decline in the economy

■ *Meanings*

Match each prefix to its meaning. Use each choice only once.

1. re- _____   a. equal

2. sub- _____   b. against

                        c. under, below, part of
3. anti-, ant- _____
                        d. again, back
4. equi-, equa- _____

■ *Words in Context*

Complete each sentence with the word that fits best. Use each choice
only once.

a. antagonism   e. equitable   i. revert
b. antidote   f. equivocal   j. subconscious
c. antithesis   g. recession   k. submissive
d. equilibrium   h. revelation   l. subordinate

1. When I am on vacation I _____ to my old habit of
   sleeping late.

2. The company president, Ms. Lopez, was so busy that her

   _____ had to handle many details for her.

3. Car and home sales have dropped because of the

   _____ .

4. The _____ decision enabled everyone to feel that
   justice had been served.

5. Citizens were shocked by the _____ that the
   trusted public official had spied on his own country.

6. The man took a(n) _____ to lead poisoning.

7. The housewife kept her _____ and was able to deal calmly with three crying children and a broken window.

8. People are not aware of _____ desires.

9. Slater's compliment was _____, and we were afraid that it was actually an insult.

10. The slaves were forced to be _____ to the will of their master.

■ *Using Related Words*

Complete each sentence using a word from the group of related words above it. You may need to capitalize a word when you put it into a sentence. Use each choice only once.

1. antagonistic, antagonism, antagonists, antagonized,

   There was much _____ among the rulers of ancient Rome. In 60 B.C., a "triumvirate," or ruling group of three men—Crassus, Pompey, and Julius Caesar—was set up to rule Rome. Since Pompey was married to Caesar's daughter, it was

   hard to believe that the two men would be _____ of each other. However, Caesar's foreign conquests made him

   popular with the people, and he soon _____ jealous Pompey. They fought, and Caesar won. Later members

   of the Senate grew _____ toward Caesar because of his growing power, and they murdered him.

2. submit, submissive

   Although the Romans conquered many peoples, other groups re-

   fused to _____ to their rule. Queen Boudicca, a tribal leader of Britain, revolted after the Romans betrayed her. She attacked London in A.D. 61. Although she was eventually

   defeated, the queen refused to be _____, and she poisoned herself rather than surrendering.

3. antithesis, antithetical

The city of Rome was destroyed in a series of barbarian invasions. With their lack of culture, the barbarians were

_____ to the highly civilized Romans. Their vio-

lent and destructive behavior was the _____ of the principles on which the Roman Empire stood. After many invasions, the last Roman emperor was forced to resign in A.D. 467.

4. equivocating, equivocal

My feelings toward studying Latin were _____.
I knew that Latin would help me to become a cultured person and improve my English vocabulary. However, I feared that it would

not be as useful as Spanish. After _____ for a few weeks, I decided to take courses in both Latin and Spanish.

■ *Which Should It Be?*

Complete the following sentences by choosing the letter of the phrase that makes better sense.

1. To help you recover from poisoning, you would _____ .

   a. refuse to submit to a doctor's examination
   b. take an antidote

2. A hostile person _____ .

   a. is antagonistic toward others
   b. maintains equilibrium

3. Psychiatrists may _____ .

   a. try to make you revert to your childhood habits
   b. explore the revelations of your subconscious mind

4. A clear statement is _____ .

   a. equivocal
   b. the antithesis of an unclear one

5. The governor of a province would be pleased if _____ .

   a. his subordinates acted in an equitable manner
   b. his province went into a recession

Prefixes

Part 2

The following three prefixes are introduced in Part 2.

auto- (self)
> This prefix comes from the Greek word for "self." The word *automobile* comes from *auto-* and *mobile*, meaning "moving." When the automobile was invented, it was named for the amazing sight of something moving all by itself.

ex-, e-, ec- (out of; former)
> When *ex-* is combined with base words, it usually means "former." The words *ex-wife* (former wife) and *ex-president* (former president) show *ex-* used in this sense. The hyphens in these words give a hint that the "former" meaning is being used. When *ex-* is used with combining roots, it usually means "out of," as in *exhale* (to breathe out). The words introduced in this lesson join *ex-* to combining roots, and so *ex-* means "out of" in all of these words. However, you should remember that *ex-* can have two meanings.

im-, in- (not; in)
> This prefix is spelled in two different ways, and either spelling may have two different meanings. The most common meaning of *im-* and *in-* is "not," as in the words *impure* (not pure) and *invalid* (not valid). *Im-* and *in-* can also mean "in," as in *inhale* (to breathe in) and *import* (to carry into a country). The prefix is spelled *ir-* or *il-* before roots that begin with *r* or *l*, such as in *irregular* and *illogical*. The *il-* and *ir-* spellings always mean "not."

Words to Learn

Part 2

auto-

13. **autobiography** (noun)   ô'tō-bī-ŏg'rə-fē

> From Greek: *auto-* (self) + *bio* (life) + *graph* (to write)

> account of a person's life written by himself or herself

>> Many movie stars have written revealing **autobiographies.**

> ▶ *Related Word*
>> **autobiographical** (adjective) The novel was *autobiographical.*

14. **automaton** (noun)   ô-tŏm′ə-tən

From Greek: *auto-* (self) + *matos* (willing)

robot; person acting in a mechanical fashion

> People who work on assembly lines sometimes feel like **automatons** because they go through the same motions hundreds of times a day.

> A TV cartoon series features Robocop, an **automaton** who serves on the Detroit police force.

The word *robot,* which is one definition of *automaton,* comes from the Czech *robota,* meaning "hard labor." Karel Capek, a Czech playwright, gave the name *robot* to the obedient machine-man he invented for a play he wrote in 1923.

---

15. **autonomous** (adjective)   ô-tŏn′ə-məs

From Greek: *auto-* (self) + *nomos* (law)

self-governing; independent

> After World War II, many colonies of the British Empire became **autonomous.**

> People usually need to be self-supporting before they can truly be **autonomous.**

▶ *Related Word*
   autonomy (noun)   Slaves have no *autonomy.*

ex-

16. **eccentric** (adjective)   ĕk-sĕn′trĭk

From Greek: *ek-* (out) + *kentron* (center)

odd; different from normal or usual

> The **eccentric** man had an apartment littered with crumpled newspapers.

▶ *Related Word*
   eccentricity (noun)   (ĕk′sĕn-trĭs′ə-tē)   The man's *eccentricities* annoyed his wife.

17. **exorbitant** (adjective)   ĭg-zôr′bə-tənt

From Latin: *ex-* (out) + *orbita* (path)

expensive; unreasonable; exceeding proper limits

> Prices at the shop were so **exorbitant** that I refused to buy anything there.

> Management refused to meet the football player's **exorbitant** contract demands.

18. **exploit** (verb) ĭk-sploit'; (noun) ĕks'ploit'

From Latin: *ex-* (out) + *plicāre* (to fold), making *explicāre* (to unfold) (When we *exploit* something, we "fold it out" and make it work for us.)

to take advantage of; to use (verb)

> In the early twentieth century, American laborers were **exploited** and often worked long hours for little pay.

> Alaska **exploited** its rich oil and natural gas reserves without harming the environment.

great adventure; great deed (noun)

> Homer's *Odyssey* related the **exploits** of the Greek hero Odysseus as he returned home from the Trojan War.

NOTE: 1. *Exploit*, when used as a verb, often suggests taking unfair advantage (as in the exploitation of women or minorities). However, it can mean simply "to take advantage of" or "to use wisely."
2. Notice the difference in pronunciation stress between *exploit'* (verb) and *ex'ploit* (noun).

▶ *Related word*
exploitation (noun) (ĕks'ploi-tā'shən) The *exploitation* of the workers resulted in a strike.

19. **extricate** (verb) ĕk'strĭ-kāt'

From Latin: *ex-* (out) + *tricae* (difficulties), making *extricāre* (to disentangle, to free)

to free from difficulty; to disentangle

> We **extricated** the bleeding rabbit from the trap.

> Roy **extricated** himself from an embarrassing situation by leaving the room.

▶ *Common Phrase*
to extricate from

Harry Houdini (1874–1926) was a world-famous escape artist. Houdini extricated himself from many seemingly escape-proof devices, including ten pairs of handcuffs, jail cells, nailed crates, and an airtight tank filled with water. Once, tied into a straitjacket and hung upside-down from the top of a tall building, he extricated himself within minutes.

im-, in-

20. **impartial** (adjective)   ĭm-pär′shəl

From Latin: *im-* (not) + *pars* (part)

fair; just; not biased

It is important for a basketball referee to be **impartial**.

Mother maintained an **impartial** attitude in the fight between my brother and sister.

▶ *Related Word*
impartiality (noun)   (ĭm′pär-shē-al′ə-tē)   Mary Jo's *impartiality* helped to settle the argument fairly.

21. **ingenious** (adjective)   ĭn-jēn'yəs

    From Latin: *in-* (in) + *gen* (born), making *ingenium* (inborn talent)

    clever; inventive

    > The **ingenious** inventor Thomas Edison was responsible for both the phonograph and the motion picture projector.

    > The **ingenious** slogan "snap, crackle, pop" has sold many boxes of Rice Krispies.

    ► *Related Word*
    ingenuity (noun)   (ĭn'jə-nōō'ə-tē)   Computer programmers are known for their *ingenuity*.

    Benjamin Franklin, a Philadelphian who lived in the 1700s, produced many ingenious inventions, including the lightning rod, bifocals (glasses with two visual corrections), and the Franklin stove (which stood in the middle of a room, heating all parts evenly). Franklin also developed some valuable public services, such as the public library and the volunteer fire department.

    ---

22. **interminable** (adjective)   ĭn-tûr'mə-nə-bəl

    From Latin: *in-* (not) + *terminus* (end, boundary)

    endless; too long

    > The lecture seemed **interminable,** but we were afraid to get up and leave.

    NOTE: Interminable has a negative connotation. It often describes something that seems endless rather than actually is endless.

23. **invariably** (adverb)   ĭn-vâr'ē-ə-blē

    From Latin: *in-* (not) + *variabilis* (changeable)

    consistently; always

    > My brother **invariably** loses his temper when we ask him to do the dishes.

24. **invoke** (verb)   ĭn-vōk'

    From Latin: *in-* (in) + *voc* (to call) (*Invocāre* means "to call upon.")

    to call for assistance; to call upon

The minister **invoked** the help of God in troubled times.

The President **invoked** the aid of the National Guard to stop the rioting.

▶ *Related Word*
invocation (noun) (ĭn′və-kā′shən) The minister gave an *invocation*. (*Invocation* means "prayer.")

The Fifth Amendment of the U.S. Constitution states that those accused of a crime cannot be forced to testify against themselves. Thus, when asked to explain something that may injure their case or make them appear guilty, accused people may "invoke the Fifth Amendment" and refuse to answer.

Exercises

Part 2

■ Definitions

Match each word in the left-hand column with a definition from the right-hand column. Use each choice only once.

1. autobiography _____   a. robot
2. eccentric _____   b. the story of one's own life
                             c. odd
3. impartial _____   d. clever
4. exorbitant _____   e. consistently; always
5. exploit _____   f. to call for assistance
                             g. to take advantage of
6. invoke _____   h. to free from difficulty
7. ingenious _____   i. not biased
8. autonomous _____   j. self-ruling
                             k. very expensive

9. extricate _____   1. endless

10. invariably _____

■ *Meanings*

Match each prefix to its meaning. Use each choice only once.

1. ex-, e-, ec- _____   a. self

2. im-, in- _____   b. in; not

                              c. out; former

3. auto- _____

■ *Words in Context*

Complete each sentence with the word that fits best. Use each choice only once.

a. autobiography	e. exorbitant	i. ingenious
b. automaton	f. exploit	j. interminable
c. autonomous	g. extricate	k. invariably
d. eccentric	h. impartial	l. invoke

1. Since the drive from Philadelphia to Portland can seem

   _____, many people prefer to fly there.

2. Scientists have devised a(n) _____ car window glass that blocks heat and reduces the need for air conditioning.

3. It is important not to _____ migrant workers by making them work long hours for very low pay.

4. In his _____, Lee Iacocca revealed the secrets of his success.

5. Under President Vytautas Landsbergis' leadership, Lithuania has

   become more _____ and under less strict Russian control.

6. The defending lawyer tried to _____ the court's mercy for her client.

7. Most people feel that $100,000 is a(n) _____ price to pay for a car.

8. The _____ lady kept ninety-nine cats in her home.

9. People _____ close their eyes when they sneeze, since it is not possible to keep them open.

10. The _____ was not capable of independent thought.

■ *Using Related Words*

Complete each sentence using a word from the group of related words above it. You may need to capitalize a word when you put it into a sentence. Use each choice only once.

1. impartial, impartiality

   Socrates, whose teachings inspire many young people, was among the most famous citizens of Athens. Unfortunately, he criticized many city leaders, and in 399 B.C., he was brought to trial for corrupting youth. Emotions were so strong that it was difficult to

   be _____ in the debate. Socrates was condemned to die by drinking the poison hemlock. Although the city elders

   thought they had acted with _____, others disagreed. Among Socrates' most famous pupils was the philosopher Plato, author of *The Republic*.

2. autonomy, autonomous

   In 490 B.C., Darius, King of the enormous Persian empire, decided

   to conquer the city-state of Athens and end its _____ . Against all odds, Athens defeated the Persian army on the Plain

   of Marathon, and remained _____. Pheidippides ran 26 miles to deliver news of the victory to Athens. Since then, a race of 26 miles, or any long, difficult contest, has been called a "marathon."

3. ingenious, ingenuity

   Euclid, who lived in Alexandra at about 500 B.C., was a mathematician of great _____ . His _____ system of teaching geometry through proofs is still used in classrooms today.

4. exploited, exploitation

Despite the great culture that Greece produced, it was a civilization based on _____. Slaves provided the basis of much of the labor. Even free women were _____ , since they were considered to be the property of their families, rather than citizens.

5. extricated, extricate

After several years of fighting the Trojan war, the Greeks had not conquered the Trojans. Finally, the Greeks used a trick to

_____ themselves from their difficulties. Greek soldiers hid inside a large wooden horse just outside the city gates. Assuming the horse was a gift, the Trojans brought it inside. When night fell, the Greeks _____ themselves from the horse, attacked, and conquered Troy.

■ *True or False?*

Each of the following statements contains at least one word from this section. Read each statement and then indicate whether you think it is probably true or probably false.

____ 1. A person writing an autobiography tells about his or her own life.

____ 2. An eccentric person behaves like everyone else.

____ 3. An interesting, well-acted play would seem interminable.

____ 4. Knitting a sweater can be described as an exploit.

____ 5. Ingenious inventions are clever.

____ 6. We would want to extricate ourselves from a good situation.

____   7. One hundred dollars is an exorbitant price to pay for a nice house.

____   8. Rain is invariably wet.

____   9. We might want to invoke the aid of an impartial person to settle an argument.

____   10. An automaton is autonomous.

Chapter Exercises

■ *Practicing Strategies: New Words from Word Elements*

See how your knowledge of prefixes can help you to understand new words. Complete each sentence with the word that seems to fit best. Use each choice only once.

a. antifreeze   e. equipoise   i. refill
b. antibacterial   f. impression   j. retry
c. autoinoculation   g. income   k. subliminal
d. equator   h. irresponsible   l. subcontractors

1. The scientists will _____ the space launch next week, since it failed to take off today.

2. After I drank all of my coffee, the waiter offered to

   _____ my cup.

3. The _____ solution helped to protect the wound from germs.

4. The _____ person did not fulfill her duties.

5. Something _____ is beneath the limits of your hearing or vision.

6. A(n) _____ is made when feet press into soft cement.

7. The process in which chemicals from your own body are injected

   back into you to fight disease is called _____ .

8. Several _____ may work under a contractor.

9. The _____ divides the earth equally into the Northern and Southern hemispheres.

10. When two forces are poised equally against each other, they are in

    a state of _____ .

■ *Practicing Strategies: Combining Context Clues and Word Elements*

Combining the strategies of context clues and word elements is a good way to figure out unknown words. In the following sentences, each italicized word contains a word element that you have studied in this chapter. Using the meaning of the prefix and the context of the sentence, make an intelligent guess at the meaning of the italicized word. Your instructor may ask you to check the meaning in your dictionary after you have finished.

1. The *subcellar* was the first room to flood during the storm.

   Subcellar means _____ .

2. Using the *autofocus* feature of the camera, even an amateur can take a clear picture.

   Autofocus means _____ .

3. The criminal was *extradited* from England and sent to the United States.

   Extradited means _____ .

4. At the time of an *equinox*, there are twelve hours of daylight in the twenty-four-hour day.

   Equinox means _____ .

5. Since the computer is *infallible*, the mistake must be due to human error.

   Infallible means _____ .

■ *Practicing Strategies: Using the Dictionary*

Read the following definition and then answer the questions below it.

> **pha·lanx** (fā′lăngks′) *n., pl.* **pha·lanx·es** or **pha·lan·ges**
> (fə-lăn′jēx, fā-) **1.** A formation of infantry carrying overlap-
> ping shields and long spears, developed by Philip II of Macedo-
> nia and used by Alexander the Great. **2.** A close-knit or
> compact body of people: *"formed a solid phalanx in defence
> of the Constitution and Protestant religion"* (G.M. Trevelyan).
> **3.** *pl.* **phalanges.** *Anat.* A bone of a finger or toe. [Lat. < Gk.]

1. Which common word in the dictionary key contains a vowel pro-

   nounced like the second *a* in *phalanx?* _____

2. What is the plural form of *phalanx* when used in an anatomical

   sense? _____

3. Which writer is quoted to help define *phalanx?*

   _____

4. Give the number and the part of speech of the definition that best
   fits this sentence: "The community formed a phalanx to urge their

   representative to pass the law." _____

5. Give the number and the part of speech of the definition which best
   fits this sentence: "The phalanx marched into battle."

   _____

■ *Companion Words*

Complete each sentence with the word that fits best. Choose your answers from the words below. You may use each word more than once.

Choices: in, to, toward, of, from

1. The revelations _____ dishonesty among city politicians
   shocked us.

2. The tribal chief invoked the aid _____ the central government.

3. The University of Michigan and The Ohio State University were an-

   tagonists _____ the football game.

4. Please don't revert _____ childish behavior.

5. The vice president is subordinate _____ the president.

6. The vice president is a subordinate _____ the president.

7. Please maintain an impartial attitude _____ both sides.

8. We enjoyed hearing about the exploits _____ Dr. Livingstone.

9. Kindness is the antithesis _____ cruelty.

10. Please extricate us _____ this situation.

■ *Writing with Your Words*

This exercise will give you practice in writing effective sentences using the vocabulary words. Each sentence is started for you. Complete it with an interesting phrase that also indicates the meaning of the italicized word.

1. When I lose my *equilibrium* _____

_____ .

2. An *antidote* to envy is _____

_____ .

3. The *exploits* of the adventurer included _____

_____ .

4. The world needs an *ingenious* solution to the problem of _____

_____ .

5. Since the wait seemed *interminable*, we _____

_____ .

6. Because of the shocking *revelations*, _____

_____ .

7. I *invariably* have difficulty _____

_____ .

8. The *exorbitant* price of the car _____

_____ .

9. In a *recession,* _____

_____ .

10. A man would be considered *eccentric* if _____

_____ .

Passage

*Alchemy—Gold from Tin and Aluminum**

To achieve wealth without work is a common desire. If only we could become rich by turning our tin cups and aluminum pans into precious metals!

Alchemists were early experimenters who tried to turn common metals into gold. They searched for a mythical ingredient called the "philosopher's stone," which was thought to be the key to the change. Some thought the **revelation** would come through experiments; others searched in ancient books; still others looked for **subconscious** guidance from their own dreams. Alas, no one ever succeeded in making gold!

The first well-known alchemist was Abou Moussah Djafar, the Wise. Born in Mesopotamia (now Iraq) in the eighth century, he believed that gold would cure all illnesses. **(1)** Djafar's **ingenious** experiments led to the discovery of several compounds.

Alchemists were often credited with strange powers. Albertus Magnus, a German born in 1193, was said to have brought a statue to life and then destroyed it when it annoyed him. **(2)** According to legend, his other **exploits** included changing winter into summer so that his prince could enjoy an outdoor feast. Not content with this, Albertus made the season **revert** to winter, just in time for his prince to suffer from the cold as he journeyed home.

Nicholas Flamel, born in France in the 1200s, by chance bought an old book written in Latin. He decided that it had been composed by

*Adapted from Charles MacKay, *Memoirs of Extraordinary Popular Delusions* (London: Richard Bently, 1841).

the biblical figure, Abraham. It did not occur to Flamel that Abraham had been born almost three thousand years before Latin was spoken. The book contained specific directions for making gold. But there was one problem: it assumed that the reader already had the philosopher's stone! This was like giving a starving man a recipe for cooking a steak without supplying the money to buy one. For the rest of his life, Flamel searched for the precious stone. **(3)** It is rumored that he found it, but was so **eccentric** that he chose to continue living in poverty. **(4)** Although Flamel's reputation for making gold is **equivocal,** some people must have believed it. Six centuries later, a man rented Flamel's house and tore it up, searching for gold dust. Unfortunately, his search resulted only in payment for damages.

How did alchemists work? First, they decided upon the ingredients of the philosopher's stone. Wine, salt, garbage (highly purified), sea water, and eggshells were often used. After adding these to some tin or aluminum, the alchemist told his **subordinates** to heat the mixture. **(5)** They stirred it for what seemed like an **interminable** time, emptied the pot, and searched for gold dust. **(6)** The experiment **invariably** failed.

"If only my pot had not cracked," one would cry. "If only I could find more dark brown eggshells," said another. "If only I had used a round container," complained a third. **(7)** The **exorbitant** cost of these experiments reduced many an alchemist to poverty.

Alchemists never succeeded in producing gold.

(8) Yet **impartial** witnesses sometimes believed that they had seen gold being made. How did this happen? Some phoneys and crooks would give public displays of their skills. Standing dramatically by a large pot, they would slowly add "secret" ingredients, **invoking** the aid of spirits. Then they would quietly throw in some real gold. They often used hollow wands filled with gold and sealed with butter. When the wand was put in the hot mixture, the butter melted and the gold was mixed into the liquid. Thus, it appeared that gold had been made.

John Dee and Edward Kelly, Englishmen of the 1500s, were good examples of such swindlers. They told Polish nobleman Albertus Laski that they would find the philosopher's stone for him if he would only support their experiments. (9) Laski was persuaded to **submit** to their demands. He gave huge amounts of money for experiments, which always failed, just at the last minute. (10) Finally, Laski became **antagonistic** and ordered them out. Ending his days in poverty, Dee was given royal permission to beg by Queen Elizabeth I.

Not all alchemists were as lucky as Dee. It is said that some were locked in prisons and required to make thousands of pounds of gold in order to **extricate** themselves.

And thus, we leave the story of alchemy. Although alchemists made some important scientific discoveries, they never succeeded in producing gold. Today we know that making it, although possible, would require complex atomic reactions and involve expenses greater than the value of the gold itself. Hard word is a surer road to riches than the philosopher's stone.

■ *Exercise*

Each numbered sentence below corresponds to a sentence in the Passage. Fill in the letter of the choice that makes this sentence mean the same thing as the corresponding sentence in the Passage.

1. Djafar's _____ experiments led to the discovery of several compounds.

   a. elaborate   b. slow   c. clever   d. scientific

2. Among his other _____ he reportedly changed winter into summer.

   a. adventures   b. disasters   c. hobbies   d. experiments

3. It is rumored that he found it, but was so _____ that he chose to continue living in poverty.

   a. wise   b. nice   c. humble   d. odd

4. Although Flamel's reputation for making gold is _____, some people must have believed it.

   a. false   b. evil   c. doubtful   d. crazy

5. They stirred it for a _____ period of time.

   a. short   b. long   c. reasonable   d. wonderful

6. The experiment _____ failed.

   a. always   b. rarely   c. usually   d. never

7. The _____ cost of these experiments reduced many an alchemist to poverty.

   a. unnecessary   b. ridiculous   c. large   d. small

8. Yet _____ witnesses sometimes believed that they had seen gold being made.

   a. intelligent   b. blind   c. careless   d. fair

9. Laski was persuaded to _____ to their demands.

   a. listen   b. reply   c. return   d. surrender

10. Finally, Laski became _____ and ordered them out.

    a. tired   b. foolish   c. rich   d. unfriendly

■ Discussion Questions

1. Why is it impossible for Abraham to have written Flamel's book?

2. Why do you think alchemists continued with their experiments even after so much failure?

3. Name another phony get-rich-quick scheme and defend your choice.

Word Elements: People and Names

Many words in English are derived from descriptions of people and names. Characters from classical myths, as well as the names of famous people, have been a rich source of words. The first part of this chapter introduces four word roots that relate to people. The second part adds two prefixes that were taken from names of characters in Greek mythology and introduces some additional words formed from the names.

Chapter Strategy: Word Elements about People

Chapter Words:

Part 1			
anthrop	anthropomorphism	*nom*	nominal
	misanthrope		pseudonym
	philanthropist		renown
gen	congenital	*viv*	viable
	genesis		vital
	genocide		vivacious
Part 2			
pan-	panorama	*Name Words*	boycott
	pandemonium		chauvinism
psych-	psyche		martial
	psychosomatic		maverick
			quixotic
			spartan
			tantalize
			vandalism

Did You Know?

Which Words Come from Names?

Many English words are formed from names in classical mythology. The Greeks and Romans had a well-developed and colorful mythology, whose legends reflected the violence and passion of life in a time when natural forces and disease could not be controlled.

According to myth, Jupiter, king of the gods, ruled thunder, a fearful force to the ancient people. His many exploits included dethroning his father, and turning himself into a swan in order to seduce a young girl. He loved to play nasty pranks on others. The word *jovial*, meaning "merry," was taken from Jove, another name for Jupiter.

Mercury, often shown in paintings with wings on his feet, was the speedy messenger of the gods. The metal *mercury*, used in most thermometers, is a quickly-moving liquid at room temperature. A quick-tempered person is often called *mercurial*.

Venus, or Aphrodite, was the goddess of love. An *aphrodisiac* is a drug or food that increases sexual desire.

Two English words derive from the Titans, giants who ruled the earth before Jupiter's thunderbolts conquered them. Something of enormous size and power is called *titanic*. Since one Titan, Atlas, was condemned to support the world on his shoulder, a book containing maps is now called an *atlas*.

Many real people have also given their names to words. U.S. Union Civil War general Ambrose Burnside, a fashion leader, allowed his hair to grow down the side of his face, inventing a style we still call *sideburns*.

At the time of the California gold rush (1848–60), Levi Strauss bought large amounts of denim canvas to make tents, but found that he could not sell them. In order to use the material, Strauss began to manufacture sturdy pants with copper rivets at the pockets to hold gold samples. To this day, the pants are called *levis*, and Levi Strauss and Company still operates in San Francisco.

Some words come from names of religious organizations. The coffee drink *cappucino* comes from the Italian order of Capuchin, a group of Roman Catholic monks.

Finally, places have donated their names. The word *dollar* comes from *taler*, short for *Joachimstalther*, the city in Bohemia where it was first used. The *tuxedo*, men's formal wear, comes from Tuxedo Park in New York State. Scotch liquor comes from Scotland. The *peach* was the Latin word for Persia (now Iran) where this fruit originated.

Even names of some imaginary places have been used. In about 1500, a Spanish novelist described a beautiful, imaginary island inhabited by strong women. When exploring the new world, one of Cortez's captains used the novelist's word to name a real place of great natural beauty, at first thought to be an island. The name, *California*, is still used today.

You will be learning several words derived from names and places in this chapter. Perhaps one day a word will be named after you!

Learning Strategy

Word Elements About People

This first part of the chapter discusses word roots and how they function in words. Four specific roots dealing with people are used as examples. The second part continues with prefixes and presents two prefixes taken from names.

Element	Meaning	Origin	Function	Chapter Words
		Part 1		
anthrop	human	Greek	root	anthropomorphism, misanthrope, philanthropist
gen	birth; type	Latin; Greek	root	congenital, genesis, genocide
nom, nym	name	Latin; Greek	root	nominal, pseudonym, renown
viv, vit	life	Latin	root	viable, vital, vivacious
		Part 2		
pan-	all	Greek	prefix	panorama, pandemonium
psych-	mind; soul	Greek	prefix	psyche, psychosomatic

A root is the word element that carries the most meaning. Although prefixes and suffixes may alter the meaning of a root, they never carry as much meaning as the root itself.

There are two kinds of roots—base words and combining roots. Base words can stand alone as English words. They may or may not have prefixes and suffixes attached to them. *Work* is an example of a base word.

Combining roots cannot stand alone as English words. They require a prefix, a suffix, or at least a change in spelling in order to form a word. Most of the roots you will study in this book are combining roots that come from ancient Greek and Latin. Although they were words in these ancient languages, they appear in modern English only as root word elements.

The root *anthrop* (human) is an example of a combining root. It can form a word when it is attached to a prefix *(misanthrope)* or a suffix *(anthropomorphism)*.

Nom or *nym*, meaning "name," is another example of a combining root. This root has more than one spelling because it comes from both Latin and Greek. It forms over thirty English words. Slight changes in spelling give us the words *name* and *noun*; adding a suffix gives us *nominate*; adding different prefixes gives us *antonym* and *synonym*.

Each of the words formed from the root *nom* or *nym* carries a meaning related to "name." Sometimes the meaning is directly related to "name"; at other times the word root gives a hint about a word's meaning rather than supplying a direct meaning. The word *name* has the same meaning as the root *nom* or *nym*; the word and the root are directly related. Other words have an indirect relationship to *nom* and *nym*.

A *noun* is a word that names something.

To *nominate* is to name somebody to a position, or to name somebody as a candidate in an election.

A *synonym* means the same thing as another word; two synonyms "name" the same thing. (*Sym* means "same.")

An *antonym* is a word opposite in meaning to another word; two antonyms "name" opposite things. (As you learned in Chapter 5, *ant-* means "opposite.")

Word Roots

Part 1

The four roots presented in Part 1 of this chapter all deal with people and their lives.

anthrop (human)

The root *anthrop* comes from the Greek word for "human," *anthropos*. This root is often used in words from college courses on biology and human society. Perhaps you have taken a course in *anthropology*, the study of human society.

gen (birth; type)

Because it forms over fifty English words, *gen* is an extremely useful root. *Gen* has two meanings: "birth" and "type." The ancients felt that these meanings were related because, when someone was born, he or she was a certain "type" of person. *Gen* means "birth" in the word *gene*, which refers to the hereditary information in each cell of a living plant or animal. We are all "born with" our genes.

Gen means "type" in the word *gender*, which tells what type of person you are, male or female. Perhaps you buy *generic* foods at the grocery. These have no brand names and are of a "general type." The use of context clues will help you to determine whether *gen* means "birth" or "type" when you see it in a word.

nom, nym (name)

This root word comes from both Latin and Greek. *Nomen* is Latin for "name" and the word originally appeared in Greek as *onoma*.

Naming customs differ throughout the world. In the Far East, one's first name follows one's family (or last) name. For example, the last name of the famous Chinese leader Mao Tse-tung was "Mao." Russians use *patronymics*, names from a father's first name, as middle names. For example, Sonya Fekson, the daughter of Ivan, would be known as Soyna Ivanovna Fekson. David, Ivan's son, would be David Ivanovich Fekson. It is considered very respectful to call a person by a first name and patronymic, without using a last name.

---

viv, vit (life)

In Latin *vita* means "life." *Vit* forms such words as *vitamin*, a chemical necessary for human life. Manufacturers have used this root to make brand names, such as the hair product "Vitalis," which is supposed to add life to your hair.

Words to Learn

Part 1

anthrop

1. **anthropomorphism** (noun)   ăn'thrə-pō-môr'fĭz'əm

   From Greek: *anthrop* (human) + *morphē* (form)

   giving human characteristics to nonhumans

   > The cartoon character Mickey Mouse is an example of **anthropomorphism.**

   > People indulge in **anthropomorphism** when they call bees "busy" and flies "lazy."

   ▶ *Related Word*
   anthropomorphic (adjective)   The Greeks and Romans had *anthropomorphic* gods.

2. **misanthrope** (noun)   mĭs'ən-thrōp'

   From Greek: *misein* (to hate) + *anthrop* (human)

   a person who hates or distrusts other people

The **misanthrope** allowed his workers to suffer from low wages and unhealthy conditions.

▶ *Related Words*
　misanthropic (adjective)   (mĭs′ən-thrŏp′ĭk)   The *misanthropic* behavior of Ebenezer Scrooge caused unhappiness.

　misanthropy (noun)   (mĭs-ăn′thrə-pē)   Scrooge learned that his *misanthropy* had made him and others unhappy.

One famous literary character exemplifies misanthropy. Ebenezer Scrooge, created by Charles Dickens in the classic novel *A Christmas Carol*, mistreats his employees and wishes ill to everybody. He will not let anyone enjoy Christmas if he can make it miserable. His famous line "Bah, humbug!" has become a motto for the misanthrope.

---

3. **philanthropist** (noun)   fĭ-lăn′thrə-pĭst

From Greek: *philos* (loving) + *anthrop* (human)

one who wishes to help others; a person who makes large gifts to charity

　The **philanthropist** donated $100,000 to aid the homeless.

▶ *Related Words*
　philanthropic (adjective)   (fĭl′ən-thrŏp′ik)   The *philanthropic* gift helped the hospital to fund new research.

　philanthropy (noun)   Mexican workers who make money in the U.S. often demonstrate *philanthropy* by donating money to improve their hometowns.

gen

4. **congenital** (adjective)   kən-jĕn′ə-təl

From Latin: *com-* (together; with) + *gen* (birth) (If something is *congenital*, you are born with it.)

existing at birth

　Because of a **congenital** ear defect, the man had been completely deaf since birth.

　According to recent studies, fingerprint patterns can often reveal **congenital** health problems.

naturally being a certain way; habitual

　He was a **congenital** liar who could not tell the truth, no matter how much pressure was put on him.

5. **genesis** (noun)   jĕn′ə-sĭs

From Greek: *gen* (birth) (*Genesis* meant "birth" or "origin" in ancient Greek.)

origin; beginning

> The **genesis** of the steam engine dates back to the ancient Greeks.

> Many scientists think that the **genesis** of our universe was an enormous explosion called the "big bang."

Genesis, the first book of the Bible, tells the story of a great flood which only Noah, his family, and two of each type of animal survived. Many other religions and cultures have tales of a large flood. In southern Mesopotamia (now largely Iraq), references to a flood are recorded on a stone tablet (dated at 2100 B.C.) and in the Babylonian Epic of Gilgamesh (about 700 B.C.). Other references are found in India, Burma, Australia, and among native American Indian tribes. Was there ever a great flood? In 1929, Sir Leonard Woolley, after exploring lower Mesopotamia, concluded that a widespread area had been badly flooded in about 3000 B.C.

---

6. **genocide** (noun)   jĕn′ə-sīd′

From Greek: *gen* (type) + Latin: *-cidium* (killing) (*Genos* meant "race" in ancient Greek, so *genocide* means "the killing of an entire race.")

the planned murder of an entire group

> The **genocide** of Armenians during World War I resulted in over a million deaths.

One of the most horrible recent examples of genocide occurred from 1939 to 1945, when the leader of Nazi Germany, Adolph Hitler, planned the destruction of all of Europe's Jews. This dreadful plan, often called the Holocaust, resulted in the deaths of over six million people. Another six million civilians were murdered in countries occupied by the Nazis because of their ethnic origins, beliefs, or resistance to Nazi ideas.

---

nom; nym

7. **nominal** (adjective)   nŏm′ə-nəl

From Latin: *nom* (name)

in name only

> Although Queen Elizabeth is the **nominal** ruler of England, the prime minister actually holds most of the power.

a very small amount

> The nonprofit organization paid the city a **nominal** rent of one dollar a year.

8. **pseudonym** (noun)   sōō′də-nĭm′

From Greek: *pseudes* (false) + *nym* (name)

assumed name; pen name

> Stephen King has published many successful novels under the **pseudonym** Richard Bachman.

NOTE: The word *pseudonym* often refers to authors or artists. In contrast, *alias* usually refers to names assumed by criminals and has a negative connotation.

9. **renown** (noun)   rĭ-noun′

From Latin: *re-* (again) + *nom* (to name) (A person who is "named repeatedly" becomes famous.)

honorable fame; celebrity

> Robert E. Lee, head of the Confederate army in the Civil War, gained **renown** for his strategic ability and sense of honor.
> Bruce Lee won great **renown** for his ability in judo.

▶ *Related Word*
renowned (adjective)   Mexican tenor Placido Domingo is a *renowned* opera star.

vit; vit

10. **viable** (adjective)   vī′ə-bəl

From Latin: *vit* (life), becoming French *vie* (life)

capable of living; capable of success; workable

> Although this seed is several years old, it is still **viable** and will grow if we plant it.
> A second career has become a **viable** alternative to retirement.

Many species of parrots that once covered North and South America have died out or are in danger of becoming extinct. As their homelands have been destroyed, millions have perished. In 1982, there were only 15 Hispaniolan Parrots left in the world. By breeding birds in captivity and releasing them into the wild, scientists help the species to continue. Scientists hope that released birds will be *viable* in the wild and will survive to breed future generations.

11. **vital** (adjective)   vī**′**təl

From Latin: *vit* (life)

referring to life

The doctor measured her pulse, blood pressure, and other **vital** signs.

necessary; essential

Endurance is **vital** to a champion swimmer.

The information supplied by the spy was **vital** to the national defense.

▶ *Common Phrase*
vital to

▶ *Related Word*
vitality (noun)   (vī-tăl**′**ə-tē)   The plumber's *vitality* enabled him to work long hours. (*Vitality* means "life energy.")

12. **vivacious** (adjective)   vǐ-vā**′**shəs

From Latin: *viv* (to live) (*Vivax* meant "lively.")

lively; full of spirit

The girl's **vivacious** temperament and sense of fun made her popular at school.

▶ *Related Word*
vivacity (noun)   (vǐ-văs**′**ə-tē)   The hostess's **vivacity** helped to make the restaurant popular.

The word *vivacious* is related to *vivace*. Written above a piece of music, it tells the musician to play it in a lively way. Most musical terms are written in Italian, the modern descendant of Latin. Other examples are *largo* (slowly), *andante* (at a walking pace), and *moderato* (moderately).

Exercises

Part 1

■ Definitions

Complete each sentence in the left-hand column by choosing a word or phrase from the right-hand column. Use each choice only once.

1. A congenital condition is _____ .
2. Genocide is _____ .
3. A pseudonym is _____ .
4. A person in nominal control is

   _____ .
5. A person of renown is _____ .
6. A philanthropist is _____ .
7. Anthropomorphism means

   _____ .
8. Genesis is _____ .
9. Something vital to a person is

   _____ .
10. A viable idea is _____ .

a. a beginning

b. a person who distrusts others

c. giving human characteristics to a nonhuman

d. murder of an entire group

e. charitable

f. a false name

g. famous

h. workable

i. lively

j. not really in power

k. present at birth

l. necessary

■ Meanings

Match each word element to its meaning. Use each choice only once.

1. nom, nym _____
2. viv, vit _____

a. life

b. human

c. birth; type

3. gen _____   d. name

4. anthrop _____

■ *Words in Context*

Complete each sentence with the word that fits best. Use each choice only once.

a. anthropomorphism   e. genesis   i. renown
b. misanthrope   f. genocide   j. viable
c. philanthropist   g. nominal   k. vital
d. congenital   h. pseudonym   l. vivacious

1. The _____ of writing dates back to 3500 B.C.

2. Some people are born with spinal bifida, a(n) _____ condition that affects their ability to walk.

3. The heart is a(n) _____ organ to the human body.

4. Rick Santiago won _____ throughout the city for his beautiful masonry work.

5. The small chick was not _____ and it soon died.

6. The _____ woman loved to socialize at parties.

7. Samuel Clemens published under the _____ Mark Twain.

8. The evil creatures from Mars planned the _____ of the entire human race.

9. Since she was only an honorary mayor of the city, she was paid a(n)

   _____ salary of five dollars a year.

10. Only a(n) _____ would turn away from this scene of human happiness.

■ *Using Related Words*

Complete each sentence using a word from the group of related words above it. You may need to capitalize a word when you put it into a sentence. Use each choice only once.

1. anthropomorphic, anthropomorphize

   The Greeks and Romans had an _____ religion in which they represented their gods as having the physical features and emotions of human beings. This anthropmorphism is far removed from most modern concepts of religion. However the

   authors of modern children's books often _____ their characters. In the book *Charlotte's Web,* by E.B. White, Charlotte, a spider, and Tempelton, a rat, plot to save Wilbur, a pig, from slaughter.

2. vital, vitality

   In Greek mythology, the efforts of the hero, Achilles, were

   _____ to the success of the Greeks over Troy. At his birth, Achilles' mother, a goddess, wanted to make her son immortal, so she dipped him in the River Styx to preserve his

   _____ . Unfortunately, she held him by his heel, and the protective water failed to touch it. As battle raged in Troy, an arrow struck Achilles in his heel, killing him. A vulnerable point, which can be easily harmed is now called an "Achilles heel."

3. renown, renowned

   When the legendary hero Odysseus went to fight in the Trojan war, he entrusted the education of his son to the

   _____ tutor, Mentor. In modern sports and busi-

   ness, a coach or adviser of great _____ is often called a "mentor."

4. philanthropist, philanthropy

   Andrew Carnegie was a _____ who donated many libraries to towns throughout the United States. His

   _____ helped to educate many people.

5. vivacious, vivacity

   The law enforcement officer was a _____ woman who loved to talk with friends, go to parties, and dance.

Her _____ at social occasions showed those who worked with her that she could be charming in social situations. Yet on the job, she was tough and effective in dealing with those who broke the law.

■ *Reading the Headlines*

This exercise presents five headlines that might have been taken from newspapers. Read each headline and then answer the questions that follow. (Remember that small words, such as *a* and *the*, are often left out of newspaper headlines.)

VIVACIOUS PHILANTHROPIST HELPS TO BRING ABOUT GENESIS OF PROGRAM

1. Is the person generous? _____

2. Is the program ending? _____

CITIZENS PAY NOMINAL AMOUNT FOR VITAL CITY SERVICES

3. Is the amount of payment small? _____

4. Are the services important? _____

MAN WINS RENOWN UNDER PSEUDONYM

5. Is the man famous? _____

6. Do most people know the man's real name? _____

MISANTHROPE SUSPECTED OF PLAYING PART IN GENOCIDE

7. Does the suspected person like other people? _____

8. Did murder take place? _____

SCIENTIFIC ADVANCE MAKES BABY WITH CONGENITAL HEART DEFECT VIABLE

9. Will the baby live? _____

10. Was the defect caused by events after the baby was born?

_____

Prefixes and Name Words

Part 2

Part 2 of this chapter deals mostly with words taken from names. The two prefixes presented also occur as names in Greek mythology. Four words using these prefixes and eight words taken directly from names are introduced.

pan- (all)

The prefix *pan-* is the Greek word for "all." It appears in two names in Greek mythology. Pan was the god of woods, fields, and shepherds. He had the lower body of a goat and the upper body of a man. He got his name "because he delighted all," wrote Homer. Pandora (*pan-*, all, + *dora*, gifts) was the first woman. The gods sent her to earth and gave her a box that she was told not to open. Curiosity got the better of her, she disobeyed, and out flew all the world's troubles. Only Hope remained shut up in the box. Like Eve in the Bible, Pandora was a woman blamed for causing all the world's problems. The prefix *pan-* is used in such words as *pan-American*, which refers to all of America: North, South, and Central.

psych-; psycho- (mind; soul)

The Greek word *psyche* originally meant "breath," and thus means the soul or the spirit of a person. It is personified in Greek mythology as Psyche, a beautiful mortal, who was loved by Eros (Cupid), the god of love. He visited her every night, but told her never to look at him. One night, overcome by curiosity, Psyche held a lamp up to Eros as he slept. A drop of oil dripped on his shoulder, waking him, and he fled. Psyche searched frantically for Eros and performed many difficult tasks to win the favor of the gods. As a reward, the gods made her immortal and allowed her to marry Eros. In this story, Psyche, with her beauty and dedication, symbolizes the soul. When she is made immortal, Psyche shows how the human soul finally goes to heaven. In modern words, *psych-* usually means "mind" rather than "soul." *Psychobiology* is the study of biology that affects the mind. In some words, *psych* functions as a root. Perhaps you have taken a class in *psychology,* the study of the mind.

Words to Learn

Part 2

pan-

13. **pandemonium** (noun)   păn'də-mō'nē-əm

    From Greek: *pan-* (all) + *daimōn* (demon)

    chaos, wild disorder, and noise

    > **Pandemonium** broke loose when people realized that someone was trying to hijack the airplane.

    In John Milton's poem *Paradise Lost,* written in 1667, *Pandaemonium* was the principal city of Hell, where "all the demons" lived.

    ---

14. **panorama** (noun)   păn'ə-răm'-ə

    From Greek *pan-* (all) + *horan* (to see)

    a clear view over a wide area

    > From the Jungfrau mountain top, we had a **panorama** of the Swiss countryside.

    a wide-ranging survey

    > The professor presented a **panorama** of the Middle Ages in his first lecture.

    ▶ *RELATED WORD:*
    panoramic (adjective) The office window displayed a *panoramic* view of the Denver skyline.

    NOTE: Panorama can refer either to a physical view of something or a "view" in one's mind, as in a wide-ranging presentation of a subject.

psych-

15. **psyche** (noun)   sī'kĕ

    From Greek: *psych-* (soul)

mind; soul; mental state

> Bad dreams troubled Luis's **psyche.**

> Psychologists believe that the human **psyche** is governed by primitive needs for food and love.

16. **psychosomatic** (adjective)   sī′kō-sō-măt′ĭk

From Greek: *psych-* (mind; soul) + *soma* (body)

referring to physical disorders that are caused by the mind

> Many **psychosomatic** illnesses disappear after people come to understand their causes.

Name Words

17. **boycott** (verb, noun)   boi′kŏt′

to refuse to use or buy something as an act of protest (verb)

> The official golf tournament decided to **boycott** country clubs that did not admit minorities.

the act of boycotting (noun)

> A **boycott** of grapes helped migrant workers to unionize.

The Irish potato famine of the mid 1800s had made the farmers so poor that a law was passed in 1881 to reduce rents. Captain Charles C. Boycott, a cruel English land agent, angered the Irish people by insisting on the old payments, thus forcing many farmers out of business. In response, the Irish Land League "boycotted" him by refusing to deal with him in any way.

---

18. **chauvinism** (noun)   shō′vən-ĭz′əm

prejudiced devotion to a group or country

> Fernando's **chauvinism** was so strong that any bad word about his native country would anger him.

▶ *Related Words*

chauvinist (noun)   Michael angered us because he was a male *chauvinist.*

chauvinistic (adjective)   The city of Sacramento helped to eliminate *chauvinistic* labels by renaming a "manhole" as a "maintenence hole."

NOTE: The commonly used term *male chauvinism* refers to the view that men are superior to women, and a *male chauvinist* shows by his words and behavior that he shares this view.

Nicholas Chauvin was a legendary lieutenant in the French army who was extremely devoted to his general, Napoleon Bonaparte. Even after Napoleon's defeat, Chauvin continued in his blind loyalty. Such excessive devotion is now called *chauvinism*.

19. **martial** (adjective)   mär'shəl

referring to war or soldiers

The army did **martial** exercises to prepare for combat.

Japanese **martial** arts, such as judo, are popular forms of self-defense in North America.

▶ *Common Phrase*
martial law   The dictator imposed *martial law*. (Martial law is rule by military authorities imposed on a civilian population.)

Mars was the Roman god of war after whom the month of March is named. His name is also honored as the name of a planet, Mars, which appears to be faintly red, suggesting the color of blood. Each of the names of planets in our solar system is named for a Greek or Roman god. Closest to the sun is *Mercury*, the quickly rotating planet named for the messenger god. *Venus*, named for the god of love, is followed by *Earth* and *Mars*. *Jupiter* is named for the king of the gods. *Saturn* is Jupiter's father, and *Uranus* is his grandfather. *Neptune* is ruler of the sea. Finally, *Pluto*, the planet furthest from the sun, honors the gloomy god of the underworld, the region of the dead.

20. **maverick** (noun)   măv'ər-ĭk

an independent-minded person who does not conform or adhere to rules

Tom was a **maverick** who refused to wear the school uniform.

NOTE: Maverick is a stronger word than *nonconformist*, since a maverick openly defies rules.

In the nineteenth century, cattlemen began branding their calves to indicate ownership. Samuel Maverick was a Texan rancher of independent spirit who refused to do so. This annoyed the other ranchers and they called all unbranded cattle "mavericks." Maverick led a colorful life, fighting duels, spending time in prison, and serving in the Texas legislature.

21. **quixotic** (adjective)   kwĭk-sŏt′ĭk

noble, but not practical; having unreachable ideals

> We admired the mayor's **quixotic** behavior in defending an unpopular cause that he knew was right.

Don Quixote is the major figure in Cervantes's book of the same name. As an old man, Don Quixote decides to become a wandering knight and does noble but strange deeds that no one else quite understands. For example, he has a duel with a windmill that he thinks is a giant. He mistakes an inn for a castle, and a peasant girl for a noble lady. His squire (helper), Sancho Panza, sees how ridiculous all of this is, but remains loyal to his master.

Originally written in Spanish, many famous phrases from *Don Quixote* are used in modern-day English. They include "in a pickle," "too much of a good thing," "a wink of sleep," "a stone's throw," "smell a rat," "honesty is the best policy," "turn over a new leaf," and "faint heart never won a fair lady."

22. **spartan** (adjective)   spärt′n

lacking in comfort; requiring self-discipline

> The **spartan** room was furnished with only a cot.

The ancient city of Sparta was known for its devotion to athletics and fighting, just as Athens was known for its intellectual life. Spartans valued physical stamina, rough living, and bravery.

---

23. **tantalize** (verb)   tăn′tə-līz′

to tempt and then to deny satisfaction

> The sight of cookies in the bakery window **tantalized** the hungry child.

▶ *Related Word*
tantalizing (adjective)   The *tantalizing* jewels glittered in the store window.

Tantalus was a mythical Greek king who was popular with the gods until he began telling their secrets to mortals. Then he was punished by being put in water up to his chin, with a fruit tree above his head. When he bent down to drink, the water would sink too low for him to reach. Similarly, the fruit moved above his reach when he grasped for it. Although he could see food and water, he was always thirsty and hungry.

---

24. **vandalism** (noun)   vănd′l-ĭz′əm

willful, vicious destruction of property

> In large cities, many parks and libraries have been destroyed by **vandalism.**

▶ *Related Words*
vandal (noun)   The *vandal* tore the house apart.
vandalize (verbs)   The intruders *vandalized* the house.

The Vandals were one of the many uncivilized Germanic tribes that invaded the decaying Roman empire. Their destructive behavior when they captured Rome in A.D. 455 gave the word *vandal* its current meaning.

Exercises

Part 2

■ Definitions

Complete each sentence in the left-hand column by choosing a word or phrase from the right-hand column. Use each choice only once.

1. A psyche is _____ .

2. Psychosomatic illness has

   _____ .

3. A chauvinist is _____ .

4. Pandemonium is _____ .

5. To boycott is _____ .

6. A panorama is _____ .

7. A maverick is _____ .

8. A martial nation is _____ .

9. A quixotic person is _____ .

10. A spartan life is _____ .

a. a mind or mental state

b. ruining property

c. without comforts

d. independently minded

e. warlike

f. idealistic

g. a wide view

h. to tempt

i. not to buy or use

j. a mental cause

k. filled with prejudiced devotion

l. confusion

■ Meanings

Match each word element to its meaning. Use each choice only once.

1. pan- _____

2. psych- _____

a. mind; soul

b. all

■ Words in Context

Complete each sentence with the word that fits best. Use each choice only once.

a. panorama   e. boycott   i. quixotic
b. pandemonium   f. chauvinism   j. spartan
c. psyche   g. martial   k. tantalize
d. psychosomatic   h. maverick   l. vandal

1. Lan's _____ headaches disappeared when she got a good job.

2. Norm's troubled _____ made him very nervous.

3. The riot caused _____ in the city.

4. People decided to _____ the store until it lowered its unfair prices.

5. The short book presented a(n) _____ of major world religions.

6. The _____ man defended his idealistic opinion.

7. The sunny beaches in these ads _____ me, but I know I could never afford such an expensive vacation.

8. Dressed in armor and carrying his sword, the knight had a splen-

   did _____ appearance.

9. The political _____ refused to follow the policies of his party.

10. Scott had trouble adjusting to the _____ existence in the lumber camp.

■ Using Related Words

Complete each sentence using a word from the group of related words above it. You may need to capitalize a word when you put it into a sentence. Use each choice only once.

1. vandalism, vandalize, vandals

   In many city neighborhoods, an abandoned home is a target for

   _____ . _____ often strip the house of all of the furniture and appliances. Sometimes they

_____ the house itself, spraying graffiti both inside and outside.

2. tantalized, tantalizing

The mythological king Midas, granted a wish from the gods, was

_____ by the idea of great wealth. Thus, his wish was that everything he touched be turned to gold. He was delighted when his palace and all of the metal in it turned to gold. However, when his food also became gold, he found that he could

not eat even the most _____ morsel. A person who easily amasses a fortune is often referred to as having "the Midas touch."

3. chauvinism, chauvinists, chauvinistic

Football aficionados are often _____ toward their home teams. One's opinion on whether the 49ers or the Giants is a better football team often depends on whether one

lives in San Francisco or New York. _____ from

San Francisco will choose the 49ers, and the _____ of New Yorkers will make them root for the Giants.

4. martial, martial law

In some nations, a group of soldiers will seize power and declare

_____ . However, many such governments have returned to civil rule. People are often afraid of the unlimited

powers of a _____ government.

■ *Reading the Headlines*

This exercise presents five headlines that might have been taken from newspapers. Read each headline and then answer the questions that follow. (Remember that small words, such as *a* and *the*, are often left out of newspaper headlines.)

STUDY FINDS CHAUVINISM CAN DAMAGE PSYCHE

1. Can prejudiced devotion cause the damage? _____

2. Is the body damaged? _____

SPARTAN LIVING CONDITIONS FOUND TO CURE PSYCHOSOMATIC ILLNESSES

3. Are the living conditions luxurious? _____

4. Are the illnesses based in the mind? _____

MUSEUM EXHIBIT PRESENTS PANORAMA OF MARTIAL HISTORY

5. Is an overview presented? _____

6. Does the exhibit deal with peaceful times? _____

QUIXOTIC MAVERICK NOT TANTALIZED BY RICHES

7. Is the person idealistic? _____

8. Is the person independent? _____

ANNOUNCEMENT OF BOYCOTT CAUSES PANDEMONIUM AT COMPANY MEETING

9. Are people going to buy the company's product? _____

10. Was the meeting calm? _____

Chapter Exercises

■ *Practicing Strategies: New Words from Word Elements*

See how your knowledge of roots and prefixes can help you to understand new words. Complete each sentence with the word that seems to fit best. Use each choice only once.

a. anthropoids e. nomenclature i. psychopath
b. genealogy   f. pan-Asian   j. rename
c. generation   g. pandemic   k. revive
d. homogenize h. psychotherapy l. vivid

1. Therapy used to restore health to the mind is called

   _____ .

2. When referring to plants and animals, scholars often use scientific

   _____ .

3. Since -*logy* means "study of," _____ is the study of
   your heredity, or the family into which you were born.

4. When people faint and then awaken, they are said to

   _____ , or "live again."

5. A picture may be so _____ that it appears to be
   living.

6. The word _____ refers to all of Asia.

7. A worldwide epidemic of a disease is _____ .

8. The root *path* can mean "sick," so a person with a sick mind is a(n)

   _____ .

9. The prefix *homo-* means "same," so to _____ milk
   is to make it the same type, or mixture.

10. Apes that resemble human beings are called

    _____ .

■ Practicing Strategies: Combining Context Clues and Word Elements

Combining the strategies of context clues and word elements is a good
way to figure out unknown words. In the following sentences, each italicized word contains a word element that you have studied in this chapter. Using the meaning of the word element and the context of the
sentence, make an intelligent guess at the meaning of the italicized word.
Your instructor may ask you to check the meaning in your dictionary
after you have finished.

1. Conditions of poverty can *engender* criminal behavior.

   Engender means _____ .

2. It would be difficult to find a *panacea* for all the problems of humanity.

   Panacea means _____ .

3. Defenders of animal rights oppose the *vivisection* of animals to look at their organs.

   Vivisection means _____ .

4. It is a *misnomer* to call only citizens of the United States "Americans," for America consists of North, Central, and South America.

   Misnomer means _____ .

5. *Psychosis* is a serious illness.

   Psychosis means _____ .

■ COMPANION WORDS

Complete each sentence with the word that fits best. Choose your answers from the words below. You may use each word more than once.

Choices: of, for, to

1. Ilya paid only a nominal amount _____ his apartment.

2. The genesis _____ the steam engine dates back to the Greeks.

3. Ulcer medicine is vital _____ my father's health.

4. Albert Einstein is renowned _____ his work on relativity.

5. The boycott _____ hand guns greatly reduced sales.

■ *Writing with Your Words*

This exercise will give you practice in writing effective sentences using the vocabulary words. Each sentence is started for you. Complete it with an interesting phrase that also indicates the meaning of the italicized word.

1. A *pseudonym* I would like to use _____

_____ .

2. The *quixotic* man _____

_____ .

3. A *misanthrope* might _____

_____ .

4. The *martial* music _____

_____ .

5. We *boycotted* the store because _____

_____ .

6. I would be *tantalized* by _____

_____ .

7. Your plan is not *viable* so _____

_____ .

8. *Spartan* living conditions _____

_____ .

9. *Pandemonium* broke loose when _____

_____ .

10. The *nominal* ruler _____

_____ .

Passage

The Greek Myth of Winter

The ancient Greeks and Romans lived in a world that was very different from the one we inhabit. Having few protections against harsh weather, earthquakes, or disease, they were awed by these forces. Perhaps to gain a feeling of power, the Greeks invented a story to account for the cold weather of winter. Since human beings are **congenitally** self-centered, it was natural for them to assume that nature was controlled by gods who thought and behaved in human ways. **(1)** The story of winter is an example of Greek **anthropomorphism.**

(2) The legend of the **genesis** of winter concerns Persephone, the daughter of Demeter, the goddess of agriculture. **(3)** The story also illustrates a common problem of the human **psyche,** a mother-in-law's resentment of her son-in-law.

(4) One day, the lovely and **vivacious** Persephone was running through fields of flowers in Sicily. Unfortunately, she was seen by Hades, king of the underworld, **(5)** who was viewing the **panorama** of scenery on earth. **Tantalized** by her beauty, he was unable to resist temptation. He seized her, dragged her into his chariot, and carried her off to the underworld, where he made her his bride.

Back on Mount Olympus, the home of the gods, there was **pandemonium** as Persephone's mother, Demeter, frantically tried to get her daughter back. She asked Zeus, the **renowned** king of the gods, to help her, **(6)** but Hades was a **maverick** whom not even Zeus could control.

In desperation, Demeter assaulted the usual victim—the earth. She declared that there would be eternal winter. **(7)** She replaced the sunlight and warmth **vital** to growing plants with darkness and cold. The world was soon on the brink of starvation.

Zeus appealed to Hades, who finally agreed to let Persephone return to her mother, as long as the bride had not eaten anything.

But what had Persephone been doing while Demeter was trying to release her? **(8)** Sitting unhappily in the underworld, she had led a **spartan** existence, refusing all the luxuries that Hades offered. She had eaten no food—except for seven pomegranate seeds. Alas! **(9)** Persephone had eaten only a **nominal** amount, but she had eaten. Hades did not have to let her go.

(10) Zeus and Demeter quickly thought of another arrangement, which proved to be **viable.** For nine months of the year, Persephone would live with her mother and for three months she would live with Hades. Just as Persephone's life was divided, Demeter decreed that for nine months the earth would have warm weather, and for three months it would have winter. Although this arrangement was not perfect, it was a relief from endless winter.

And that is how, according to the ancient Greeks, winter and summer came to alternate.

■ *Exercise*

Each numbered sentence below corresponds to a sentence in the Passage. Fill in the letter of the choice that makes this sentence mean the same thing as the corresponding sentence in the Passage.

1. The story of winter is an example of Greek _____ .
   a. making things difficult   b. making things human   c. making things ancient   d. making things wintry

2. The legend of the _____ of winter concerns Persephone.
   a. snow   b. weather   c. hatred   d. beginning

3. The story also illustrates a common problem of the human

   _____.
   a. family   b. life   c. body   d. mind

4. One day, the lovely and _____ Persephone was running through fields of flowers.
   a. beautiful   b. silly   c. lively   d. graceful

5. Hades was looking at the _____ of scenery on earth.
   a. beauty   b. view   c. fields   d. crime

6. But Hades was a(n) _____ whom not even Zeus could control.
   a. independent individual   b. miserable individual   c. clever individual   d. strong individual

7. She replaced the sunlight and warmth _____ to growing plants with darkness and cold.
   a. necessary   b. helpful   c. provided   d. useless

8. Sitting unhappily in the underworld, she had led a(n) _____ existence.
   a. sad   b. uncomfortable   c. lonely   d. married

9. Persephone had eaten only a _____ amount, but she had eaten.
   a. fair   b. small   c. reasonable   d. huge

10. Zeus and Demeter quickly thought of another arrangement, which

    proved to be _____ .
    a. pleasant   b. perfect   c. friendly   d. workable

■ *Discussion Questions*

1. What reasons explain why the Greeks thought of their gods as being cruel humans?

2. Was Zeus's power limited? Explain your answer.

3. Describe a human situation that would bring forth the same types of emotions Demeter felt.

Word Elements:
Movement

Many word elements originally referred to physical movement. Each of the six roots and two prefixes in this chapter describes actions such as pulling and turning. These word elements have combined with others to form many useful English words.

Chapter Strategy: Word Elements: Movement

Chapter Words:

Part 1

duct	abduction	*stat*	static
	conducive		status quo
	deduction		staunch
ject	dejected	*ten*	abstain
	eject		tenable
	jettison		tenacious

Part 2

tract	distraught	*circum-*	circumscribe
	extraction		circumspect
	retract		circumvent
vert	adversary	*trans-*	transformation
	inadvertently		transgress
	perverse		transitory

Did You Know?

How Did Inventions Get Their Names?

The last two hundred years have been a time of great progress in the fields of invention and discovery. If we were put back on earth in the 1700s, we would hardly recognize the way of life. Travel, food, and medicine were vastly different from what we experience today.

People traveled on foot or used horses, on unpaved roads with deep ruts. A twenty-mile trip from an English country village to London took all day. Today the same trip takes less than half an hour by automobile or subway.

Because there were no stoves or refrigerators, food was prepared differently in the 1700s. People cooked over open fires and just hoped that the temperature would be suitable. Meat could not be kept by cooling or freezing. It was either eaten immediately or preserved as sausage or salted meat. In Europe and America, pepper and other spices were very valuable, for they were used to keep meat from spoiling. Nevertheless, people sometimes had to eat rotten meat.

The medical science of the 1700s was primitive. There were few methods of disease prevention and control. In fact, fewer than half of all children survived to adulthood. Operations were often carried out by barbers, who were unclean and had few healing techniques. Doctors treated sick patients by applying leeches to suck the "bad blood" from them. Medical historians now think that such "bleeding" caused George Washington's death.

Society has made great advances since those times. Today, science and technology have greatly improved our travel, diet, and health. Automobiles, trains, and airplanes provide rapid transportation. We use freezers and refrigerators to preserve our food and stoves to cook it with precision. Many diseases have been controlled, and average life expectancy has almost doubled.

The astonishing number of inventions in the last three hundred years has both improved the quality of life and brought many new words into English as each new device received a name. Often scientists and inventors have composed these names from ancient Greek and Latin word elements. This tradition started in 1611 when a Greek poet suggested a name for Galileo's new invention, using two Greek word elements, *tele-* (far) and *-scope* (look). The invention is called the *telescope*.

Modern inventors continue to create names from ancient Greek and Latin word elements. This makes a knowledge of classical word elements more useful than ever.

The following inventions and discoveries have made your life easier. Each contains at least one classical prefix, root, or suffix. You will be studying some of these elements in this book.

Invention	Classical Word Elements	Approximate Date of Invention
microscope	*micro-* (small) + *-scope* (look)	1665
antiseptic	*anti-* (against) + *sepsis* (rotten)	1745
photography	*photo-* (light) + *-graph* (written)	1780
anesthetic	*an-* (without) + *aisthēsis* (feeling)	1850
bicycle	*bi-* (two) + *kuklos* (wheel)	1862
phonograph	*phono-* (sound) + *-graph* (written)	1875
telephone	*tele-* (far) + *-phone* (sound)	1880
automobile	*auto-* (self) + *movēre* (to move)	1885
refrigerator	*re-* (again) + *frigus* (cold)	1890
television	*tele-* (far) + *visus* (sight)	1925
computer	*com-* (together) + *-putāre* (to reckon)	1940
microwave	*micro-* (small) + *wave*	1963

Learning Strategy

Word Elements: Movement

Each of the word elements in this chapter describes a type of movement, such as leading *(duct)*, pulling *(tract)*, and turning *(vert)*. A surprising number of word elements are taken from classical words referring to movement. Every one of these elements forms at least fifty English words, so learning them will help you increase your vocabulary word power.

Element	Meaning	Origin	Function	Chapter Words
		Part 1		
duc, duct	lead	Latin	root	abduction, conducive, deduction
ject	throw	Latin	root	dejected, eject, jettison
stans, stat	standing; placed	Latin; Greek	root	static, status quo, staunch
tain, ten	hold	Latin	root	abstain, tenable, tenacious
		Part 2		
tract	pull	Latin	root	distraught, extraction, retract
vers, vert	turn	Latin	root	adversary, inadvertently, perverse
circum-	around	Latin	prefix	circumscribe, circumspect, circumvent
trans-	across	Latin	prefix	transformation, transgress, transitory

Words formed from movement word elements often have interesting histories. Such words may have started out describing physical movement, but over the years many have gained an abstract, nonphysical meaning. Although they may no longer describe movement itself, the elements in these words will still give you hints about their meanings.

One word element you are studying, *ject* (throw), illustrates how word elements and meanings relate. Each of the *ject* words in this chapter consists of a prefix and a root. If you think about the meanings of the word elements below, you will get an imaginative physical picture of each word's meaning.

The word elements *de-* (down) and *ject* (throw) make *deject,* or "throw down." The word *dejected* actually means depressed, or how we feel when our mood is "thrown down."

The word elements *e-* (out of) and *ject* (throw) make *eject,* or "throw out of." When a candy bar is *ejected* from a vending machine, it is "thrown out."

The word elements *pro-* (forward) and *ject* (throw) make *project,* or "throw forward." A *projectile* is a bullet or missile that is "thrown forward" from a gun or rocket.

Circumstance is another word in which the elements give us a mental picture. It combines two word elements presented in this chapter, the prefix *circum-* and the root *stans. Circumstances* are things that are "standing" *(stans)* "around" *(circum-)* an event; in other words, they surround it. Circumstances that might "stand around" and keep you from studying are noise in the library or a friend who wants to talk!

Word Roots

Part 1

The four movement word roots presented in Part 1 are discussed below.

duc, duct (lead)
> This root appears in many different words. The *ducts* in a building lead air and water to different rooms. A *conductor* leads an orchestra so that all the players stay together *(con-* means "together"). European noblemen are called *dukes* because long ago their ancestors led troops into battle.

ject (throw)
> This root appears as *jet,* a stream of water or air thrown into space. *Ject* can also represent the idea of throwing rather than the physical

action itself. Although the word elements of *reject* actually mean "to throw back," the word itself has the related, but nonphysical, meaning of "not to accept."

stans, stat (standing; placed)

This root indicates a lack of movement, as in *statue. Stans, stat* can also refer to standing in an imaginative, nonphysical way. For example, one's *status* is one's "standing" or "placement" in society.

tain, ten (hold)

This root can mean "hold" in a physical sense; a can *contains*, or holds, baked beans. It can also mean "hold" in a nonphysical sense. For example, a *tenet* is a belief that somebody "holds."

Words to Learn

Part 1

duc, duct

1. **abduction** (noun)   ăb-dŭk′shən

   From Latin: *ab-* (away) + *duct* (lead)

   kidnapping

   > **Abduction** of children is a serious problem in the United States.

   ▶ *Related Word*
   abduct (verb)   The terrorists tried to *abduct* the diplomat.

2. **conducive** (adjective)   kən-dōō′sĭv

   From Latin: *con-* (together) + *duc* (lead)

   contributing to; leading to

   > A noisy library is not **conducive** to studying.
   > Candlelight and soft music are **conducive** to romance.

   ▶ *Common Phrase*
   conducive to

3. **deduction** (noun)   dĭ-dŭk′shən

   From Latin: *de-* (away) + *duct* (lead)

   something subtracted from a total

   > The monthly **deduction** in Pat's paycheck covered her health insurance.

a conclusion drawn from evidence

> From the smell in the room, we drew the **deduction** that we were in the smoking section.

▶ *Common Phrase*
draw a deduction

▶ *Related Words*
deductive (adjective)   The detective solved crimes by using *deductive* reasoning.

deduce (verb)   dĭ-doōs')   The detective was able to *deduce* the criminal's identity.

Sherlock Holmes, the fictional English detective created by Sir Arthur Conan Doyle, was a master of deductive reasoning. Holmes would amaze his companions by drawing brilliant conclusions from the smallest bits of evidence. The famous, but fictional, Holmes was based on a real-life Scottish doctor, Joe Bell, who was an expert in diagnosing disease from little evidence.

ject

4. **dejected** (adjective)   dĭ-jĕkt′əd

   From Latin: *de-* (down) + *ject* (throw)

   depressed; downcast

   > Clarence felt **dejected** after he failed the exam.

   ▶ *Related Word*
   dejection (noun)   After Ms. Tomario lost the election, her campaign workers were in a state of *dejection*.

5. **eject** (verb)   ĭ-jĕkt′

   From Latin: *ex-* (out) + *ject* (throw)

   to force to leave; to expel

   > The usher **ejected** the noisy person from the theater.

   ▶ *Related Word*
   ejection (noun)   Seconds before the plane crashed, the automatic *ejection* device saved the pilot.

6. **jettison** (verb)   jĕt′-ĭ-sĕn

   From Latin: *ject* (throw)

   To throw out forcefully; to throw overboard

   > The lifeboat was able to hold two more sailors after we **jettisoned** the extra supplies.

   > To avoid fire, the disabled airplane **jettisoned** its extra fuel before landing.

   NOTE: Jettison can also apply to nonphysical things, as in to "jettison an unworkable plan" or "jettison the unprofitable division of a company."

stans, stat

7. **static** (adjective, noun)   stăt′ik

   From Greek: *stat* (standing, placed)

   motionless (adjective)

   > The guards at Buckingham Palace must remain **static** for more than an hour at a time.

   > Standard and Poor's index of stock prices has been nearly **static** for a month.

disturbances in the air due to static electricity

> Because of **static**, we received small shocks whenever we stood on the rug.

> **Static** on our television set prevented us from watching "Twin Peaks."

NOTE: Static has a slang meaning of "negative comments, back talk." (The students gave the school cafeteria manager a lot of *static* about prices.

8. **status quo** (noun)   stā'təs kwō'

From Latin: *stat* (standing, placed) + *quo* (in which), making "the condition in which"

the existing conditions

> Those in power often want to preserve the **status quo.**

Some major events of modern history have done much to upset the status quo. The French Revolution of 1789, which established the new principle of equality, is considered the beginning of modern history. The Russian Revolution of 1917 brought Communism to Russia, abolishing private business. Now the Communist status quo is, in turn, being upset by a move back to capitalism.

In the late 1940s and 1950s, the European colonial system collapsed, and countries such as Nigeria, Rwanda, Algeria, Sri Lanka, India, and Pakistan have become self-governing. More recently the status quo in East and West Germany was affected when the Berlin Wall was torn down and the two countries were united.

---

9. **staunch** (adjective)   stônch

From Latin: *stans* (standing), through the French word *estanche* (watertight, firm) (Something *staunch* stands firm and strong.)

faithful; firmly supporting

> The U.S. was a **staunch** ally of Great Britain in World Wars I and II.

healthy; strong

> My **staunch** constitution can withstand cold easily.

▶ *Related Word*

staunchness (noun)   The congresswoman's *staunchness* in supporting the equal rights proposal helped it to pass in the state senate.

tain, ten

10. **abstain** (verb)   ăb-stān′

From Latin: *abs-* (away) + *tain* (hold) ("To hold away from" is not to do.)

not to do something by choice

> Religious Jews and Muslims **abstain** from eating pork.

not to vote

> Seven people voted yes, seven voted no, and seven **abstained.**

▶ *Common Phrase*
abstain from

▶ *Related Words*
abstinence (noun)   (ăb′stə-nəns)   *Abstinence* from smoking was difficult when others continued the habit. (Abstinence usually refers to self-denial.)

abstention (noun)   (ăb-stən′shən)   Because of Teresa's *abstention*, we won the vote. (Abstention usually refers to voting.)

11. **tenable** (adjective)   tən′ə-bəl

From Latin: *ten* (hold)

capable of being defended; logical

> The theory that the universe was created by a huge explosion, called the "Big Bang," is now considered **tenable.**

> The army general chose a **tenable** position for his troops to defend.

▶ *Related Words*
tenability (noun)   Trung convinced others that his argument had *tenability.*

untenable (adjective)   The *untenable* theory was abandoned. *(Untenable* means "not tenable.")

When the great Italian scientist, Galileo, proposed that the earth rotated around the sun, many thought that his theory was untenable. It seemed ridiculous that the earth, with its heavy mass, could move around the sun, which appeared so small in the sky. Surely, they believed, the earth was the center of the universe. However, as more evidence accumulated, it became clear that Galileo's theory had great tenability. Today, it is accepted as scientific fact.

---

12. **tenacious** (adjective)   tə-nā'shəs

From Latin: *ten* (hold)

firmly holding; gripping; retaining

> The ship's captain kept a **tenacious** grasp on the wheel through-out the storm.

> The law enforcement official's **tenacious** investigation revealed the identity of the murderer.

▶ *Related Words*

tenaciousness (noun)   Winston Churchill's *tenaciousness* in be-lieving that Nazi Germany was a threat helped to prepare England for World War II.

tenacity (noun)   (tə-năs'ə-tē)   The lawyer's *tenacity* played a large part in winning the case.

Exercises

Part 1

■ Definitions

Match each word in the left-hand column with a definition from the right-hand column. Use each choice only once.

1. tenable _____
2. conducive _____
3. status quo _____
4. dejected _____
5. abduction _____
6. static _____
7. deduction _____

a. something thrown forward
b. kidnapping
c. motionless
d. logical
e. conclusion drawn from evidence
f. to throw overboard
g. gripping
h. contributing to
i. depressed

8. tenacious _____   j. the present state of things

9. abstain _____   k. faithful

10. jettison _____   l. not to do

■ *Meanings*

Match each word root to its meaning. Use each choice only once.

1. duc, duct _____   a. lead

2. tain, ten _____   b. hold

                          c. throw

3. ject _____   d. standing; placed

4. stans, stat _____

■ *Words in Context*

Complete each sentence with the word that fits best. Use each choice only once.

a. abduction   e. ejection   i. staunch
b. conducive   f. jettison   j. abstain
c. deduction   g. static   k. tenable
d. dejected   h. status quo l. tenacity

1. According to law, _____ is a crime.

2. The woman became _____ when she realized she could not possibly support her children.

3. From the evidence of space missions, scientists drew the

   _____ that it was not possible to live on Mars.

4. The knight's _____ ally would never desert him in battle.

5. To lighten the airplane, we had to _____ all the luggage.

6. The dog showed its _____ by refusing to let go of the bone.

7. It is safest to _____ from alcohol while driving.

8. The models had to remain _____ while the artist painted them.

9. Air pollution is not _____ to good health.

10. If all money were divided equally among people, there would be

quite a change in the _____ .

■ *Using Related Words*

Complete each sentence using a word from the group of related words above it. You may need to capitalize a word when you put it into a sentence. Use each choice only once.

1. abstain, abstentions, abstinence

Nonsmoking areas have been hotly debated in our town. Some

people feel that everyone should _____ from smoking in public buildings. However, it is difficult for many

smokers to practice _____ throughout their working hours. When our town council met to debate this issue, several representatives were undecided, and, therefore, there

were many _____ among the votes.

2. deductive, deduce, deduction

Dorothy Sayers, one of England's leading detective writers, created the aristocratic Lord Peter Wimsey. Lord Peter's rather

silly manner hides a _____ mind of great brilliance. In *The Nine Tailors*, for example, a man is found dead in the bell tower of a church. There are few clues to help Lord

Peter _____ the identity of the murderer. Yet, he

is able to draw the correct _____ and find out how the man was killed.

3. ejection, eject

Should guards have the right to _____ from a public gathering people who are making nasty comments? On the one hand, their _____ helps keep meetings orderly. On the other hand, such people may only be exercising the right to speak their minds.

4. tenacity, tenacious

Human beings have been fighting an age-old battle with the

_____ mosquito. Each time scientists develop a new chemical to combat them, mosquitos develop new re-

sistances. Scientists are puzzled by the _____ of the small pest.

■ True or False?

Each of the following statements contains one or more words from this section. Read each sentence carefully and then indicate whether you think it is probably true or probably false.

____   1. A statue is static.

____   2. A staunch friend would help people to abduct you.

____   3. Preserving the status quo is conducive to change.

____   4. Deductions should be based on evidence.

____   5. When we jettison cargo, a ship becomes heavier.

____   6. You would be hungry after you abstained from food for a week.

____   7. You would be dejected if you won a prize.

____   8. A rocket that ejects a missile throws off the missile.

____   9. Tenable opinions are ridiculous.

____   10. People with tenacious opinions are likely to change them.

Word Elements

Part 2

Part 2 continues with more word elements that show movement; first, two additional roots, *tract* (pull) and *vert* (turn); then two prefixes, *circum-* (around) and *trans-* (across).

tract (pull)

    Tractor, a machine that pulls plows and other equipment through the earth, is an example of a common word formed from this root. Like many movement roots, *tract* is used in words that no longer carry the physical meaning of pull. For example, when we *distract* someone's attention, we "pull it away" in a mental rather than in a physical sense.

vers, vert (turn)

    Vert can mean "turn" in a direct sense. When we *invert* a cup, we turn it upside down. The root can also hint at a nonphysical meaning of "turn." When we *advertise*, we "turn attention toward" a product.

circum- (around)

    Circum- is a prefix with the movement meaning of "around." The distance around a circle is called its *circumference*. Like other movement word elements, *circum-* can indicate the idea, rather than the physical action, of "around." For example, a library book that *circulates* "goes around" and is used by many different people.

Circus is the Latin word for "circle." A circus was originally a large circular area surrounded by seats used for viewing shows. Roman emperors were said to stay in power by giving the people "bread and circuses," that is, food and entertainment. In modern English, a "three-ring circus" is a commonly used expression. This originally meant a very large circus, but it has come to mean any event that causes a great deal of excitement.

---

trans- (across)

> *Transcontinental* jets cross a continent, say, from New York to Los Angeles. The prefix *trans-* can also suggest the idea of "across" rather than physical movement. When we *translate* something, it goes "across" languages, or from one language to another.

Words to Learn

Part 2

tract

13. **distraught** (adjective)   dĭs-trôt'

From Latin: *dis-* (apart) + *tract* (pull) (*Tract* changed to *traught* in Middle English.)

crazy with worry

> When the mother found out that her son was missing, she became **distraught** and could not eat or sleep.

> Wayne was **distraught** when he realized that the bank holding his life savings had gone out of business.

NOTE: Distracted, which comes from the same word elements as *distraught,* has a less extreme meaning. It can be used simply for "confused" or "not attentive."

14. **extraction** (noun)   ĭk-străk'shən

From Latin: *ex-* (out) + *tract* (pull)

pulling out; drawing out

> Scientists are working on the economical **extraction** of oil from shale.

origin; ancestry

> Many people of Philippine **extraction** now live in the United States and Canada.

▶ *Related Words*
  extract (verb) (ĭk-străkt') The dentist wanted to *extract* my tooth.
  extract (noun) (ĕk'străkt) Vanilla *extract* is used for flavoring cakes and pies.

NOTE: The pronunciation of *extract* indicates whether the verb or the noun is being used.

15. **retract** (verb)   rĭ-trăkt**'**

From Latin: *re-* (back) + *tract* (pull)

to withdraw a promise or statement; to pull something back

> The newspaper **retracted** its false statements about the political candidate.
>
> The turtle **retracted** its head into its shell.

▶ *Related Word*
> **retraction** (noun)   The president issued a *retraction* of his statement.

vert

16. **adversary** (noun)   ăd**'**vər-sĕr**'**ē

From Latin: *ad-* (toward) + *vert* (turn) (When we "turn toward" an enemy or adversary, we prepare to fight.)

opponent; foe

> After a hard-fought tennis match, the two **adversaries** shook hands.
>
> The Republican party is the traditional **adversary** of the Democratic party.

NOTE: 1. *Adversary* connotes a stubborn and determined foe.
2. The plural form is *adversaries.*

What contests were these adversaries engaged in?

1. George Bush and Michael Dukakis

2. Julius Caesar and Pompey

3. Mike Tyson and Alex Stewart

4. Shredder and Splinter

(*Answers:* 1. The 1988 U. S. presidential race   2. Control of the ancient Roman republic   3. The 1990 heavyweight boxing world championship   4. Ninja fighting in the movie "Teenage Mutant Ninja Turtles")

17. **inadvertently** (adverb)   in′əd-vûr′tənt-lē

From Latin: *in-* (not) + *ad-* (toward) + *vert* (turn) (When you are "not turned toward" something, events often happen inadvertently, or accidentally.)

unintentionally; by accident

Tom **inadvertently** locked his keys in the car.

Sheila **inadvertently** forgot to cook the sweet potatoes for Thanksgiving dinner.

▶ *Related Word*
inadvertent (adjective)   The *inadvertent* right turn Hattie made caused her to lose her way.

18. **perverse** (adjective)   pər-vûrs′

From Latin: *per-* (completely) + *vert* (turn) (A perverse person is "completely turned away" from what is natural.)

contrary; determined not to do what is expected or right

My **perverse** mother-in-law ordered us to cook her favorite meal and then refused to eat it.

▶ *Related Words*
perverseness (noun)   Because of his *perverseness*, the child refused to wear a coat in the freezing weather.

perversity (noun)   The patient's *perversity* caused him to refuse to speak to the nurse who had saved his life.

circum-

19. **circumscribe** (verb)   sûr′kəm-skrīb′

From Latin: *circum-* (around) + *scrib* (to write)

to limit; to restrict; to enclose

The general's rivals **circumscribed** his authority.

The European cities of Paris and London were originally **circumscribed** by a protecting wall.

20. **circumspect** (adjective)   sûr′kəm-spĕkt′

From Latin: *circum-* (around) + *spec* (to look) (To be circumspect is "to look around" or be careful.)

cautious; careful; considering results of actions

Public figures should be **circumspect** in their personal lives, since scandal has ruined many careers.

▶ *Related Word*
   circumspection (noun)   The official's *circumspection* prevented him from meeting privately with the man accused of offering bribes.

21. **circumvent** (verb)   sûr′kəm-vĕnt′

From Latin: *circum-* (around) + *venīre* (to come)

to avoid; to outwit

Students can **circumvent** long lines by using the telephone to register.

The man tried to **circumvent** payment of his debts by moving to another state.

▶ *Related Word*
   circumvention (noun)   *Circumvention* of child support payments has become more difficult in recent years.

trans-

22. **transformation** (noun)   trăns′fər-mā′shən

From Latin: *trans-* (across) + *forma* (shape), making *transformāre* (to change shape)

a complete change

The sudden **transformation** of the awkward girl into a beautiful woman surprised everyone.

The second-graders where amazed when they saw the **transformation** of the caterpillar into a butterfly.

▶ *Related Word*
   transform (verb)   (trăns-fôrm′)   By hard work, family members *transformed* the losing business into a profitable company.

23. **transgress** (verb)   trăns-grĕs′

From Latin: *trans-* (across) + *gradi* (to step)

to violate; to go beyond what is proper or good

It was sometimes hard not to **transgress** my mother's strict rules.

The drunken driver was put in jail for **transgressing** the law.
The girl's short skirt **transgressed** the boundaries of good taste.

▶ *Related Words*

> **transgression** (noun)   The drunken driver was punished for his *transgression.*

> **transgressor** (noun)   The *transgressor* received his just due.

NOTE: The religious meaning of *transgress* is "to sin."

24. **transitory** (adjective)   trăn'sə-tôr'ē

From Latin: *trans-* (across) + *īre* (to go), making *transīre* ("to go across" or to pass through quickly)

short-lived; existing briefly; passing

> People hope their sorrows will be **transitory.**

Exercises

Part 2

■ Definitions

Match each word in the left-hand column with a definition from the right-hand column. Use each choice only once.

1. perverse _____   a. to limit

2. transitory _____   b. complete change

3. circumspect _____   c. drawing

4. inadvertently _____   d. short-lived

5. distraught _____   e. to violate

6. circumvent _____   f. to withdraw

                            g. opponent

7. transgress _____   h. to avoid

                            i. contrary

8. retract _____   j. cautious

9. circumscribe _____   k. crazy with worry

10. adversary _____   l. accidentally

■ *Meanings*

Match each word element to its meaning. Use each choice only once.

1. trans- _____   a. around

2. vers, vert _____ b. pull

3. circum- _____   c. turn

4. tract _____   d. across

■ *Words in Context*

Complete each sentence with the word that fits best. Use each choice only once.

a. distraught	e. inadvertently	i. circumvent
b. extraction	f. perverse	j. transformation
c. retract	g. circumscribe	k. transgress
d. adversary	h. circumspect	l. transitory

1. I was _____ after I realized that the diamond earrings my friend had loaned me were missing.

2. Some people think that rap groups _____ the boundaries of good taste with their references to sex and violence.

3. People saw a _____ of the area as farms were replaced by city streets.

4. The child's sadness was _____ , and he soon was smiling again.

5. My _____ uncle complained constantly about his illnesses, yet refused to call a doctor.

6. I _____ tripped when I got out of the car.

7. The government agency was _____ in dealing with foreign firms and checked them carefully.

8. Leshan tried to _____ the traffic jam by taking a side street.

9. The United States Constitution acts to _____ the authority of the president so that he does not have absolute power.

10. The president of the company decided to _____ the error-filled profit statement.

■ *Using Related Words*

Complete each sentence using a word from the group of related words above it. You may need to capitalize a word when you put it into a sentence. Use each choice only once.

1. extract, extraction

   Commercial plants _____ oxygen, hydrogen, and argon from the air. These gases have many industrial uses. The

   _____ and separation of these gases is a highly technical process.

2. adversary, adversarial

   Russia and Germany had an _____ relationship during World War II. Although they began as allies, Germany's army invaded Russia, putting the two countries at war. Germany

   tried to defeat its _____ by blockading the Russian city of Leningrad. Although many Russians starved, the city did not surrender.

3. circumspect, circumspection

   Banking is a profession that requires great _____ . Since bankers handle other people's money, they must be

_____ in avoiding even the appearance of ir-
regularity in their own business or personal dealings.

4. transgress, transgression

    In his daily life, the holy man felt that it was important not

    to _____ religious laws. He believed that even

    the slightest _____ could bring great sorrow.

5. transformed, transformations

    The city of Santa Fe has undergone several _____
    since it was founded in 1610 to serve as a capital of Spain in the
    New World. In 1912 it became part of the U. S. and the capital
    of the state of New Mexico. Recently its carefully protected an-

    cient ruins and fine cultural institutions have _____
    it into an attractive cultural and tourist center.

■ True or False?

Each of the following statements contains one or more words from this
section. Read each sentence carefully and then indicate whether you
think it is probably true or probably false.

____   1. A transformation is a small change.

____   2. An appendix that is about to burst should be extracted from
          your body.

____   3. People hope that enjoyment will be transitory.

____   4. If a person retracts a statement, he is pleased with it.

____   5. A circumspect person does not care what others think.

____   6. Your adversary would be happy if your authority were
          circumscribed.

——   7. A small child lost in the snow would be distraught.

——   8. You might circumvent a long wait at a store by placing your order by phone.

——   9. A perverse person is likely to enjoy transgressing rules.

——   10. Most people inadvertently forget things from time to time.

Chapter Exercises

■ *Practicing Strategies: New Words from Word Elements*

See how your knowledge of prefixes and roots can help you to understand new words. Complete each sentence with the word that seems to fit best. Use each choice only once.

a. aqueduct
b. attract
c. circuit
d. conduct
e. detain
f. interject
g. statement
h. stationary
i. tenor
j. traction
k. trans-Atlantic
l. vertigo

1. The _____ cable carries phone calls across the Atlantic Ocean.

2. A (n) _____ object stands still.

3. When your leg is broken, _____ , or a pulling motion, may help to mend the bones properly.

4. You suffer from _____ when you get dizzy and things around you seem to turn.

5. When the police _____ someone, they hold that person in jail.

6. *Aqua* means "water"; the ancient Romans built _____ to lead water to their cities.

7. To _____ a remark is to "throw it between" other remarks. *(Inter-* means "between.")

8. *Ad-* or *at-* can mean "toward," so to _____ is to draw someone toward you.

9. The _____ voice was named because these singers held the melody in a part-song.

10. A(n) _____ refers to a circular, or closed, path that carries electricity.

■ *Practicing Strategies: Combining Context Clues and Word Elements*

Combining the strategies of context clues and word elements is a good way to figure out unknown words. In the following sentences, each italicized word contains a word element that you have studied in this chapter. Using the meaning of the word element and the context of the sentence, make an intelligent guess at the meaning of the italicized word. Your instructor may ask you to check the meaning in your dictionary when you have finished.

1. In a terrible *subversion* of justice, the man's innocent words were twisted to seem evil.

   Subversion means _____ .

2. The headlight of the car *projected* on to the road.

   Projected means _____ .

3. For hundreds of years, alchemists sought methods to *transmute* iron and copper into gold.

   Transmute means _____ .

4. In 1522 the ships of Magellan became the first to *circumnavigate* the world.

   Circumnavigate means _____ .

5. The company offered many *inducements* to attract qualified computer operators.

   Inducements means _____ .

■ *Practicing Strategies: Using the Dictionary*

Read the following definition. Then answer the questions that follow.

> **march** (märch) *v.* **marched, march·ing, march·es.** *-intr.*
> **1. a.** To walk in a formal military manner with measured steps at a steady rate. **b.** To begin to move in such a manner: *The troops will march at dawn.* **2.** To advance or proceed with steady movement. *-tr.* **1.** To cause to march: *march soldiers into battle.* **2.** To traverse by marching: *They marched the route in a day.* *-n.* **1.** The act of marching, esp.: **a.** The steady forward movement of a body of troops. **b.** A long tiring journey on foot. **2.** Forward movement; progression: *the march of time.* **3.** A regulated pace: *quick march.* **4.** The distance covered by marching: *a week's march away.* **5.** *Mus.* A musical composition in regularly accented usually duple meter to accompany marching. **—idioms.** **on the march.** Advancing; progressing: *Science is on the march.* **steal a march on.** To get ahead of, esp. by quiet enterprise. [ME *marchen* < OFr. *marchier*, prob. of Germanic orig.]

1. Give the number and part of speech of the definition of *march* most used in music?

   _____

2. What is the third-person singular form of *march* when it is used as

   a verb? _____

3. Give the number and the part of speech of the definition that best

   fits this sentence: Science is on the march. _____

4. How many definitions does *march* have as a transitive verb?

   _____

5. Give the number and the part of speech of the definition that best fits this sentence: "The guard marched the prisoners into their cell."

   _____

■ *Companion Words*

Complete each sentence with the word that fits best. Choose your answers from the words below. You may use each word more than once.

Choices: in, of, to, draw, from

1. We have witnessed a tranformation _____ aircraft from small propeller planes to jet carriers.

2. The prime minister is circumspect _____ his personal life.

3. Circumvention _____ long lines is pleasant.

4. The professor issued a retraction _____ his statement when he realized it was based on faulty evidence.

5. The American Civil Liberties Union is a staunch defender _____ free speech.

6. The chemistry students will _____ a deduction from the results of the experiment.

7. Abduction _____ children is a horrible crime.

8. Personal freedom is conducive _____ creativity.

9. I must abstain _____ eating for 24 hours before my medical test.

10. The extraction _____ juice from oranges is often done by machine.

■ *Writing with Your Words*

This exercise will give you practice in writing effective sentences using the vocabulary words. Each sentence is started for you. Complete it with an interesting phrase that also indicates the meaning of the italicized word.

1. My *adversary* _____

   _____ .

2. During my lifetime, there has been a *transformation* _____

   _____ .

3. The *circumspect* woman _____

   _____ .

4. People should *abstain* from _____

   _____ .

5. I *inadvertently* _____

   _____ .

6. People were *distraught* when _____

   _____ .

7. The three-year-old felt *dejected* because _____

   _____ .

8. I *retracted* my complaint when _____

   _____ .

9. The jury drew the *deduction* that the man was guilty of the robbery

   when _____

   _____ .

10. People often try to *circumvent* lines for ticket sales by _____

    _____ .

Passage

What Body Language Tells Us

The posture of your body, where you place your arms, and how you walk
may reveal more to others than the words you are speaking. Many people do not realize how effectively body language communicates.

A first-grade teacher stands by the door smiling and greeting the
children with friendly words. **(1)** If her arms are crossed, however, she
is **inadvertently** communicating another message. Crossed arms can indicate negative feelings, and the children will probably see her as a foe
rather than a friend.

In a nearby high school, a student sits in math class, his body
straight, his hands folded, fixing a **tenacious** stare on the teacher. Is
he paying attention? No! His lack of movement indicates that his
thoughts are far away (perhaps on his girlfriend). If the student were
interested in the lesson, he would move and react. **(2)** Only an inexperienced teacher would make the **deduction** that a student who remains
static is thinking about math.

In contrast to the math student's rigid posture, tilting one's head
indicates friendliness and interest. A student who tilts her head and sits
on the edge of her chair is paying attention to a lecture. People often
tilt their heads or bodies forward slightly to show interest in members

of the opposite sex. Enlarged pupils in one's eyes also indicate this interest.

Smiling is a body language behavior with a hidden message. Most people believe that smiling indicates happiness. **(3)** But scientists observing animals have found that another conclusion may be more **tenable**: smiling indicates apology, or the wish to avoid an attack. A gorilla often smiles when showing stronger animals that it doesn't want to fight. A person who has accidentally **transgressed** social custom by hitting a stranger with an elbow **(4)** will give a **transitory** smile that requests the injured person not to become angry.

Hands communicate much body language. **(5)** An open-handed gesture is **conducive** to friendliness. Perhaps this is the origin of the handshake, in which people open their hands to each other.

Arms folded on the chest, however, indicate defensiveness. **(6)** Baseball fans have seen this behavior many times when an umpire makes a call that a team manager wants him to **retract. (7).** As the manager approaches, the formerly neutral umpire undergoes a **transformation** into an **adversary** simply by folding his arms. **Abstaining** from movement, he listens to the manager's arguments. Finally, the umpire shows his rejection just by turning his back. The **dejected** manager walks back to the dugout, shrugging his shoulders.

Walking styles can also communicate messages. **(8)** We all have seen the controlled and measured walk of a person trying to appear digni-

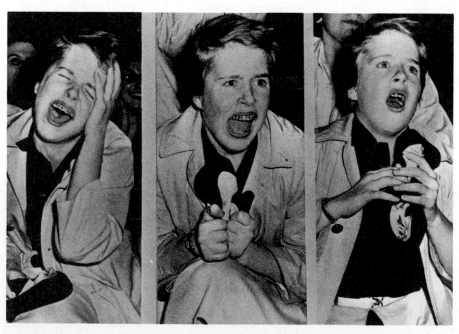

Body language sends out powerful messages.

fied and **circumspect**. People who are **distraught** often walk with their heads down and their hands clasped behind their backs. The person with energy and will power moves rapidly, hands swinging freely from side to side. **(9)** Those who walk with their hands in their pockets may be **perverse** and critical of others. **(10)** People who look toward the ground may be trying to **circumvent** the glances of others.

Body language sends out powerful messages. The next time you shake hands, tilt your head, or fold your arms, think about what you are wordlessly telling another person.

■ *Exercise*

Each numbered sentence below corresponds to a sentence in the Passage. Fill in the letter of the choice that makes this sentence mean the same thing as the corresponding sentence in the Passage.

1. If her arms are crossed, however, she is _____ communicating another message.
   a. hopefully b. accidentally c. strongly d. probably

2. Only an inexperienced teacher would make the deduction that a student who remains _____ is thinking about math.
   a. still b. careless c. present d. seated

3. Another conclusion may be more _____ .
   a. logical b. negative c. desirable d. ridiculous

4. A person will give a _____ smile that requests the injured person not to start a fight.
   a. happy b. false c. brief a. friendly

5. An open-handed gesture is _____ to friendliness.
   a. opposed b. leading c. obvious d. given

6. An umpire makes a call that a team manager wants him to _____ .
   a. take back b. be firm about c. discuss intelligently
   d. slightly delay

7. As the manager approaches, the formerly neutral umpire undergoes a(n) _____ .
   a. reform b. illness c. inspection d. change

8. We have all seen the controlled and measured walk of a person try-

   ing to appear dignified and _____ .
   a. unfriendly b. worried c. busy d. cautious

9. Those who walk with their hands in their pockets may be

   _____ and critical of others.
   a. contrary b. unhappy c. observant d. lonely

10. People who look toward the ground may be trying to _____ the
    glances of others.
    a. capture b. greet c. avoid d. notice

■ *Discussion Questions*

1. According to the passage, what is the "hidden message" of smiling?

2. Identify two situations in which the position of a person's arms indicate an attitude.

3. Suggest three ways in which dogs communicate using body language.

Word Elements: Together and Apart

People come together in classes, clubs, concerts, parties, and sports events. Yet disagreements and disputes can also force them apart. This chapter concentrates on word elements meaning "together" and "apart," presenting three prefixes and two roots. The chapter also introduces several words that came into English from other languages, showing how languages come together. As English speakers came into contact with people speaking different languages, English borrowed foreign words.

Chapter Strategy: Word Elements: Together and Apart

Chapter Words:

Part 1

co-, com-, con-	coherent	dis-	discord
	collaborate		disparity
	communal		disreputable
	compatible	sym-, syn	synchronize
	concur		synopsis
	contemporary		synthesis

Part 2

greg	congregate	Borrowed Words	bravado
	gregarious		charisma
	segregate		cliché
sperse	disperse		cuisine
	intersperse		nadir
	sparse		zenith

Did You Know?

What Are Two Sources of English?

Modern English has roots in two languages, Old French and Old English. Old French was a Romance language; that is, it descended from Latin, which was spoken by the Romans. Old French was an ancestor of the French spoken today. Old English, spoken in England from about the beginning of the eighth century to the middle of the twelfth century, was a Germanic language, similar in many ways to the German used today. The two languages first came into contact in 1066.

In 1066 William the Conqueror crossed the English Channel from northwestern France, conquered England, and made himself king. He replaced the English nobility with his fellow Norman countrymen, who spoke a version of Old French. For many years, then, the ruling class of England spoke Old French, and the rest of the people continued to speak Old English.

Gradually the two languages merged into Middle English, which was spoken until about the fifteenth century, when it became what we know as Modern English. But to this day, many rare, fancy words of English (like the ones you find in vocabulary books) tend to be of Old French origin. The common words of English are from Old English.

What does this mean to you? Perhaps you speak or have studied Spanish, Italian, French, or Portuguese. If so, you may realize that these languages are related to the Old French that William the Conqueror brought to England. They are all Romance languages. If you speak a Romance language, you can easily learn many difficult English words. All you need to do is to think of a *cognate*, a word that sounds the same and has the same meaning, from a Romance language. As an example, *furious* is an uncommon English word descended from Old French. The Spanish cognate is *furioso*. The common English word derived from Old English is *mad*.

Modern English is full of pairs of words that have the same or similar meanings. In these cases, one word is often derived from Old French and the other from Old English. Several of these word pairs are listed below. Notice that the words descended from Old French are often longer and less common.

Old English (Germanic Origin)	Old French (Romance Origin)
eat	devour
talk	converse
give	donate
earth	terrain
top	pinnacle
late	tardy

During the 1400s and the 1500s, interest in the ancient Greeks and Romans resulted in another great expansion in English. Writers simply coined new words from ancient Greek and Latin ones. In this way, words such as *compatible, congenital,* and *conspicuous* (all found in this book) entered the English language. The great English playwright, Shakespeare, was the first to use the words *misanthrope* and *frugal.*

Finally, English has borrowed words from many other languages, including Arabic, Hindi, Urdu, Italian, German, and Spanish. If you know another language, you'll probably recognize many words that are similar in English. In this chapter you will study several words that English has borrowed. These words are a spoken and written record of the explorations that brought English speakers together with people of other cultures and languages.

Learning Strategy

Word Elements: Together and Apart

Part 1 of this chapter presents three common prefixes that refer to being together or apart: *com-* and *syn-* mean "together"; *dis-* means "apart." These prefixes are very useful, since each one is used to form more than one hundred words in English.

Part 2 presents two roots that are related to the idea of together and apart, *greg* (flock, herd) and *sperse* (scatter).

Element	Meaning	Origin	Function	Chapter Words
		Part 1		
co-, col-, com-, con-, cor-	together	Latin	prefix	coherent, collaborate, communal, compatible, concur, contemporary
dis-	apart; not	Latin; Greek	prefix	discord, disparity, disreputable
sym-, syn-	together; same	Greek	prefix	synchronize, synopsis, synthesis
		Part 2		
greg	flock	Latin	root	congregate, gregarious, segregate
sperse	scatter	Latin	root	disperse, intersperse, sparse

Prefixes

Part 1

The three prefixes presented in Part 1 are discussed in more detail below.

co-, col-, com-, con-, cor- (together)
   This prefix is used in several hundred English words. Its five spelling variations help us to pronounce it more easily when it is attached to various roots, as in these examples: *coworker, collect, communicate, contact,* and *correspond.* Each of these words carries some sense of "together." For example, when people *communicate* they come together through speech or writing. When two electrical wires establish *contact,* they come together by touching. A *coworker* is someone who works together with another worker. The word *companion* is also formed from *com-* (together) and the Latin word *panis* (bread). Originally, a companion was a person with whom one shared bread or other food.

dis- (apart; not)
   Dis- means "apart" in some words. For example, students often *dissect* (cut apart) frogs in biology classes. A noisy student may *disrupt* (break apart into confusion) a class. *Dis-* can also mean "not." The word *distrust,* formed from the prefix *dis-* and the base word *trust,* means "not to trust." A person in *disgrace* is not in the grace, or favor, of others.

sym-, syn- (together; same)
   The two meanings of *syn-* and *sym-* are related, making them easy to remember. For example *sympathy* is composed from *sym-* (same) and the root *path* (feeling). *Synagogue,* a place where Jewish people meet to worship, is composed from *syn-* (together) and *agein* (to lead).

Words to Learn

Part 1

co-, com-, con-

   1. **coherent** (adjective)   kō-hîr'ənt

      From *co-* (together) + *haērere (to cling or stick)*

      logical; consistent; clearly reasoned

Marisa's **coherent** argument for changing school rules impressed the president of the university.

The **coherent** lecture was easy for students to understand.

▶ *Related Words*
  coherence (noun)   The *coherence* of his reasoning proved that he had considered the problem carefully.
  cohere (verb)   In the cold weather, ice *cohered* to the surface of the road. (Cohere means "to stick.")

2. **collaborate** (verb)   kə-lăb′ə-rāt′

From Latin: *col-* (together) + *labōrāre* (to work)

to work together

  A team of physicists and chemists **collaborated** under the leadership of Enrico Fermi to produce the first nuclear chain reaction in 1942.

  Andrew Lloyd Weber and David Cullen **collaborated** on the orchestration of the musical *Phantom of the Opera*.

▶ *Related Word*
  collaboration (noun)   Working in *collaboration*, Jose, Phillip, and Suzuki produced an award-winning science project.

NOTE: The word *collaborator* can have the negative meaning of "one who aids an enemy occupying one's country."

3. **communal** (adjective)   kə-myōōn′əl

From Latin: *com-* (together) *(Communis* meant "shared," "public.")

referring to a community or to joint ownership

  People from all six apartments ate **communal** dinners.

  The courtyard of the apartment building is **communal** property.

▶ *Related Word*
  commune (noun)   (kŏm′yōōn′)   The ten people living in the *commune* shared all expenses.

A *commune* is a place where people live as a group, sharing their incomes. Two types of well-established communes are monasteries (religious communities) and kibbutzim (collective farms in Israel).

---

4. **compatible** (adjective) kəm-păt'ə-bəl

   From Latin: *com-* (together) + *path* (feeling)

   harmonious; living in harmony

   > A messy person and a neat person would not make **compatible** roommates.

   > Since the partners' objectives were **compatible,** their business grew rapidly.

   ▶ *Common Phrase*
   compatible with

   ▶ *Related Word*
   compatibility (noun) *Compatibility* is an important factor in a happy marriage.

5. **concur** (verb) kən-kûr'

   From Latin: *con-* (together) + *currere* (to run)

   to agree

   > The court of appeals **concurred** with the decision of the district court.

   > My wife and mother **concurred** that my yellow and green striped tie was not suitable for the business meeting.

   to happen at the same time

   > The times that the two of us left the house **concurred** exactly.

   ▶ *Common Phrase*
   concur with

   ▶ *Related Words*
   concurrence (noun) There is a general public *concurrence* that recycling is worth the effort to help our environment.
   concurrent (adjective) The criminal was serving two *concurrent* jail sentences.

6. **contemporary** (noun, adjective) kən-tĕm'pə-rĕr'ē plural: contemporaries

   From Latin: *com-* (together) + *tempus* (time)

   a person living at the same time as another person (noun)

   > My great-grandmother was a **contemporary** of Abraham Lincoln.

   > Great artists are often not appreciated by their **contemporaries.**

existing at the same time (adjective)

> The American Revolutionary War and the French Revolution were almost **contemporary** events.

current; modern (adjective)

> According to **contemporary** beliefs, it is healthy for mothers to breastfeed their babies.

▶ *Related Word*
contemporaneous (adjective) (kən-tĕm′pə-rā′nē-əs) George Washington's life was *contemporaneous* with the life of Thomas Jefferson.

dis-

7. **discord** (noun)   dĭs′kôrd′

From Latin: *dis-* (apart) + *cor* (heart, mind)

strife; lack of agreement

> According to experts, money is the most common cause of **discord** in marriage.

▶ *Related Word*
discordant (adjective) (dĭs-kôr′dənt) The horns of cars stuck in traffic made a *discordant* noise.

A Greek legend tells the story of the apple of discord. The goddess Discord had not been invited to a wedding at which all the other gods were to be present. Enraged, she arrived at the party and threw onto the table a golden apple intended "for the most beautiful." Three goddesses, Juno, Minerva, and Venus, all claimed it. Paris, prince of Troy, was asked to settle the dispute. He chose Venus. As a reward, Venus promised him the most beautiful woman in the world, Helen, who was, however, married to the Greek king Menelaus. When Paris abducted her, a Greek army went to Troy to get her back. This military expedition resulted in the Trojan War, the subject of Homer's *Iliad*.

---

8. **disparity** (noun)   dĭs-păr′ə-tē

From Latin: *dis-* (not) + *par* (equal)

inequality; difference

> According to economists, income **disparity** in the United States has increased in the last twenty years.

> There was a **disparity** between the words and actions of the hypocrite.

▶ *Related Word*
   disparate (adjective) (dĭs′pər-ĭt)   The *disparate* viewpoints of the two foremen caused problems for the workers.

9. **disreputable** (adjective)   dĭs-rĕp′yə-tə-bəl

From Latin: *dis-* (not) + *re-* (again) + *putāre* (to think) (Literally, this means "not worth a second thought.")

not respectable; having a bad reputation

   The student's appearance was so **disreputable** that we thought he was a beggar.

   If you deal with a **disreputable** merchant, you risk being cheated.

▶ *Related Word*
   disrepute (noun) (dĭs′rĭ-pyoot′)   The chemist who had reported false results was held in *disrepute*.

sym-, syn-

10. **synchronize** (verb)   sĭn′krə-nīz′

From Greek: *syn-* (same) + *khronos* (time)

to adjust to the same time

   The movie was difficult to watch because the soundtrack and the picture were not **synchronized.**

▶ *Related Word*
   synchronization (noun)   The *synchronization* of the city's church bells ensured that they all rang on the hour.

11. **synopsis** (noun)   sĭ-nŏp′sĭs

From Greek: *syn-* (together) + *opsis* (view) (In a synopsis, something is viewed "all together.")

a short summary

   The newspaper critic gave a **synopsis** of the movie.

   The **synopsis** told the plot of the book in a few short paragraphs.

▶ *Related Word*
   synopsize (verb)   The critic *synosized* the plot of the movie.

NOTE: The plural form of *synopsis* is *synopses*.

12. **synthesis** (noun)   sĭn′thə-sĭs

From Greek: *syn-* (together) + *tithenai* (to put)

something made from combined parts

> The new book was a **synthesis** of the best ideas in psychology and philosophy.

▶ *Related Words*
synthesize (verb)   He *synthesized* many ideas in his lectures.

synthetic (adjective)   (sĭn-thĕt′ĭk)   Nylon and polyester are examples of *synthetic* materials made from petroleum.

synthetically (adverb)   The fabric was *synthetically* produced.

NOTE: 1. *Synthetic* and *synthetically* can refer to products produced chemically, or by other artificial means, rather than those of natural origin.
2. The plural form of *synthesis* is *syntheses*.

A synthesis is the creation of a whole from many parts. One of the funniest syntheses on record was the writing of the book *Naked Came the Stranger*. Twenty-five newspaper reporters got together to write the worst novel they could. Each person contributed one bad chapter. The result was a bestseller!

Exercises

Part 1

■ Definitions

Match each word in the left-hand column with a definition from the right-hand column. Use each choice only once.

1. communal _____
2. disreputable _____
3. disparity _____
4. synopsis _____
5. collaborate _____

a. to work together
b. to agree
c. not respectable
d. jointly owned
e. harmonious
f. summary

6. compatible _____
7. discord _____
8. synthesis _____
9. synchronize _____
10. coherent _____

g. strife; lack of agreement
h. something made from combined parts
i. to adjust to the same time
j. logical
k. current, modern
l. inequality

■ Meanings

Match each prefix to its meaning. Use each choice only once.

1. syn- _____
2. dis- _____
3. con- _____

a. apart; not
b. together; same
c. together

■ Words in Context

Complete each sentence with the word that fits best. Use each choice only once.

a. coherent   e. concur   i. disreputable
b. collaborate   f. contemporary   j. synchronize
c. communal   g. discordant   k. synopsis
d. compatible   h. disparity   l. synthesis

1. Presenting your reasons in a _____ manner will help persuade others that you are correct.

2. I was annoyed by the _____ noise from five radios playing different music.

3. Since we are the same age, Alice is my _____

4. The two students will _____ and produce one final paper.

5. Reading a _____ of the plot helped us to understand better what happens in Shakespeare's, *Macbeth*.

6. There is a great _____ of power between a master and a slave.

7. Nobody would deal with the _____ lawyer.

8. Many people _____ with the decision to limit nuclear arms.

9. The swimming pool was _____ property, and everyone in the neighborhood owned a share in it.

10. Popular people tend to be _____ with others.

■ Using Related Words

Complete each sentence using a word from the group of related words above it. You may need to capitalize a word when you put it into a sentence. Use each choice only once.

1. contemporaries, contemporaneous, contemporary

   Wolfgang Amadeus Mozart, who lived from 1751 to 1792, was a

   _____ of the Austrian Emperor, Franz Joseph. Mozart was a child prodigy, who with the help of his father, performed throughout Europe at the age of six. However, as an adult,

   he had many problems. His _____ often ignored

   his best music. _____ reports tell us that he lost the sponsorship of royalty. He died in poverty when he was thirty-one years old, but his great music lives on today.

2. synposis, synopses, synopsize

   It is often tempting for a student to read a _____ of a novel, rather than the entire book. However, reading is a major source of vocabulary growth. Therefore, people who continu-

   ally read _____ rather than full novels are limiting their opportunities to learn new words. Despite the fact that

   people writing study aids _____ novels, it is best to read the entire work.

3. synthesized, synthetically

Many vitamins are now _____ produced in factories. Vitamins A and B12 are among those that can be commercially _____ .

4. concur, concurrence

It takes many years to reach _____ on policies that unify regional economies. In 1992, most countries of Western Europe combine into a trade cooperative, with no duties on goods traveling between them. In the same year, four Andean nations, Venezuela, Columbia, Peru, and Bolivia, also eliminate duties. Most economic experts _____ in the opinion that economies profit from this unification.

■ *Reading the Headlines*

This exercise presents five headlines that might have been taken from newspapers. Read each one carefully and then answer the questions that follow. (Remember that little words, such as *a* and *the*, are often left out of headlines.)

PSYCHOLOGISTS CONCUR THAT COMPATIBLE COUPLES OFTEN TALK

1. Do the psychologists agree? _____

2. Do these marriages have problems? _____

CONTEMPORARY BUSINESS PRACTICES CALLED DISREPUTABLE BY INVESTIGATING TEAM

3. Did the practices take place in the past? _____

4. Are the business practices honorable? _____

COLLABORATING CITY OFFICIALS ANNOUNCE COHERENT PLAN FOR IMPROVING CITY TRAFFIC

5. Did the officials work together? _____

6. Is the plan logical and consistent? _____

DISPARITY OF INCOME IN COUNTRY CAUSES DISCORD

7. Do most people in the country have equal incomes? _____

8. Are people arguing? _____

PLAY PRESENTED IN SYNOPSIZED FORM AT PARTY TO SUPPORT COMMUNAL RECYCLING CENTER

9. Was the play fully presented? _____

10. Does one person own the recycling center? _____

Word Roots

Part 2

The learning strategy for Part 2 presents two word roots that are concerned with together and apart, but do not carry these meanings directly. These roots are *greg* and *sperse*.

Finally, Part 2 presents some words borrowed from other languages when English speakers came together with speakers of these languages.

greg (flock; herd)
   Greg once referred to a flock of sheep or a herd of cattle. By extension, *greg* has come to be used as a word element meaning the action of coming, or "flocking," together. For example, one word you will learn, *gregarious*, describes people who like to be with other people.
sperse (scatter)
   When we scatter things, we move them apart. Thus the root *sperse* is concerned with being apart. *Disperse*, one of the words in this lesson, means "to scatter widely."

Words to Learn

Part 2

greg

13. **congregate** (verb)   kŏng'grə-gāt'

    From Latin: *con-* (together) + *greg* (flock, herd)

    to meet; to assemble

    > Both houses of Congress **congregated** to hear the president's State of the Union address.

    > Everyone at the party **congregated** in one corner of the room.

    ▶ *Related Word*
      congregation (noun)   The *congregation* listened intently to the minister's sermon.

    Congregation is a religious word, meaning the members of a religious organization such as a church or synagogue. Many other religious words have interesting origins.

    Catholic, from the meaning "universal"   When it is spelled with a small c, *catholic* still means "universal," rather than the religion.
    Protestant, from *protest*   In the early 1500s, Martin Luther and his followers protested against certain Catholic practices. They formed a new set of "protesting" religions.
    Jewish, from the Hebrew word *Judah,* the ancient Jewish Kingdom
    Muslim, from the Arabic word *aslama,* meaning "he surrendered," referring to people who are obedient to God's will
    Hindu, from the Persian word for India, *Hind*

    ---

14. **gregarious** (adjective)   grĭ-gâr'ē-əs

    From Latin: *greg* (flock; herd)

    sociable; fond of company

    > Since Thelma was **gregarious,** she loved to talk to clients while she styled their hair.

    ▶ *Related Word*
      gregariousness (noun)   Because of their *gregariousness,* the elderly couple enjoyed large parties.

15. **segregate** (verb)   sĕg′rə-gāt′

From Latin: *sē-* (apart) + *greg* (flock; herd) *(Sēgregāre* meant "to separate from the flock.")

to separate

It is wrong to **segregate** disabled people from the rest of society.

▶ *Related Word*
  segregation (noun)   The *segregation* of children and adults seemed strange to us.

The words *segregated* and *segregation* have come to mean the forced separation of religious and ethnic groups from the mainstream of society. At times in the past, segregated minorities were forced to use separate and inferior facilities. The U. S. Congress has passed several Civil Rights Acts prohibiting these unjust practices.

---

sperse

16. **disperse** (verb)   dĭs-pûrs′

From Latin: *dis-* (apart) + *sperse* (scatter)

to scatter; to distribute widely

The individual call of each parakeet enables other birds to identify it, even when the flock is **dispersed.**

The crowd **dispersed** after the movie ended.

▶ *Related Word*
  dispersion (noun)   The students observed the *dispersion* of light through a prism.

17. **intersperse** (verb)   ĭn′tər-spûrs′

From Latin: *inter-* (between) + *sperse* (scatter)

to scatter here and there; to distribute among other things

The lecturer **interspersed** some personal views into a presentation of the facts.

The paved highway was **interspersed** with stretches of dirt road.

▶ *Common Phrase*
  intersperse with

► *Related Word*
   interspersion (noun) The *interspersion* of jokes made the
   speech amusing.

18. **sparse** (adjective) spärs

From Latin: *sperse* (scatter)

thinly scattered or distributed

   In the 1800s there was only **sparse** settlement in the newly explored territory of Wyoming.

   Gorillas are now **sparse** in Africa, however at one time they
   existed in large numbers.

► *Related Word*
   sparsity (noun) There is a *sparsity* of trees on high mountain
   tops.

Borrowed Words

19. **bravado** (noun) brə-vä**'**-dō

From Spanish

false bravery; showy display of courage

   In a show of **bravado,** the young tenderfoot challenged the gun-
   slinger to a shootout.

20. **charisma** (noun) kə-rĭz**'**mə

From Greek

quality of leadership that attracts other people

   The **charisma** of Lech Walesa has made him a symbol of freedom in Poland.

► *Related Word*
   charismatic (adjective) (kăr**'**ĭz-măt**'**ĭk) The *charismatic* personality of Nelson Mandela has attracted many followers and
   admirers.

Although the special quality of *charisma* is hard to define, history
records many charismatic leaders.

   Napoleon Bonaparte became emperor of France in 1804, less
than ten years after the French had beheaded King Louis XVI and
declared the country a republic. It is said that Napoleon's charisma
was so strong that anybody who met him would be captured by his

personality. Napoleon united the French behind him and managed to conquer half of Europe before he was defeated by England and Austria in 1815.

In his powerful speeches, the modern black leader Martin Luther King, Jr., inspired all who heard him with the justice of his great cause. King employed nonviolent peace marches to win rights for black people in the United States.

21. **cliché** (noun)   klē-shā'

From French

an overused, trite expression

> An example of a **cliché** often used in sports is "no pain, no gain."
> The official's speech was full of **clichés** and promises, but it gave no plan of action.

Many clichés stay with us over the years. In 1878, W. S. Gilbert and Arthur Sullivan wrote a song featuring clichés in their operetta, "H. M. S. Pinafore." Many are still in use today, including "All that glitters is not gold," "Only brave deserve the fair," "Who spares the rod spoils the child," and "Here today and gone tomorrow."

22. **cuisine** (noun)   kwĭ-zēn′

From French

a style of food or cooking

> Puerto Rican **cuisine** features delicious pasteles, which are made of cornmeal and stuffed with meat, raisins, olives, capers, and almonds.

> It takes years to master the techniques of preparing French **cuisine.**

NOTE: Generally a *cuisine* refers to food prepared by skilled cooks or chefs.

Cuisines of different regions feature various specialities. Can you match each food item with its country or group of origin?

1. curry	a. Arab
2. sushi	b. Japanese
3. crepes	c. Mexican
4. phò tai	d. French
5. fajitas	e. Vietnamese
6. hummos	f. Indian

(*Answers:* 1. f 2. b 3. d 4. e 5. c 6. a)

---

23. **nadir** (noun)   nā′dər

from Arabic: *nazīr as-samt* (the lowest point; opposite the zenith)

the lowest point

> Human behavior reaches its **nadir** in the act of genocide.

24. **zenith** (noun)   zē′nĭth

From Arabic: *samt ar-ra's* (the path overhead; the highest point in the heavens)

the highest point

> The British empire was at the **zenith** of its power under Queen Victoria.

Arabic astronomers have made many important contributions. As early as 800 B.C. Babylonians and Assyrians had calculated new moons and composed a seasonal calendar. The Chaldeans (about 500

B.C.) had a table of lunar eclipses and knew the cycles of five planets around the sun. The work of Abû Ma'shar (born in A.D. 787), who calculated the length of the year and catalogued the stars, was translated from Arabic into Latin and was one of the first books ever printed in Germany.

Exercises

Part 2

■ Definitions

Match each word in the left-hand column with a definition from the right-hand column. Use each choice only once.

1. sparse _____   a. to distribute among other things

2. cliché _____   b. a quality that attracts others

3. intersperse _____   c. sociable

4. congregate _____   d. lowest point

5. charisma _____   e. highest point

6. nadir _____   f. showy display of bravery

7. disperse _____   g. to scatter; to distribute widely

8. bravado _____   h. to gather together

9. segregate _____   i. style of cooking

10. gregarious _____   j. thinly scattered

                           k. to separate

                           l. overused expression

■ Meanings

Match each word root to its meaning. Use each choice only once.

1. sperse _____   a. flock; herd

2. greg _____   b. scatter

■ *Words in Context*

Complete each sentence with the word that fits best. Use each choice only once.

a. congregate   e. intersperse   i. cliché
b. gregarious   f. sparse   j. cuisine
c. segregate   g. bravado   k. nadir
d. disperse   h. charisma   l. zenith

1. People will _____ in the church to hear the address of the archbishop.

2. In the college dormitory, they will _____ the rooms into men's living spaces and women's living spaces.

3. When the crowd started to become violent, the police ordered it

   to _____ .

4. At the _____ of his remarkable career, Genghis Khan ruled a vast Asian empire.

5. Indian _____ includes many tasty vegetables and interesting spices.

6. _____ rainfall has caused a lack of water in southern California.

7. The expression "save for a rainy day" is a(n) _____ that most of us have heard many times.

8. He displayed true _____ when he dared his enemy to shoot at him.

9. Farmers often _____ rows of corn with rows of other crops.

10. Homeless and starving, she had reached the _____ of her fortunes.

■ *Using Related Words*

Complete each sentence using a word from the group of related words above it. You may need to capitalize a word when you put it into a sentence. Use each choice only once.

1. gregarious, gregariousness

   Politicians are often _____ people, who enjoy

   meeting others. The _____ of politicians enables them to mingle with crowds comfortably and remember names easily.

2. disperse, dispersion

   The wind will often _____ seeds throughout a

   large area. The _____ of seeds helps ensure that plants are fertilized and reproduce.

3. interspersed, interspersion

   The great playwright Shakespeare often _____ a

   few comic scenes into his tragic plays. This _____ allowed the audience some comic relief from the dramatic tension.

4. sparse, sparsity

   In many portions of Canada, settlement is _____ . One can go for hundreds of miles without seeing people. This

   _____ of settlement is due to mountains and cold weather.

5. charisma, charismatic

   With his riveting blue eyes and mysterious manner, the Russian

   figure Rasputin, (1871?–1916), was extremely _____ .

   His _____ attracted many followers, including Queen Alexandra. Her devotion to Rasputin was deeply resented by the Russian people and may have been a factor leading to the Russian Revolution.

■ Reading the Headlines

This exercise presents five headlines that might have been taken from newspapers. Read each one carefully and then answer the questions that follow. (Remember that little words, such as *a* and *the*, are often left out of headlines.)

PEOPLE CONGREGATE TO HEAR CHARISMATIC SPEAKER

1. Do the people stay apart? _____

2. Does the speaker appeal to people? _____

CLOUDS TOO DISPERSED TO FORM RAIN IN AREA WITH SPARSE CROP GROWTH

3. Are the clouds gathered together? _____

4. Are there many crops? _____

GREGARIOUS GROUP INTERSPERSES BUSINESS TALK WITH SOCIALIZING

5. Do the members of the group like to be alone? _____

6. Do the members socialize as well as talk business? _____

REBELS DISPLAY BRAVADO AT NADIR OF THEIR FORTUNES

7. Do the rebels seem courageous? _____

8. Are they enjoying good luck? _____

VIETNAMESE CUISINE CALLED ZENITH OF TASTE

9. Is food referred to? _____

10. Is it good? _____

Chapter Exercises

■ *Practicing Strategies: New Words from Word Elements*

See how your knowledge of word elements can help you to understand new words. Complete each sentence with the word that seems to fit best. Use each choice only once.

a. aggregate   e. compress   i. dislocated
b. coexist   f. conform   j. disuse
c. collide   g. disconnect   k. symmetrical
d. community   h. discourteous   l. sympathize

1. When something is no longer used, it has fallen into

                    _____ .

2. Someone who is not courteous is _____ .

3. A _____ consists of many people living together.

4. When we separate parts from a connection, we

                    _____ them.

5. If an accident pushes your arm or hip bone out of the correct loca-

tion, you have _____ your arm or leg.

6. When all of something is herded together, the total is called the

                    _____ .

7. If two cars bump together in an accident, they

                    _____ .

8. When a person takes the same forms of behavior and dress as

others, we say that person is trying to _____ .

9. To press together is to _____ .

10. *Meter* means "measure," so a figure with two equal sides is called

                    _____ .

■ Practicing Strategies: Combining Context Clues and Word Elements

Combining the strategies of context clues and word elements is a good way to figure out unknown words. In the following sentences, each italicized word contains a word element that you have studied in this chapter. Using the meaning of the word element and the context of the sentence, make an intelligent guess at the meaning of the italicized word. Your instructor may ask you to check the meaning in your dictionary when you have finished.

1. We *dismantled* the machine into twenty-five pieces.

   Dismantled means _____ .

2. At the *confluence* of the stream with the Colorado River, the color of the water revealed both sources.

   Confluence means _____ .

3. Thanks to the total *concordance* of the aims of the delegates, the meeting was a complete success.

   Concordance means _____ .

4. The man was so *disheartened* by his failure to find a job that he soon stopped his search.

   Disheartened means _____ .

5. In many movie musicals, stars *lip-synch* lyrics that are actually sung by other people.

   Lip-synch means _____ .

■ Companion Words

Complete each sentence with the word that fits best. Choose your answers from the words below. You may use each word more than once.

Choices: with, on, between, of, in

1. My taste in clothing is compatible _____ my sister's taste.

2. We concur _____ your decision.

3. There is a disparity _____ income distribution.

4. The Beatles were contemporaries _____ my professor.

5. My friend presented a synopsis _____ the long paper.

6. The style is a synthesis _____ many fashion trends.

7. In the evening, people congregate _____ the town square.

8. I like to intersperse working _____ socializing.

9. There is a disparity _____ good and evil.

10. Two people collaborated _____ the project.

■ *Writing with Your Words*

This exercise will give you practice in writing effective sentences using the vocabulary words. Each sentence is started for you. Complete it with an interesting phrase that also indicates the meaning of the italicized word.

1. We read the *synopsis* so that _____

_____ .

2. To avoid *discord,* _____

_____ .

3. The taste of ketchup is *compatible* with _____

_____ .

4. Most people *concur* that _____

_____ .

5. People like to *intersperse* studying with _____

_____ .

6. The cornered outlaw showed his *bravado* by _____

_____ .

7. A *disreputable* person might _____

_____ .

8. Because the plot of the movie was not *coherent,* _____

_____ .

9. You would know a person was *gregarious* if _____

_____ .

10. My favorite *cuisine* is _____

_____

Passage

Situation Comedies: Changes In Images

The situation comedies we watch on television are powerful representations of the American family. **(1)** Critics **concur** that changes shaping American society have been reflected in these TV programs.

It is said that at any given time, somewhere throughout the world, the show *I Love Lucy* is being shown on television. This 1950s comedy features the happily married Lucy and her Cuban-born husband, Ricky Ricardo, who owns a nightclub. Unfortunately, Lucy's urge to be a performer sometimes causes **discord.** To give the **synopsis** of a typical show, Lucy, disguised as a glamorous performer, decides to dance in Ricky's nightclub. However, a series of disasters during her performance causes panic **(2)** and ruins the **convivial** atmosphere. Ricky vents his frustrations in Spanish, or with English words liberally **interspersed** with such expressions such as "ay, yay, yay, yay, yay!" They fight, then kiss and make up at the end of the show.

The classic comic acting of *I Love Lucy* has assured its popularity for more than forty years, yet some of its attitudes are now outdated. Lucy's frequent attempts to establish a career are seen in a negative light, reflecting the 1950s idea that a woman's career goals are less worthy than those of a man. **(3)** This **disparity** in the treatment of men and women would not be tolerated today.

Like most sitcoms of its day and age, *I Love Lucy* presented the **clichés** of the middle class: a clean home headed by a woman who loved to cook and raise children, and a man who earned a comfortable living. The married couples may have gotten angry, but they never swore. Divorce was unheard of.

A happy household also appears in the most successful comedy of the 1980s, *Cosby*. **(4)** The **compatible** couple has an almost ideal family of five bright children. Physician Heathcliff Huxtable presides over a spotless house and a family that radiates love and cheer. Although the Cosbys resemble a classic TV family from the sitcoms of the 1950s, this is a ground-breaking comedy for two particular reasons: the mother is an attorney, and the family is African American. **(5)** The people who **collaborated** to produce the *Cosby* show experienced rejection by two major networks. Once on the air, however, the **charisma** of comedian Bill

Cosby ensured its success. **(6)** The **gregarious** Cosby always has a house full of neighborhood children whom he is always willing to entertain.

The show is a beautifully crafted **synthesis** of middle-class values, a minority family, and extraordinary talent. **(7)** It is easy to see why it maintained a position at the **zenith** of TV ratings for several years.

In the late 1980s and into the 1990s, situation comedies changed once again, as families shown on TV became poorer and less traditional. In *Married with Children,* Peg and her husband constantly fight. Unlike Dr. Cliff Huxtable, Al Bundy is a "regular guy" who works in a shoe store. The clothing of Peg and her daughter flaunt their sex appeal. **(8)** Their behavior with men is often **disreputable.** Mom's **cuisine** seems limited to boiled eggs, beans, and store-bought pizza.

In the situation comedy *Roseanne,* Dad works on an assembly line, and Mom is often jobless. A **sparse** supply of money is the subject of many family arguments. The show presents many informal poses: lying together on the messy couch, Roseanne and her husband eat junk food and rub each other's feet! Lucy Ricardo or Cliff Huxtable would be horrified.

I Love Lucy is still popular, even with outdated attitudes.

The Simpsons are very different from TV families of the 1950s.

(9) Perhaps the **nadir** of housekeeping is presented in *The Simpsons*. This animated feature cartoon shows staircases littered with toys, skateboards, and electrical wires. Dressed in his underwear, dad Homer watches football on TV while drinking beer. Bart, a self-proclaimed underachiever, delights in talking back to teachers. He is usually doing something he shouldn't, like throwing his sister's Thanksgiving centerpiece into the fire. When threatened with punishment, he displays **bravado,** defying the power of his school or family. His favorite expression, "Don't have a cow, dude," has become a **cliché.**

(10) **Contemporary** comedies have, indeed, changed as different lifestyles have become acceptable. However, the one thing that remains constant, as families **congregate** in front of the television, is a happy ending.

■ *Exercise*

Each numbered sentence below corresponds to a sentence in the Passage. Fill in the letter of the choice that makes this sentence mean the same thing as the corresponding sentence in the passage.

1. Critics _____ that changes in America are reflected in our situation comedies.

   a. agree b. feel c. know d. believe

2. A series of disasters ruins the _____ atmosphere of the club.
   a. peaceful   b. quiet   c. social   d. relaxing

3. This _____ in the treatment of men and women would not be tolerated today.
   a. silliness   b. cruelty   c. difference   d. snobbishness

4. The _____ couple has an almost ideal family.
   a. rich   b. attractive   c. harmonious   d. minority

5. The people who _____ to produce the show experienced rejection by two networks.
   a. worked together   b. met together   c. spoke together
   d. traveled together

6. The _____ Cosby always has a house full of neighborhood children.
   a. helpful   b. lonely   c. sociable   d. affectionate

7. It maintained a position at the _____ of TV ratings.
   a. bottom   b. lower half   c. upper half   d. top

8. Their behavior with men is often _____ .
   a. essential to happiness   b. not respectable   c. not noticeable
   d. helpful to them

9. The _____ of housekeeping is presented on *The Simpsons*.
   a. model   b. best   c. worst   d. dangerousness

10. _____ comedies have changed as different lifestyles have become acceptable.
    a. Modern   b. Funny   c. Warm   d. Popular

■ *Discussion Questions*

1. How does the housekeeping in the Huxtable household contrast with that of the Simpsons?

2. Why is the Cosby show both a traditional and a ground-breaking show?

3. Name and describe at least two ways in which situation comedies have reflected changes in American lifestyles.

Review

Chapters 5–8

■ Reviewing Words in Context

Complete each sentence with the word that fits best. Use each choice only once.

a. abstain   g. communal   l. ingenious
b. antidote   h. contemporary   m. panorama
c. autobiography i. extricate   n. revert
d. automaton   j. genesis   o. tantalize
e. charisma   k. impartial   p. transitory
f. circumspect

1. A warm hug from mother can often be a(n) _____ to a child's tears.

2. From the mountain top, we could see a(n) _____ of the countryside.

3. The park was _____ property that belonged to everyone in the neighborhood.

4. It is often easy to _____ to old, bad habits.

5. People usually try to _____ themselves from embarrassing situations.

6. A robot is a(n) _____ .

7. The _____ of the religious leader drew thousands to his speeches.

8. The crook wanted to _____ us with the prospect of getting rich quickly.

9. The antique furniture looked strange in the _____ house.

10. The _____ of farming dates back to the ancient Egyptians.

11. A _____ person carefully considers what others think of him.

12. The _____ inventor made thousands of dollars through sales of her machine.

13. Her sadness was _____ , and she soon felt happy again.

14. Many people _____ from drinking coffee before bedtime because it keeps them awake.

15. As a(n) _____ observer, I cannot favor one side of the dispute.

■ *Passage for Word Review*

Complete each blank in the Passage with the word that makes the best sense. The choices include words from the vocabulary lists and related words. Use each choice only once.

a. autobiography   e. equilibrium   i. submissive
b. compatible   f. equitable   j. subconscious
c. concur   g. interminable   k. synchronized
d. deduced   h. psyche   l. vivacity

My First and Worst Job Interview

Every working person remembers the frightening experience of interviewing for a job. Before my first interview, I had a feeling there would be a disaster, and I was almost right!

Before the interview, I wondered about what the person interviewing me would be like. Would it be a man or a woman? Would he or she

be a **(1)** _____ person whom I could get along with, or someone I could not like or trust?

I tried to dress in good taste for the interview. I didn't want to look too unusual, but I did want to get some attention. I thought about how

to behave. I wanted to display some **(2)** _____ , but I didn't want to overshadow the person who was interviewing me. I

wanted to seem willing to be **(3)** _____ in some situations, but still make it clear that I have a mind of my own.

Finally the big day arrived, and I went off for the interview. As I waited nervously in the reception room, the telephone rang. An emergency had come up. Just my luck! It seemed that an evil fate had care-

fully **(4)** _____ my interview with some unfortunate event.

After what seemed an **(5)** _____ wait (it was really half an hour), the boss signaled me to come into her office. The first thing she did was to ask me what had made me choose this career. I panicked! Five years of training, and I couldn't even remember why I wanted to be an engineer. I became nervous and felt like I had com-

pletely lost my **(6)** _____ . Finally, I thought up a silly answer, which I'm sure wasn't satisfactory. "I like engineering."

When my interviewer saw that I was incapable of replying, she decided to talk about the company. It was well known, and she described its excellent opportunities for advancement as well as the

(7) _____ way it treated all employees. Trying to involve me in conversation, she asked me things like "What do you think?"

and "Do you **(8)** _____ with my point of view?"

After a while, she glanced at her watch and said, "Well, it looks like we are at the end of our time. Nice talking with you, and you will hear from us."

Filled with gloom, I crawled home. My **(9)** _____

was in a terrible state. Naturally, I **(10)** _____ that I had not been chosen for the job.

The next day I got a call. I had gotten the job! It seems that my excellent grades in school had persuaded the woman to hire me. All that studying had rewarded me with a good position.

But I never want to interview for a job again!

■ *Reviewing Learning Strategies*

New words from word elements   Below are some words you have not studied that are formed from classical word elements. Using your knowledge of these elements, write in the letter of the word that best completes each sentence. Use each choice only once.

a. attract
b. coactor
c. distaste
d. equiangular
e. ex-member
f. immobile
g. injection
h. intractable
i. regenerates
j. sympathy
k. synonym
l. vivarium

1. My _____ and I performed the play together.

2. A(n) _____ person is stubborn or "cannot be pulled."

3. A person who used to belong to a club is a(n) _____ .

4. If you are not moving, you are _____ .

5. When a plant grows new leaves or is "born again," after appearing

   to be dead, it _____ .

6. If you do not like a particular food, you may have a(n)

   _____ for it.

7. A word with the "same name," or same meaning, as another is a(n)

   _____ .

8. A triangle with three equal angles is a(n) _____ triangle.

9. When a nurse gives you a(n) _____ , something is "thrown in" to your body.

10. Animals might live in a(n) _____ .

Word Elements: Numbers and Measures

In ancient Egypt, Greece, and Rome, the lives of most people were organized around farming. They needed number words to tell them "when" planting should take place, "how many" bushels of grain the soil yielded, and "how much" money they would get for their crops. From these words were developed our modern words for quantities. This chapter presents Latin and Greek word elements for numbers and measurement, which will help you with the meanings of thousands of words.

Chapter Strategy: Word Elements: Numbers and Measures

Chapter Words:

Part 1

uni-	unanimity	di-, du-	dilemma
	unilateral		duplicity
mono-	monopoly	tri-	trilogy
	monotonous		trivial
bi-	bilingual	dec-	decade
	bipartisan		decimate

Part 2

cent-	centennial	integer	disintegrate
	centigrade		integrity
ambi-, amphi-	ambiguous	magn-, mega	magnanimous
	ambivalence		magnitude
ann, enn	annals	meter	metric
	perennial		symmetrical

Did You Know?

How Were the Months of the Year Named?

Did you ever wonder how the months got their names? Many of our months are based on number word elements. It took civilization thousands of years to develop an accurate calendar. Ancient calendars were so inaccurate that people often found themselves planting crops when the calendar claimed that winter was approaching. A famous Roman, Julius Caesar, helped to reform the calendar about two thousand years ago, and we have had many other changes since then. Even now, however, we must adjust the length of our years by adding an extra day (February 29) in every fourth, or leap, year. Since the Romans enacted a major calendar reform, our months bear Latin names.

January gets its name from the god Janus, the doorkeeper of the gate of heaven and the god of doors. Since doors are used to enter, Janus represented beginnings, and the first month of the year is dedicated to him. Janus is pictured with two faces, looking back to the past year as well as forward to the new year.

February comes from Februa, the Roman festival of purification. *March* is named for Mars, the Roman god of war. *April* has an uncertain origin. It may have been from *apero*, which means "second," for at one time it was the second month of the year, or from *aperīre* (to open) since it is the month in which flowers and trees open out in bloom.

May comes from the goddess of fertility, Maia. It was natural to name a spring month for the goddess who was thought to control the crops. *June* was named either for the Junius family of Roman nobles or for the goddess Juno, wife of Jupiter. *July* is named for Julius Caesar, the famous Roman we have mentioned. You will read about him in the Passage for this chapter.

August is named for Augustus Caesar, the nephew of Julius Caesar and the first emperor of Rome. His actual name was Octavian, but he took the title of Augustus (distinguished). The word *august* still means "distinguished" when the second syllable in the word is stressed.

The last four months all contain number prefixes: *September, sept* (seven); *October, oct* (eight); *November, nov* (nine); *December, dec* (ten). As you can see, the number roots are wrong! How did the ninth, tenth, eleventh, and twelfth months get the elements of seven, eight, nine, and ten?

Until 153 B.C. the new year was celebrated in March, so the months corresponded to the correct numbers. Then a change in the calendar left these months with the wrong meanings.

Learning Strategy

Word Elements: Numbers and Measures

Every word element in this chapter has a meaning of number or measurement. A list of the prefixes for the first ten numbers is given below. Although you won't be studying all of them in this chapter, you will find this list a handy reference for textbooks and everyday reading. English uses these number prefixes frequently; in fact, we are still making new words from them.

Prefix	Meaning	Example Word
*uni-	one	unidirectional (in one direction)
* mono	one	monologue (speech by one person)
*bi-	two	bidirectional (in two directions)
*di-, du	two	diatomic (made up of two atoms)
*tri-	three	trio (a musical group of three)
quad-, quar-	four	quartet (a musical group of four)
quint-, quin	five	quintet (a musical group of five)
sex-	six	sextet (a musical group of six)
sept-	seven	septet (a musical group of seven)
oct-	eight	octet (a musical group of eight)
nov-	nine	novena (a prayer offered for nine days)
*dec-	ten	decade (ten years)

*You will study these word elements intensively in this chapter.

To test your understanding of these number word prefixes, fill in the blanks in the following sentences.

a. A duplex is an apartment with _____ floors.

b. A trilingual person speaks _____ languages.

c. A quadruped is an animal that walks on _____ feet.

d. When quintuplets are born, _____ children are born.

e. Sextuple means to multiply by _____ .

f. If something is produced in septuplicate, there are

_____ copies of it altogether.

(*Answers:* a. 2 b. 3 c. 4 d. 5 e. 6 f. 7)

All the word elements you will study in this chapter are either number prefixes *(uni-, mono-, bi-, di-, tri-, dec-, cent-)* or measurement roots and prefixes *(ambi-, ann, integer, magn-, meter).*

Element	Meaning	Origin	Function	Chapter words
		Part 1		
uni-	one	Latin	prefix	unanimity, unilateral
mono-	one; single	Greek	prefix	monopoly, monotonous
bi-	two	Latin	prefix	bilingual, bipartisan
di-, du-	two	Greek; Latin	prefix	dilemma, duplicity
tri-	three	Greek; Latin	prefix	trilogy, trivial
dec-	ten	Greek; Latin	prefix	decade, decimate
		Part 2		
cent-	hundred	Latin	prefix	centennial, centigrade
ambi-, amphi-	both; around	Latin; Greek	prefix	ambiguous, ambivalence
ann, enn	year	Latin	root	annuals, perennial
integer	whole; complete	Latin	root	disintegrate, integrity
magn-, mega-	large	Latin; Greek	prefix	magnanimous, magnitude
meter, -meter	measure	Greek; Latin	root suffix	metric, symmetrical

This chapter presents a large number of word elements for study, twelve in all. However, since the number prefixes follow a clear pattern, you will find them easy to learn. They are arranged in order of the numbers they represent, rather than in alphabetical order. The first six are discussed below.

Prefixes

Part 1

uni- (one)

The Latin prefix for one, *uni-*, is used in many English words. To *unite*, for example, is to make several things into one. *Unisex* clothing uses one design, which is suitable for both men and women.

5

The *unicorn* was a mythical animal of great grace and beauty. Named for its one horn, it was supposed to have the legs of a buck, the tail of a lion, and the body of a horse. It is often represented as white with a red head and a horn of white, red, and black. Certainly, this animal would have had an interesting appearance!

---

mono- (one, single)

The Greek prefix for one, *mono-*, is usually joined to Greek combining roots. For example, *monogamy* is marriage to one person. A *monologue* is a speech given by one person. *Mono-* is also used to form many technical words in scientific fields.

bi- (two)

The Latin prefix for two, *bi-*, forms words such as *bifocals*, glasses that contain two visual corrections. When the *bicycle* was invented in the 1860s, it was named for its two wheels.

di-, du- (two)

This Greek prefix for two is often used in scientific and technical words. so you will find it useful in your college courses. For example, the word *dichromatic* refers to animals that change their colors in different seasons and, therefore, have two colors.

tri- (three)

A *triangle* is a three-sided figure. A *tricornered* hat has the brim turned up on three sides. A *tricycle* has three wheels.

dec- (ten)

Dec- is used in many words. The *decimal* system uses the base ten. The common word *dime*, a tenth part of a dollar, is also taken from the prefix *dec-*.

Words to Learn

Part 1

uni-

1. **unanimity** (noun)   yo͞o′nə-nĭm′ə-tē

   From Latin: *uni-* (one) + *animus* (soul) (When people agree, they seem to have one soul.)

   complete agreement

   > Few issues receive **unanimity** of opinion.

   > The nation demonstrated **unanimity** in facing the aggressor's threat.

   > The city council showed **unanimity** when each member voted to require recycling of paper, glass, and metal.

2. **unilateral** (adjective)   yo͞o′nə-lăt′ər-əl

   arbitrary; relating to only one side or part

   > Without consulting any one else, the owner made a **unilateral** decision to move the company from Chicago to Los Angeles.

   NOTE: Unilateral often refers to an arbitrary decision or action.

mono-

3. **monopoly** (noun)   mə-nŏp′ə-lē

   From Greek: *mono-* (single) + *pōlein* (to sell) (When only one company or person can sell something, a monopoly exists.)

   exclusive possession or control

   > Many states in the U.S.A. have a **monopoly** on the sale of liquor.

   > It is dangerous for one person to have a **monopoly** of power in a country.

► *Related Words*

monopolistic (adjective) England once maintained *monopolistic* control over the sale of salt in India.

monopolize (verb) The teenager *monopolized* the family telephone.

4. **monotonous** (adjective) mə-nŏt′n-əs

From Greek: *mono-* (single) + *tonos* (musical tone)

unvarying; repetitious; dull

Although repetition is **monotonous,** it is an effective method of learning.

► *Related Words*

monotone (noun) (mŏn′ə-tōn′) The teacher spoke in a *monotone.* (*Monotone* means an unvarying pitch of voice.)

monotony (noun) The *monotony* of the factory job bored Tranzel.

bi-

5. **bilingual** (adjective) bī-lĭng′gwəl

From Latin: *bi-* (two) + *lingua* (tongue, language)

having or speaking two languages

Since Chen was **bilingual,** he was a valuable employee of the import firm.

The **bilingual** prayer book was printed in Hebrew and English.

► *Related Word*

bilingualism (noun) Oswaldo's *bilingualism* was useful when he vacationed in Mexico.

Recent estimates indicate that a large number of people in the United States and Canada are bilingual. The 1980 U.S census found that 24 million out of 186 million people spoke a second language. Of these bilingual people, 11 million speak Spanish. According to 1987 estimates, 7 million of the 26 million Canadians speak French. In addition, languages from every corner of the world are spoken in both countries. These include Farsi, Vietnamese, Cantonese, Hindi, Urdu, Amharic, and Swahili.

---

6. **bipartisan** (adjective)   bī-pär′tə-zən

From Latin: *bi-* (two) + *pars* (part)

supported by members of two parties

> In a **bipartisan** motion, both Republicans and Democrats showed support for the education bill.

▶ *Related Word*
> **bipartisanship** (noun)   The president's *bipartisanship* gained him many supporters.

di-, du-

7. **dilemma** (noun)   dĭ-lĕm′ə

From Greek: *di-* (two) + *lēmma* (proposition) (A choice between two propositions or alternatives puts us in a dilemma.)

problem; difficult choice between equally bad things

> Dorothy was faced with the **dilemma** of having either to drop the course or to flunk it.

8. **duplicity** (noun)   dōō-plĭs′ə-tē

From Latin: *du-* (two) + *plicāre* (to fold or complicate) (A person who is involved in duplicity is not straightforward, but is "folded in two ways.")

deceitfulness; double-dealing

> The spy's **duplicity** was revealed to a shocked nation.
> I was hurt by the **duplicity** of the boyfriend who cheated on me.

▶ *Related Word*
> **duplicitous** (adjective)   Her friend's *duplicitous* behavior upset Tracy.

tri-

9. **trilogy** (noun)   trĭl′ə-jē

From Greek: *tri-* (three) + *log* (word; to speak)

a group of three books, plays or stories

> *The Lord of the Rings* by J.R.R. Tolkien is a **trilogy** about a ring that gives boundless powers.

10. **trivial** (adjective)   trĭv'ē-əl

From Latin: *tri-* (three) + *via* (road) (In Latin, *trivium* meant "where three roads meet," the public square where people would gossip.)

unimportant; silly

> The fact that the teenager wasn't invited to the party upset him, but seem **trivial** to his parents.

ordinary; commonplace

> It was a **trivial** task for the experienced electrician to install a new plug.

▶ *Related Words*
> **trivia** (noun)   Stan was an expert on rock music *trivia*.
> **triviality** (noun)   This *triviality* is not worth our attention.

dec-

11. **decade** (noun)   dĕk'ād'

From Greek: *dec-* (ten) *(Dekas* meant "group of ten.")

a ten-year period

> The **decade** of the 1920s is often called the "Roaring Twenties."
> Due to the demands of supporting a family, it took Mr. Markman almost a **decade** to complete his college degree.

12. **decimate** (verb)   dĕs'ĭ-māt'

From Latin: *dec-* (ten) *(Decimāre* meant "to take the tenth." This was the severe practice of killing every tenth soldier, chosen by lot, in order to punish a mutiny.)

to destroy or kill a large part of

> Starvation **decimated** the ship's crew.
> The crop was **decimated** by insects.

▶ *Related Word*
> **decimation** (noun)   After its *decimation* by bombing during World War II, the Dutch city of Rotterdam was completely rebuilt.

Exercises

Part 1

■ Definitions

Match each word in the left-hand column with a definition from the right-hand column. Use each choice only once.

1. unilateral _____

2. monopoly _____

3. trilogy _____

4. unanimity _____

5. dilemma _____

6. decade _____

7. monotonous _____

8. bilingual _____

9. trivial _____

10. bipartisan _____

a. ten-year period

b. complete agreement

c. relating to one part or side

d. deceitfulness

e. unimportant

f. speaking two languages

g. supported by both sides

h. three books or plays

i. to destroy most of something

j. control by one person or company

k. dull

l. problem

■ Meanings

Match each word element to its meaning. Two of the choices in the right-hand column must be used twice.

1. mono- _____

2. bi- _____

3. tri- _____

4. uni- _____

5. di- _____

6. dec- _____

a. ten

b. three

c. one

d. two

■ *Words in Context*

Complete each sentence with the word that fits best. Use each choice only once.

a. unanimity e. bilingual i. trilogy
b. unilateral f. bipartisan j. trivial
c. monopoly g. dilemma k. decade
d. monotonous h. duplicity l. decimate

1. Mystery writer P. D. James' "_____ of Death" in-cludes *Death of an Expert Witness, Innocent Blood,* and *The Skull Beneath the Skin.*

2. The board members showed their _____ when all of them agreed to take a pay cut to save the company.

3. Krisha was faced with the _____ of living in ex-treme poverty or going to an unfamiliar country.

4. Without telling anyone, the general made a(n) _____ decision to attack.

5. Don't bother me with this _____ matter.

6. The _____ music repeated the same melody again and again.

7. The government had a(n) _____ on the sale of grain, and no one else was allowed to supply it.

8. The _____ between 1900 and 1910 was marked by many inventions.

9. Liberals and Conservatives alike supported the

_____ measure.

10. Because of his _____, people felt they could not trust him.

■ *Using Related Words*

Complete each sentence using a word from the group of related words above it. You may need to capitalize a word when you put it into a sen-tence. Use each choice only once.

1. duplicity, duplicitous

   There is no more shocking _____ than that of a
   general who betrays his own country. Entrusted with defending
   a fort during the American Revolution, Benedict Arnold prepared
   to betray it to the British. His plans were discovered, and he fled

   to England. To this day the name of the _____
   Arnold symbolizes a traitor.

2. monopolized, monopoly

   For many years, one company had _____ long-
   distance telephone services. During the 1970s and 1980s, an anti-
   trust suit determined that there was an illegal

   _____ on this service. Now, the public is free to
   choose a long distance carrier from many different companies.

3. decimated, decimation

   The Black (or Bubonic) Plague of the 1300s _____

   Europe's population. The _____ was so terrible
   that one of every three Europeans died.

4. trivial, triviality

   It seems that the thumb is too _____ a part of
   the human body to be important to human beings. Yet this unique

   finger is hardly a _____ . It enables us to grasp
   things together in our hands and inspect them in a way that is
   unique in the animal world.

5. bilingual, bilingualism

   Many people living in India are _____ . They
   speak both their native language and English. So while people
   may speak Urdu, Hindi, or another language as their native

   tongue, they often find that _____ is a necessity
   in order to communicate in different areas of the country.

■ *Reading the Headlines*

This exercise presents five headlines that might have been taken from newspapers. Read each headline and then answer the questions that follow. (Remember that small words, such as *a* and *the,* are often left out of newspaper headlines.)

WELL-KNOWN AUTHOR'S TRILOGY PROVES MONOTONOUS

    1. Did the author write three books? _____

    2. Are the books interesting to read? _____

IN UNILATERAL DECISION, DEPARTMENT HEAD CUTS BILINGUAL PROGRAMS

    3. Did the department head consult others? _____

    4. Will there be more education in two languages? _____

BIPARTISAN SUPPORT SHOWN FOR BREAKING UP A DECADE OF GOVERNMENT MONOPOLY ON SALES OF LIQUOR

    5. Did only one party support this? _____

    6. Did many agencies control the sale of liquor? _____

LOCAL GOVERNMENTS DISPLAY UNANIMITY ON METHODS OF DEALING WITH DILEMMA OF ILLEGAL DRUG SALES

    7. Do the governments agree? _____

    8. Is the problem easy to solve? _____

DUPLICITY OF GENERAL LEADS TO DECIMATION OF TROOPS

    9. Was the general an honorable man? _____

    10. Did troops die? _____

Word Elements

Part 2

Part 2 represents the last number prefix, *cent-*, and five roots and prefixes that refer to quantities.

cent- (one hundred)
The prefix *cent-* is used in many common words. A *century* is a period of one hundred years. A *cent* is a coin worth one-hundredth of a dollar.

ambi-, amphi- (both; around)
This prefix has two meanings. The meaning of "both" occurs in the word *ambidextrous*, meaning "able to use both hands." The meaning of "around" is found in *amphitheater*, a theater with seats on all sides of, or around, the stage. This prefix comes from ancient Greek and Latin: *amphi-* is the Greek form; *ambi-* is the Latin form.

The common word *ambitious* is derived from the Latin verb *ambīre* (to go around). In ancient Rome, an ambitious person was a candidate who "went around" asking people to vote for him. Now, of course, an ambitious person is one who desires achievement.

---

ann, enn (year)
An *annual* event occurs every year. At times, *ann* is spelled *enn*, as in the word *perennial*.

integer (whole; complete)
This root can refer to numbers, as in the English word *integer*, which means a whole number without a fraction value. Thus, 3 is an integer, but 3.5 is not. In Latin, *integer* also describes a "whole" person, who does not have serious character flaws. Such a person is said to have *integrity*.

magn-, mega- (large)
To *magnify* something is to make it bigger. Recent books have appeared about *megatrends*, meaning large trends in society. A *megalopolis* is a region including several large cities. *Magn-* is the Latin spelling; *mega-* is the Greek spelling.

meter, -meter (measure)
This element often appears as a root, but can also be used as a suffix. One word using *meter* as a root is *metronome*, an instrument for measuring musical time. *-Meter* is used as a suffix in the words *thermometer*, an instrument for measuring heat, and *speedometer*, an instrument for measuring speed.

Words to Learn

Part 2

cent-

13. **centennial** noun   sĕn-tĕn′ē-əl

    From Latin: *cent-* (one hundred) + *ann* (year)

    one-hundred-year anniversary; a period of one hundred years

    > Health care professionals celebrated the **centennial** of the hospital's founding.

    The *quincentennial*, or 500th anniversary, of the first voyage of Christopher Columbus to the Americas is celebrated in 1992. (Note that "quin" means 5 and "cent" means 100.) Financed by Spanish royalty, Columbus set off to find a path to India. Instead, he landed in the Americas, reaching San Salvador, Cuba, and Haiti in 1492.

    Although Columbus is often credited with "discovering America," it should be remembered that the Americas were first populated many thousands of years before by ancestors of the Native Americans (American Indians) — who crossed from Russia over the Bering Strait.

    ---

14. **centigrade** (adjective)   sĕn′tĭ-grād′

    From Latin: *centi-* (one hundred) + *gradus* (step)

    referring to a temperature scale based on one hundred degrees

    > A temperature of 35 degrees **centigrade** would indicate summer heat.

    NOTE: In the *centigrade* scale, 0° marks the freezing point of water and 100° marks its boiling point.

ambi-, amphi-

15. **ambiguous** (adjective)   ăm-bĭg′yōō-əs

    From Latin: *ambi-* (around) + *agere* (to lead) (When something is ambiguous, two meanings are equally possible, and one is led around rather than "straight toward" the meaning.)

    not clear; having two or more meanings

    > His **ambiguous** answer left us still confused.

▶ *Related Word*

ambiguity (noun)   (ăm ′bĭ-gyŏŏ ′ə-tē)   The *ambiguity* of the test question made it difficult to answer.

The great linguist Noam Chomsky has pointed out the ambiguity of the sentence:
> They are flying planes.

This can mean either "The planes are meant for flying" or "Those people are flying the planes."

---

16. **ambivalence** (noun)   ăm-bĭv ′ə-ləns

From Latin: *ambi-* (both) + *valēre* (to be strong) (A person who is ambivalent about something has two equally strong feelings about it.)

existence of mixed or conflicting feelings

> The child felt **ambivalence** about the roller-coaster ride, which inspired both excitement and fear.

▶ *Related Word*

ambivalent (adjective)   Ajay was *ambivalent* about the difficult, but valuable, course.

ann, enn

17. **annals** (noun)   ăn ′əlz

From Latin: *ann* (year) *Annālis* meant "yearly." (Written *annals* are often divided by the year.)

a written record of events

> The **annals** of the Constitutional Convention form the basis of many U.S. Supreme Court decisions.

general records

> The **annals** of history record that Napoleon was a great general.

18. **perennial** (adjective)   pə-rĕn ′ē-əl

From Latin: *per-* (through) + *ann* (year)

occurring again and again; constant; lasting for a long time

> Traffic control is a **perennial** problem in modern cities.

NOTE: Something *perennial* has a long life. *Perennial* flowers bloom year after year without replanting.

integer

19. **disintegrate** (verb)   dĭs-ĭn′tə-grāt′

From Latin: *dis-* (apart) + *integer* (whole) (When something disintegrates, it becomes "not whole," or falls apart.)

to separate into small parts

> The aspirin **disintegrated** when we put it in a glass of water.

to get worse

> The calm meeting **disintegrated** into a series of arguments.

▶ *Common Phrase*
   disintegrate into

▶ *Related Word*
   disintegration (noun)   We watched the *disintegration* of the aspirin.

20. **integrity** (noun)   ĭn-tĕg′rə-tē

From Latin: *integer* (whole)

honesty; good moral character

> A person of **integrity** would never cheat on an examination.

wholeness; completeness

> Despite years of exposure to severe sandstorms, the building maintained its **integrity.**

magn-, mega-

21. **magnanimous** (adjective)   măg-năn′ə-məs

From Latin: *magn-* (great) + *animus* (soul)

noble; above revenge or resentment; forgiving of insults

> Raoul was **magnanimous** and forgave the people who had called him a liar.
> Sharon was **magnanimous** toward her defeated tennis rival.

▶ *Related Word*
   magnanimity (noun)   măg′-nə-nĭm′ĭ-tē)   The victor's *magnanimity* impressed us.

22. **magnitude** (noun)   măg′nĭ-tōōd′

From Latin: *magn-* (great) (*Magnitūdō* meant "greatness.")

greatness of size or importance

> It is difficult for a human being to imagine the **magnitude** of the universe.

> In 1871, a fire of great **magnitude** destroyed most of Chicago.

NOTE: Magnitude can also refer to the brightness of stars.

meter

23. **metric** (adjective, noun)   mĕt′rĭk

From Greek: *meter* (measure)

referring to a measurement system based on kilograms and meters (adjective)

> Scientists use the **metric** system for almost all measurements.

a standard of measurement (noun)

> People once used the length of a hand as the **metric** for cloth.

For years the United States has been considering changing to the metric system, which uses kilograms and meters. This system is more logical than the current system of pounds and feet. The metric system uses multiples of ten rather than numbers like 1,760 (yards to a mile). Canada is currently using metric measurements.

---

24. **symmetrical** (adjective)   sĭ-mĕt′rĭ-kəl

From Greek: *sym* (same) + *meter* (measure) (Things that "measure the same" are balanced, or symmetrical.)

balanced in physical size or form

> The six sides of a snowflake are perfectly **symmetrical.**

▶ *Related Word*
   symmetry (noun)   (sĭm′ə-trē)   The interior designer liked to use *symmetry* in her room arrangements.

Exercises

Part 2

■ Definitions

Match each word in the left-hand column with a definition from the right-hand column. Use each choice only once.

1. magnanimous _____
2. magnitude _____
3. perennial _____
4. metric _____
5. annals _____
6. centennial _____
7. ambiguous _____
8. centigrade _____
9. disintegrate _____
10. integrity _____

a. not clear
b. referring to a temperature scale
c. a system of measurement
d. balanced
e. honesty
f. lasting a long time
g. to fall apart
h. noble
i. hundred-year anniversary
j. existence of mixed feelings
k. written records
l. greatness of size or importance

■ Meanings

Match each word element to its meaning. Use each choice only once.

1. cent- _____
2. meter _____
3. ann _____
4. ambi-, amphi _____
5. magn-, mega- _____
6. integer _____

a. measure
b. hundred
c. both; around
d. large
e. year
f. whole

■ *Words in Context*

Complete each sentence with the word that fits best. Use each choice only once.

a. centennial   e. annals   i. magnanimous
b. centigrade   f. perennial   j. magnitude
c. ambiguous   g. disintegrate k. metric
d. ambivalence   h. integrity   l. symmetrical

1. People must constantly care for their gardens, since weeds are

   a(n) _____ problem

2. It is easy to trust a person of much _____ .

3. The tall skyscraper was a building of great _____ .

4. Patrick's _____ about going to college made him delay putting in an application.

5. Many European countries use the _____ system of measuring distance and weight.

6. Since Arizona was admitted to the United States in 1912, it will cel-

   ebrate its _____ in 2012.

7. Both sides of the _____ design were exactly matched.

8. The _____ of the scientific society meetings were kept in the library.

9. When it is zero degrees _____ , it is cold outside.

10. Paper will _____ into a powder if it becomes too dry.

■ *Using Related Words*

Complete each sentence using a word from the group of related words above it. You may need to capitalize a word when you put it into a sentence. Use each choice only once.

1. magnanimity, magnanimous

   Margaret Thatcher served as the Prime Minister of Britain from 1979 to 1990. The daughter of a shopkeeper, she became the first woman Prime Minister of her country, and led it toward free enterprise and a strong alliance with the United States. When forced

   to step down, she displayed _____ , praising her

   party and her associates. Her _____ behavior helped to maintain party unity.

2. ambiguity, ambiguous

   Nothing is more annoying than _____ directions.

   When giving directions make sure there is no _____ in them.

3. symmetry, symmetrically

   The ancient Greeks were among the great architects of the world. In Athens, the Acropolis temple, which was dedicated to the goddess Athena, stands as a great architectural achievement. The Greeks perfected a series of decorated columns, which were ar-

   ranged _____ . _____ was often used in Greek architecture.

4. ambivalence, ambivalent

   Many professionals feel that neglected children develop

   _____ toward their parents. While children resent not being cared for, they often still maintain some love for

   their mother and father, which leads to _____ feelings.

5. disintegrate, disintegration

   Nothing leads to the _____ of a neighborhood as fast as abandoned houses. Left empty, the wood, bricks, and other

   materials in these homes often start to _____ ,

and the houses can become extremely unsafe. Today, there are many government programs that encourage people to improve neighborhoods by buying and fixing up abandoned homes.

■ *Reading the Headlines*

This exercise presents five headlines that might have been taken from newspapers. Read each headline and then answer the questions that follow. (Remember that small words, such as *a* and *the,* are often left out of newspaper headlines.

STATE ANNALS REVEAL NO CELEBRATION OF ILLINOIS CENTENNIAL

1. Were records kept? _____

2. Did the period of time concern ten years? _____

MAGNANIMOUS LEADER FORGIVES INSULT OF CONSIDERABLE MAGNITUDE

3. Is the leader noble? _____

4. Was the insult small? _____

ARCHITECTURAL PANEL GIVES AMBIGUOUS RULING ON BUILDING'S PLANNED LACK OF SYMMETRY

5. Is the ruling clear? _____

6. Does the ruling concern the balance of the building? _____

CONVERSION TO CENTIGRADE SCALE A PERENNIAL ISSUE IN THE U.S.A.

7. Does the scale involve temperature? _____

8. Is the problem a constant one? _____

ALLIANCE DISINTEGRATES AFTER INTEGRITY OF LEADER IS QUESTIONED

9. Is the alliance continuing? _____

10. Is the honesty of the leader being questioned? _____

Chapter Exercises

■ *Practicing Strategies: New Words from Word Elements*

See how your knowledge of word elements can help you to understand new words. Complete each sentence with the word that seems to fit best. Use each choice only once.

a. amphibious   e. dioxide   i. monorail
b. biannual   f. integrate   j. photometer
c. centimeter   g. magnify   k. trimester
d. decameter   h. monodrama   l. uniform

1. A(n) _____ is a play written for one performer.

2. A(n) _____ event takes place twice a year.

3. A(n) _____ , which measures light, is often used in photography.

4. A(n) _____ aircraft can land on both land and water.

5. A(n) _____ system divides the academic year into three terms.

6. A(n) _____ contains two oxygen molecules.

7. If you _____ something, you make it bigger.

8. Some trains move on a(n) _____ , or single rail.

9. If you _____ one thing with another, you form the two into a whole.

10. Things that are _____ all have the same, or one, appearance.

■ *Practicing Strategies: Combining Context Clues and Word Elements*

Combining the strategies of context clues and word elements is a good way to figure out unknown words. In the following sentences, each italicized word contains a word element that you have studied in this chapter. Using the meaning of the word element and the context of the sentence, make an intelligent guess at the meaning of the italicized word. Your instructor may ask you to check the meaning of each word in your dictionary when you have finished.

1. Some people feel they can prevent illness by taking *megadoses* of Vitamin C.

   Megadoses means _____ .

2. The driver was able to tell how long the journey was by using an *odometer*.

   Odometer means _____ .

3. After we counted the sides of the figure, we determined that it was a *decagon*.

   Decagon means _____ .

4. The Jewish religion was the first to practice *monotheism* and to reject the worship of many gods.

   Monotheism means _____ .

5. The *tripartite* system of U.S. government consists of executive, legislative, and judicial branches.

   Tripartite means _____ .

■ *Practicing Strategies: Using the Dictionary*

Read the following definition then answer the questions below it.

charm (chärm) *n.* **1.** The power or quality of pleasing, attracting, or fascinating. **2.** A particular quality or feature that fascinates or attracts: *"The charm of friendship is liberty"* (Gibbon). **3.** A trinket or small ornament worn on a bracelet or other jewelry. **4.** Something worn for its supposed magical effect, as in warding off evil; amulet. **5.** An action or formula thought to have magical power. **6.** The chanting of a magic word or verse; incantation. **7.** *Physics.* A quantum property of one of the quarks whose conservation explains the absence of certain strange-particle decay modes and that accounts for the longevity of the J particle. —*v.* **charmed, charm·ing, charms.** —*tr.* **1.** To attract or delight greatly or irresistibly; fascinate. **2.** To act upon with or as if with magic; bewitch. —*intr.* **1.** To be alluring or pleasing. **2.** To act as an amulet or charm. **3.** To employ spells. [ME *charme*, magic spell < OFr.< Lat. *carmen*, incantation.] —**charm'ing·ly** *adv.*

1. In which language did *charm* originate? _____

2. What is the adverb form of *charm?* _____

3. Give the number and the part of speech of the definition for which

   an example by the author Gibbon is quoted. _____.

4. Give the number and the part of speech of the definition that best
   fits this sentence: "She believed that wearing a *charm* would scare

   away witches." _____

5. Give the number and the part of speech of the definition that best
   fits this sentence: "The girl's friendliness *charmed* everyone at the

   party." _____

■ Companion Words

Complete each sentence with the word that fits best. Choose your answers from the words below. You may use each word more than once.

Choices: of, into, toward

1. Debra was upset by the duplicity _____ her friend.

2. The winner of the election was magnanimous _____ his defeated rival.

3. We are shocked by the magnitude _____ the federal deficit.

4. The ambiguity _____ her response left us confused.

5. Too much drinking caused the party to disintegrate _____ a fight.

■ Writing with Your Words

This exercise will give you practice in writing effective sentences using the vocabulary words. Each sentence is started for you. Complete it with an interesting phrase that indicates the meaning of the italicized word.

1. There is *unanimous* agreement that _____

   _____ .

2. When another person started to *monopolize* my date's attention, I

   _____ .

3. She faced the *dilemma* of _____

   _____ .

4. My father made a *unilateral* decision to _____

   _____ .

5. He showed his *duplicity* by _____

   _____ .

6. During the next *decade,* I hope that _____

   _____ .

7. After watching a *monotonous* movie for an hour, I _____

   _____ .

8. One example of a *trivial* problem is _____

   _____ .

9. One *perennial* concern of society is _____

   _____ .

10. In the past *decade,* _____

   _____ .

Passage

Julius Caesar—Hero or Villain?

Although the famous Roman Julius Caesar lived two thousand years ago, his legend lives on in the **annals** of history. Some historians see him as a power-hungry villain. Others feel he was a reformer whose brutal assassination almost destroyed Rome. **(1)** However, there is **unanimity** of opinion on one issue: Caesar was the towering figure of his age.

Born about 100 B.C., Caesar came from a noble but poor family. At the time, the rulers of Rome were divided into two parties. The aristocratic party wanted to keep power in its own hands. The radical party wanted the support of the people, many of whom had lost their lands and were living in poverty in Rome. Caesar joined the radical cause.

A successful Roman leader had to conquer new lands and help expand the republic. **(2)** Caesar made conquests of great **magnitude. (3)** He **decimated** resisting forces in Gaul (now Belgium and France) and added this territory to the Roman empire. He invaded England, where he met strange tribes who painted their bodies and worshiped trees.

Caesar was anxious to tell the Romans of his conquests. **(4)** Although the seven books he wrote about the wars in Gaul tell an interesting story, his self-praise can become **monotonous.** On the other hand, he could be brief at times, as in his most famous statement, "Veni, vidi, vici" (I came, I saw, I conquered.)

(5) A **decade** of conquest gained Caesar considerable political power. He had formed a ruling "triumvirate" in 60 B.C. with Crassus and Pompey. Later, after Crassus's death, Caesar and Pompey started to fight for the leadership of Rome. **(6)** At first Caesar felt **ambivalent** about attacking his former friend. Then he decided that he must do it. In the first act of the conflict, Caesar crossed the Rubicon River in 49 B.C. to challenge Pompey. (To this day the phrase "crossing the Rubicon" means to take an irreversible step.) Caesar's victory over Pompey is recorded in a **trilogy,** *Commentary on the Civil War.* His triumph gave him a **monopoly** on Roman leadership, and he took the title of dictator.

Despite his busy career, Caesar took time for several romantic interests, among them the Egyptian Queen Cleopatra. Caesar aroused considerable disapproval when he invited her to Rome.

In his short time as dictator, Caesar accomplished many reforms. He extended Roman citizenship to the whole of Italy. **(7)** He improved the **disintegrating** condition of farmers by giving land to soldiers who had served under him. His **integrity** in keeping promises to his soldiers gained him the loyalty of poorer citizens. However, Caesar's reform of the calendar had the most long-lasting effects. He placed an inaccurate calendar with the improved Julian version. **(8)** In a somewhat more **trivial** action, he named the month of his birth, July, after himself.

Caesar was a unique and towering figure.

Unfortunately, Caesar's successes made him many enemies. **(9)** He was a victim of the **perennial** problem of successful people: the jealousy of others. **(10)** Caesar had shown **magnanimity** in not executing old enemies, but they now started to plot against him. Jealousy increased as some thought he might crown himself as emperor. One nobleman, Cassuis, was particularly angry over his own loss of power and prestige. Cassius plotted to assassinate Caesar, and week by week his list of treacherous conspirators grew. The day of Caesar's murder was planned for March 15, 44 B.C., called the Ides of March.

Legend records that Caesar was warned to "beware the Ides of March," but decided to face his fate. The assassins gathered on the floor of the Senate building. When Caesar entered, they attacked him with daggers. Caesar resisted until he saw that his close friend, Brutus, had also turned against him. "Et tu, Brute" (You too, Brutus) was his expression of anguish as he submitted to his murderers.

■ *Exercise*

Each numbered sentence below corresponds to a sentence in the Passage. Fill in the letter of the choice that makes this sentence mean the same thing as the corresponding sentence in the Passage.

1. However, there is _____ of opinion on one issue.
   a. division b. evidence c. agreement d. history

2. Caesar made conquests of great _____ .
   a. helpfulness b. difficulty c. importance d. violence

3. He _____ resisting forces in Gaul.
   a. helped b. greeted c. fought d. destroyed

4. His self-praise can become _____ .
   a. truthful b. exciting c. lengthy d. boring

5. A _____ of conquest gained Caesar considerable political power.
   a. ten-year period b. three-year period c. twenty-year period
   d. two-year period

6. At first Caesar felt _____ about attacking his former friend.
   a. guilty b. hopeful c. enthusiastic d. conflicted

7. He improved the _____ conditions of farmers by giving land to soldiers who had served under him.
   a. poverty-stricken b. unjust c. worsening d. terrible

8. In a somewhat _____ action, he named the month of his birth, July, after himself.
   a. heroic b. dishonest c. personal d. unimportant

9. He was a victim of the _____ problem of successful people: the jealousy of others.
   a. small b. constant c. serious d. noticeable

10. Caesar had shown _____ in not executing old enemies, but they now started to plot against him.
    a. stubbornness b. wisdom c. forgiveness d. weakness

■ Discussion Questions

1. Why was Caesar considered a great soldier?

2. Why do you think Caesar was (or was not) a great leader?

3. Would you have voted to make Caesar an emperor? Why or why not?

10

Word Elements: Thought and Belief

It is our ability to think and our system of beliefs that make us human beings. The importance of thought is apparent when we reason through a difficult problem in school or at work. The things we believe to be morally right affect our behavior. Part 1 of this chapter presents word elements about thought and belief. Part 2 presents prefixes we use when we do *not* believe something, prefixes of negation. Finally, several idioms will be discussed in this chapter. An idiom carries a different meaning from what we believe it to carry when we first hear it.

Chapter Strategy: Word Elements: Thought and Belief

Chapter Words:

Part 1

cred	credibility	*ver*	veracity
	creed		verify
	incredulity		veritable
fid	defiant	*-phobia*	acrophobia
	fidelity		claustrophobia
	fiduciary		xenophobia

Part 2

de-	delude	*Idioms*	behind the eight ball
	destitute		between the devil and the
	deviate		deep blue sea
non-	nonchalant		bolt from the blue
	nonconformity		get to first base
	nonsectarian		give carte blanche
			leave no stone unturned

Did You Know?

Where Do Our Idioms Come From?

English has thousands of expressions called *idioms*. These have meanings different from the literal meanings of the words. Because idioms usually come from life experiences, it is interesting to look at their origins. For example, the following idioms come from sports. Their colorful histories have given them special meanings.

Go to bat comes from baseball. Occasionally, a coach feels that the player who is scheduled to bat in the official line-up needs a substitute. This substitute replaces, or "goes to bat for," the scheduled player. From this, "go to bat for" has come to mean to support strongly.

Take a rain check is another baseball expression. A rain check is a ticket guaranteeing that if a game is cancelled because of rain, there will be free admission to a rescheduled game. More generally, "to take a rain check" is a polite way to decline an invitation. One says no for now, but hints that the invitation will be accepted in the future.

To throw in the towel is a phrase from boxing. When a boxer is being badly beaten or bruised, his trainer may signal that he is ready to stop fighting. To do this, the trainer throws a towel into the ring. Hence, "to throw in the towel" means to give up or quit.

The ball's in your court, from tennis, indicates that it is the other person's turn to handle the ball, since it is on his or her side of a divided court. The expression has come to mean that a person has done everything possible with a situation, and now it is time for another person to act.

To punt is from football. A team has four chances to carry the ball ten yards. If it appears that the players will fail, they may decide to "punt," or pass the ball to the other team. By punting, the first team can place the ball in a favorable position. Thus, "to punt" has come to mean to pass responsibility to someone else.

As you can see, idioms add color to English. They are acceptable in everyday speech and in informal writing, but they should not be used in formal writing, such as essays and term papers. Experts on language agree that most of us use several styles of language in our speech and writing. For example, if you met a professor on the street, you might say something formal, like "Hello, Dr. Jones." In contrast, you would greet a friend with "How's it going?" or "Hi there!" One greeting is formal and the others are informal, but they are each suitable for the situation.

Many idioms use common words such as "put." Can you identify the meanings of these expressions?

1. Put your foot in your mouth

2. Put your foot down

3. Put two and two together

4. Put up with

(*Answers:*   1. Say something embarrassing or hurtful to others   2. Take a firm stand; refuse to tolerate   3. Draw a conclusion from evidence   4. Tolerate or bear)

Learning Strategy

Word Elements: Thought and Belief

The first part of this chapter concentrates on word elements relating to thought and belief. Three roots are presented: *Cred* (believe), *fid* (faith), and *ver* (truth). Part 1 also introduces the suffix *-phobia* (fear of). Part 2 of this chapter presents two important prefixes with negative meanings. We use them when we do *not* believe in something. *Non* means "not." *De-* also has a negative sense, as it indicates "removal from" or "down."

Element	Meaning	Origin	Function	Chapter words
		Part 1		
cred	believe	Latin	root	credibility, creed, incredulity
fid	faith	Latin	root	defiant, fidelity, fiduciary
ver	truth	Latin	root	veracity, verify, veritable
-phobia	fear of	Greek	suffix	acrophobia, claustrophobia, xenophobia
		Part 2		
de-	removal from; down	Latin	prefix	delude, destitute, deviate
non-	not	Latin	prefix	nonchalant, nonconformity, nonsectarian

Word Elements

Part 1 .

Information on the roots and the suffix for Part 1 is presented below.

cred (believe)
   The root *cred* is used in many English words. When we do not believe something, we may call it *incredible*. *Credit* is granted to customers because merchants believe they will be repaid.

fid (faith)

The English word *faith* is taken from this root. Because a dog is thought to be a faithful companion to a human being, it is traditionally given the name of *Fido*, meaning "faithful."

ver (truth)

The root *ver* means "truth." A *verdict*, the judgment of a jury, is made up from the root *ver* (truth) and the root *dict* (say). Even that much-used word *very*, meaning "truly" or "really," comes from *ver*.

-phobia (fear of)

As a suffix, *-phobia* describes a strong or illogical fear of something, often forming words that are used in psychology. For example, *nyctophobia* is a fear of the dark. The base word *phobia* also means "fear."

According to Greek mythology, Phobos was the son of Ares, the god of war who was similar to the Roman god Mars. Greek warriors sometimes painted the likeness of Phobos on their shields. Because he was so terrifying, it was thought that the enemy would run merely at the sight of his picture.

Words to Learn

Part 1

cred

1. **credibility** (noun)   krĕd′ə-bĭl′ə-tē

   From Latin: *cred* (believe)

   believability; ability to be trusted

   > He had ruined his **credibility** by lying too often.

   ▶ *Related Word*
   credible (adjective)   (ktĕd′ə-bəl)   Susan's account of the accident was *credible*, and the police accepted it.

2. **creed** (noun)   krēd

   From Latin: *cred* (believe) (*Crēdo* meant "I believe.")

   set of beliefs or principles

   > The five duties of reciting the words of witness, prayer, charity, fasting, and pilgrimage are central to the **creed** of the Muslim religion.

   NOTE: Creed often refers to a formal system of religious or moral beliefs.

3. **incredulity** (noun)   ĭn'krə-doo'lə-tē

From Latin: *in-* (not) + *cred* (believe)

disbelief; amazement

> In 1913, reports of the first airplane flight were treated with **incredulity.**

▶ *Related Word*
incredulous (adjective) (ĭn-krĕj'ə-ləs) People were *in-credulous* when told that the boy had survived for three years alone in the forest.

fid

4. **defiant** (adjective)   dĭ-fī'ənt

From Latin: *dis-* (not) + *fid* (faith)

refusing to follow orders or rules; resisting boldly

> The **defiant** teenage boy disobeyed school rules by refusing to cut off his ponytail.

> Many **defiant** people openly ignored the government curfew.

NOTE: Since this word begins with *de*, we might expect it to have the sense of "down." However, the Latin word had a *dis-* prefix, which became *de-* as the word *defiant* went through the French language.

▶ *Related Words*
defiance (noun)   The sergeant's *defiance* shocked his superiors.
defy (verb) (dĭ-fī') People who *defy* the law often get arrested.

5. **fidelity** (noun)   fĭ-dĕl'ə-tē

From Latin: *fid* (faith)

faithfulness to obligation or duty

> Dogs are known for **fidelity** to their masters.

exactness, accuracy

> Compact disc players reproduce music with excellent **fidelity.**

6. **fiduciary** (adjective, noun)   fĭ-doo'shē-ĕr'ē

From Latin: *fid* (faith) (One has faith in the person who handles one's money.)

pertaining to money or property held for one person by another (adjective)

> The lawyer acted as a **fiduciary** agent who held money while the two people settled their dispute.

a person holding money for another (noun)

> Under the guidance of the **fiduciary,** the inheritance grew.

ver

7. **veracity** (noun)   və-răs′ə-tē

From Latin: *ver* (truth)

truth; accuracy

> Many eyewitnesses confirmed the **veracity** of the man's statement.

8. **verify** (verb)   věr′ə-fī

From Latin: *ver* (truth) + *facere* (to make)

to determine the truth or accuracy of

> The antique dealer **verified** that the Queen Anne chair was genuine.
>
> People often use the dictionary to **verify** a word's meaning.

▶ *Related Word*
   verification (noun) Scientists obtain *verification* of their results by repeating experiments.

9. **veritable** (adjective)   věr′ə-tə-bəl

From Latin: *ver* (truth)

unquestionable, being truly so

> The busy executive was a **veritable** whirlwind of activity.
>
> Twenty-four inches of rain caused a **veritable** disaster in the town.

NOTE: The words *veritable* and *true* are often synonymous. (The plan was a *veritable* masterpiece. The plan was a *true* masterpiece.) Veritable is usually used with the phrase "a veritable _____" or "the veritable _____ ."

-phobia

10. **acrophobia** (noun)   ăk′rə-fō′bē-ə

From Greek: *acros* (highest) + *-phobia* (fear)

fear of heights

> Because of her **acrophobia** Mrs. Robinson refused to live on a high floor in the building.

▶ *Related Word*
acrophobic (adjective)   Marek's *acrophobic* feelings prevented him from riding on ferris wheels.

11. **claustrophobia** (noun)   klôs′trə-fō′bē-ə

From Latin: *claustrum* (enclosed space) + Greek: *-phobia* (fear)

fear of closed or small spaces

> Mr. Steven's **claustrophobia** made him nervous in the crowded elevator.

▶ *Related Word*
claustrophobic (adjective)   Denicia felt *claustrophobic* in the small space.

12. **xenophobia** (noun)   zĕn′ə-fōb′ē-ə

From Greek: *xenos* (stranger) + *-phobia* (fear)

fear or hatred of foreigners of strangers

> Because of his **xenophobia,** the senator wanted to pass laws that would prohibit immigration into the country.

▶ *Related Word*
xenophobic (adjective)   The *xenophobic* man refused to travel to foreign countries.

What do the following phobias refer to?

1. aviophobia

2. zoophobia

3. hemophobia

4. ailurophobia

(*Answers:*   1. fear of airplanes   2. fear of animals   3. fear of blood
4. fear of cats)

Exercises

Part 1

■ Definitions

Match each word in the left-hand column with a definition from the right-hand column. Use each choice only once.

1. xenophobia _____	a. fear of heights
2. defiant _____	b. a person holding money for another
3. acrophobia _____	c. truth
4. fidelity _____	d. being truly so
5. veritable _____	e. disbelief
6. veracity _____	f. fear of strangers
7. creed _____	g. to determine truth or accuracy
8. fiduciary _____	h. fear of small spaces
9. claustrophobia _____	i. set of beliefs
10. credibility _____	j. rebellious
	k. faithfulness
	l. ability to be believed

■ Meanings

Match each word element to its meaning. Use each choice only once.

1. fid _____	a. faith
2. ver _____	b. fear
3. cred _____	c. truth
4. -phobia _____	d. believe

■ Words in Context

Complete each sentence with the word that fits best. Use each choice only once.

a. credible   e. fidelity   i. veritable
b. creed   f. fiduciary   j. acrophobia
c. incredulity   g. veracity   k. claustrophobia
d. defiant   h. verify   l. xenophobia

1. The cheap film did not reproduce colors with _____ , so on the photograph, the bride's dress looked green.

2. The paintings in our attic proved to be a _____ treasure of old family portraits.

3. His _____ made him nervous when he was accidently locked in the closet.

4. The lawyers expected the jury to believe the story of the

   _____ witness.

5. Charity and forgiveness are central to the _____ of Christianity.

6. The credit agent wanted to call my employer in order to

   _____ that I really had a job.

7. The child's uncle acted in a(n) _____ capacity by investing her money.

8. We doubt your _____ and feel it is unlikely that your claims are true.

9. Because of his _____ , the small child became upset when taken to the mountain top.

10. At first, Yuzuko expressed _____ when she was told she had won the lottery.

■ *Using Related Words*

Complete each sentence using a word from the group of related words above it. You may need to capitalize a word when you put it into a sentence. Use each choice only once.

1. defied, defiance

   In eighteenth-century England, many robbers _____ the law by attacking and robbing stagecoaches. These people, known as "highwaymen," were both feared and admired for their

bold _____ . Alfred, Lord Tennyson wrote an romantic poem called "The Highwayman" dedicated to these glamorous, but dangerous, outlaws.

2. xenophobia, xenophobic

Although the United States has always been seen as a land of immigrants, some _____ has entered into its immigration policies. _____ feelings inspired a series of laws that increased the difficulty of immigration in the early 1900s.

3. credibility, credible

Are some old houses haunted? The editors of the *Old House Journal* have received 27 case histories of haunting, giving it new

_____ . Reported incidents included ghostly noises, rushes of cold air, and actual appearances of ghosts. The intelligence and thoughtfulness behind these reports makes them

quite _____ . By the way, most owners are delighted to be sharing their homes with ghosts.

4. incredulity, incredulous

People often react with _____ when told that they can be hypnotized. A person often remains

_____ until he or she has tried it. Hypnosis has many uses, including helping people to stop smoking, but it should be attempted only by an expert.

5. verification, verified

Several reports have _____ that falls from high altitudes need not be fatal. In 1990 a Soviet newspaper reported that a woman survived a three-mile fall after a mid-air plane collision. There has also been _____ of an incident in which a flight attendant fell six miles to the ground—and lived.

■ *True or False?*

Each of the following statements contains one or more words from this section. Read each sentence carefully and then indicate whether you think it is probably true or probably false.

____   1. People should verify a fiduciary agent's honesty.

____   2. Prayer is a part of the creed of most religions.

____   3. A man who could multiply seventy numbers in his head would be a veritable whiz at mental arithmetic.

____   4. It is easy to be the boss of a defiant person.

____   5. We would express incredulity if we heard that there was a traffic jam during rush hour in a big city.

____   6. Fidelity is a desirable quality in a friend.

____   7. Acrophobia is fear of small spaces.

____   8. A person with claustrophobia is afraid of spiders.

____   9. "It is now the year 3025," is a statement of veracity.

____   10. A person with xenophobia would lack credibility for dealing with foreigners in a fair way.

Prefixes

Part 2

Part 2 of this chapter presents two very common prefixes that have a negative meaning: *de-* means "removal from" or "down"; *non-* means "not." Both prefixes are used in thousands of English words.

This Words to Learn section also presents several idioms. These involve our thoughts and beliefs, for an idiom does not mean what we believe it to mean when we first hear it.

de- (removal from; down)

The prefix *de-* has various meanings. In some English words it has the sense of "removal from." For example, when we *decontaminate* something, we remove the contamination or impurities from it. When people *deforest* land, they remove forest growth from it. *De-* can also mean "down." When we *depress* a button, we push it down. When something *declines*, it "goes down."

non- (not)

The prefix *non-* simply means "not." *Nonsense* is something that does not make sense. A *nonjudgmental* person is one who does not make judgments. *Non-* often combines with base words (roots that can stand alone as English words).

Words to Learn

Part 2

de-

13. **delude** (verb)   dĭ-lōōd′

    From Latin: *de-* (bad) and *lūdere* (to play) (*Deludere* meant "to deceive, to mock.")

    to mislead; to cause someone to think something that is false

    > The false prophet **deluded** people into thinking the world would end by New Year's Day.

    ▶ *Related Word*
    delusion (noun)   (dĭ-lōō′zhən)   She suffered from the *delusion* that she was being followed.

14. **destitute** (adjective)   dĕs′tə-tōōt′

    From Latin: *de-* (down) + *stat* (placed)

    without money; poor

    > The **destitute** mother could not afford milk for her baby.

    NOTE: Destitute is a strong word meaning "entirely without resources, broke."

► *Related Word*
destitution (noun)   The man's *destitution* forced him to live on the street.

15. **deviate** (verb)   dē′vē-āt′

From Latin: *de-* (removal from) + *via* (road) (*Dēviāre* meant "to go away from the road.")

to vary from a path, course, or norm

Airplane pilots must not **deviate** from their planned flight route.

Topol **deviated** from tradition when he refused to let his family arrange a marriage for him.

► *Common Phrase*
to deviate from

► *Related Words*
deviate (adjective)   (dē′vē-ənt)   Many mentally ill people show *deviant* behavior. (*Deviant* means "odd in a negative way.")

deviation (noun)   *Deviation* from routine prevents boredom.

16. **nonchalant** (adjective)   nŏn′shə-länt′

From Latin: *non-* (not) + *calēre* (to be warm) (Many people feel physically warm when they get angry. Someone who is nonchalant, "not warm," does not feel angry or concerned.)

unconcerned; carefree

Although he was hurt by his friend's insulting comments, Steve assumed a **nonchalant** attitude.

The high school student took a **nonchalant** attitude toward school, barely opening a book.

NOTE: Nonchalant can be a somewhat negative word, indicating that someone should care, but does not.

► *Related Word*
nonchalance (noun)   The soldier displayed *nonchalance* in the face of danger.

17. **nonconformity** (noun)   nŏn′kən-fôr′mə-tē

From Latin: *non-* (not) + *con-* (together) + *forma* (shape)

being different; failure to conform

Nonconformity is shown in the many different styles of students' clothing.

Some countries persecute people who show **nonconformity** in religious practices.

▶ *Related Word*

nonconformist (noun)   The clergyman was a *nonconformist* who did not follow accepted religious practices.

18. **nonsectarian** (adjective)   nŏn'sĕk-târ'ē-ən

From Latin: *non-* (not) + *secta* (group)

not associated with religion

United States public schools are **nonsectarian** and do not teach religious practices.

Although Christmas is a religious celebration, Thanksgiving Day is a **nonsectarian** holiday.

Idioms

19. **behind the eight ball**

at a disadvantage; in a hopeless situation

Because she missed the first four sessions of the class, she felt she was **behind the eight ball.**

In the game of pool, the object is to hit all the balls (which are numbered 1, 2, 3, 4, etc.) into the pockets at the side of the table—except the 8 ball. If the ball you are shooting at is located behind the 8 ball, you have big troubles. In this situation, it is likely that the 8 ball will accidentally sink into the pocket, and you will get a penalty.

---

20. **between the devil and the deep blue sea**

having two bad or unattractive choices; in a dilemma

Tony felt he was **between the devil and the deep blue sea,** since he had either to miss his sister's wedding or be absent from his final exam.

This term comes from the language of sailors. The "devil" was a heavy plank on the side of a ship, which held up guns. It was difficult to get to, and, once a sailor got there, he might fall into the "deep blue sea." Thus, he had the choice of hanging uncomfortably onto the side or going into the water.

---

21. **bolt from the blue**

a sudden surprise

> The news that the stock market had crashed hit many investors like a **bolt from the blue.**

It would be very surprising to be hit by a bolt of lightning when it was not raining and the sky was blue. This is where the phrase "a bolt from the blue" originates.

---

22. **get to first base**

do the first thing successfully

> If you want to **get to first base** in a job interview, dress neatly.

In baseball, you must run to first base, second base, third base, and then to home plate in order to score. It you cannot even "get to first base," then you will never score, or get to home plate.

---

23. **give carte blanche**   kärt blänsh'

From French: a blank document

to give full, unrestricted power

> The diplomat was **given carte blanche** to reach an agreement with the foreign power.
>
> Sue Ellen's father **gave** her **carte blanche** to spend money.

A "carte blanche" was originally a piece of paper with nothing but a signature on it, used when an army surrendered. The defeated leader would sign his name and the victor could then write in the terms of surrender.

---

24. **leave no stone unturned**

to search thoroughly; to investigate thoroughly

Monica **left no stone unturned** in her search for the missing diamond.

In 477 B.C. a Greek military commander won a victory, but failed to locate a treasure that he was looking for in the defeated enemy's camp. He consulted the Delphic Oracle, a priestess who gave advice and prophecy about the future. The oracle advised him to "leave no stone unturned," and he finally found the treasure.

Exercises

Part 2

■ *Definitions*

Match each word or phrase in the left-hand column with a definition from the right-hand column. Use each choice only once.

1. nonsectarian _____
2. bolt from the blue _____
3. leave no stone unturned _____
4. between the devil and the deep blue sea _____
5. delude _____
6. destitute _____
7. nonchalant _____
8. give carte blanche _____
9. behind the eight ball _____
10. get to first base _____

a. at a disadvantage
b. to give full power
c. to do the first thing successfully
d. to make a thorough search
e. without money
f. nonreligious
g. unconcerned
h. having two bad choices
i. unexpected happening
j. being unlike others
k. to mislead
l. to vary from a path

■ *Meanings*

Match each prefix to its meaning. Use each choice only once.

1. non- _____   a. away from; down

2. de- _____   b. not

■ *Words in Context*

Complete each sentence with the word or phrase that fits best. Use each choice only once.

a. delude   e. nonconformity   i. bolt from the blue
b. destitute   f. nonsectarian   j. get to first base
c. deviate   g. behind the eight ball   k. give carte blanche
d. nonchalant   h. between the devil and   l. leave no stone
                      the deep blue sea   unturned

1. After she lost her job and savings, Dyan was left

   _____ .

2. If you _____ from the safety procedures for disposing of nuclear waste, you can cause a serious accident.

3. The sudden death of a close relative hit her like a

   _____

4. Wearing blue jeans to a formal dinner would show

   _____ .

5. The adopted woman will _____ to find her birth mother, for she wants to know.

6. The _____ charity helped people of all faiths.

7. The wealthy owner could _____ to the decorator to spend whatever money was needed to redo the penthouse.

8. We didn't expect the mother to be so _____ about her child's accident.

9. Because the football player had to miss so much important prac-

tice, he felt he was _____ .

10. Don't _____ yourself into thinking that success is just a matter of luck.

■ *Using Related Words*

Complete each sentence using a word from the group of related words above it. You may need to capitalize a word when you put it into a sentence. Use each choice only once.

1. delusions, deluded

In the 1600s, people in Holland started to buy tulip bulbs for investment, causing prices to rise in a fever of "tulipomania." Be-

cause of the bulb's popularity, people were _____ into thinking that prices would rise forever. Some suffered from

such _____ about the value of tulips that they invested everything they had in the flowers. After a few years, prices collapsed, and many people were ruined.

2. nonchalance, nonchalant

It is important to wear life preservers whenever boating. Un-

fortunately, many people show _____ toward their own safety by forgetting this simple precaution. Such a

_____ attitude may cause a tragic accident.

3. deviant, deviate

Cultures _____ from each other in their social conventions. In the Middle East, people stand close together when they talk. The lack of distance often makes North Americans and Europeans uncomfortable. In Japan, looking at a person directly can be offensive, so North Americans and Europeans must learn to avoid eye contact when visiting that country. Such social customs are not _____ , but simply reflect cultural differences.

4. nonconformists, nonconformity

Many colonies in the United States were founded by religious

_____ from England. In the new land, Pilgrims

and Puritans were free to display religious _____ without fear.

5. destitute, destitution

The Great Depression, which started in 1929, left many people

in the United States _____ . The Depression began with the fall of the stock market and bank failures. Then, terrible wind and dust storms in the southern Great Plains (or "Dust Bowl") caused crop failure, contributing to further

_____ .

■ *True or False?*

Each of the following statements contains one or more words or phrases from this section. Read each sentence carefully and then indicate whether you think it is probably true or probably false.

____   1. If you had to choose between going out on a date with your favorite movie star or your favorite athletic performer, you would be between the devil and the deep blue sea.

____   2. Getting to first base means that all of your efforts will be completed.

____   3. A nonchalant person would usually act as if she had been hit by a bolt from the blue.

____   4. If you were destitute, you would probably leave no stone unturned to stay that way.

____   5. A Protestant religious service is nonsectarian.

____   6. It is not honest to delude others.

_____   7. Deviation from a carefully planned diet may cause health problems.

_____   8. Nonconformity helps you to be like others.

_____   9. If you are winning a game, you are behind the eight ball.

_____   10. Most people would enjoy being given carte blanche.

Chapter Exercises

■ *Practicing Strategies: New Words from Word Elements*

See how your knowledge of prefixes, roots, and suffixes can help you to understand new words. Complete each sentence with the word that seems to fit best. Use each choice only once.

a. aquaphobia   e. depopulated   i. nonsexist
b. bona fide   f. detoxify   j. phobic
c. credentials   g. discredited   k. verily
d. demote   h. nonlinear   l. very

1. Something _____ is not in a straight line.

2. *Aqua* means "water," so fear of water is _____ .

3. A place becomes _____ when people are removed from it.

4. Policies that favor neither males nor females are

   _____ .

5. Since something poisonous is toxic, when we remove poison, we

   _____ .

6. A person presents _____ so that you will believe in his abilities.

7. *Bona* means "good," so something that is shown to be done or

   presented in good faith is _____ .

8. To *promote* means to move up; to _____ means to move down.

9. Somebody who is fearful is _____.

10. If you can no longer believe in somebody, that person has been

_____ .

■ Practicing Strategies: Combining Context Clues and Word Elements

Combining the strategies of context clues and word elements is a good way to figure out unknown words. In the following sentences, each italicized word contains a word element that you have studied in this chapter. Using the meaning of the word element and the context of the sentence, make an intelligent guess at the meaning of the italicized word. Your instructor may ask you to check the meaning in your dictionary when you have finished.

1. Doctors give *credence* to a new treatment for cancer only after it has been successfully used.

   Credence means _____ .

2. Because of *arachnophobia* the child panicked when he saw a spider.

   Arachnophobia means _____ .

3. Truckers carrying *nonflammable* chemicals need not fear fire.

   Nonflammable means _____ .

4. Because of the hot sun and lack of water, Moqui's body became *dehydrated*.

   Dehydrated means _____ .

5. The *deciduous* trees were bare of leaves in winter.

   Deciduous means _____ .

■ Companion Words

Complete each sentence with the word that fits best. Choose your answers from the words below. You may use each word more than once.

Choices: from, into, like, of, a

1. Don't delude yourself _____ believing silly superstitions.

2. People who deviate _____ the norm are often treated with suspicion.

3. My teacher is _____ veritable treasure of information on word origins.

4. We have faith in the veracity _____ your statement.

5. The news hit us _____ a bolt from the blue.

■ *Writing with Your Words*

This exercise will give you practice in writing effective sentences using the vocabulary words. Each sentence is started for you. Complete it with an interesting phrase that also indicates the meaning of the italicized word or words.

1. My day became a *veritable* disaster when _____

_____ .

2. Due to his *acrophobia*, he _____

_____ .

3. Because we doubt your *veracity*,_____

_____.

4. I was surprised that he remained *nonchalant* when _____

_____ .

5. People show *nonconformity* by _____

_____ .

6. I would like to have *carte blanche* to _____

_____ .

7. I felt *behind the eight ball* when _____

_____ .

8. I would be *incredulous* if I saw _____

_____ .

9. I can never *get to first base* when I try _____

_____ .

10. *Fidelity* is _____

_____ .

Passage

The Origins of Superstitions

Why is the number thirteen considered unlucky? Why do people who spill salt throw some over their shoulder? Are black cats evil? Can a mirror steal your soul? No scientist has **verified** these superstitions, yet many people once believed them without question. How did they originate?

The number thirteen has long been considered unlucky. According to legend, the number thirteen can bring the dead back to life. A magician makes a doll that represents a living person and pierces it with thirteen needles. The doll is then placed on a grave, and a dead soul supposedly rises and haunts the unfortunate person represented by it.

(1) Thirteen was believed to be a central number in the **creed** of witches. These supposedly evil souls were thought to **defy** God and to swear **fidelity** to the devil. Thirteen was the ideal number for a witches' coven, or meeting.

Many people considered Friday an unlucky day of the week, because it was the day on which Christ was crucified. When Friday coincides with the thirteenth of a month, we get an especially unlucky day. However, other Fridays have also been know to bring misfortune. **(2)** On Friday, May 10, 1886, a financial panic in London, known as Black Friday, left many people **destitute.**

Unlike the number thirteen and Friday, salt was considered lucky. Because salt was used to preserve food, people believed that it would drive away bad spirits. However, spilling salt was thought to invite evil spirits. **(3)** In fact, dropping a salt container could make a **nonchalant** diner suddenly become frantic. There was only one way to avoid disaster. The diner had to take some salt into his right hand (the side of his lucky spirit) and throw it over his left shoulder (the side of his unlucky spirit). **(4)** Any **deviation** from this procedure would invite the invasion of the unlucky spirit, who was always lurking on the left.

Cats have held a special place in our superstitions. The mysterious ability of cats to survive falls from high places led the Egyptians to believe that they had nine lives. In fact, the Egyptians worshiped cats.

Unfortunately, these animals have not always been so lucky. In Europe, during the Middle Ages, the fact that cats' eyes reflect light in the dark caused many to believe that they were evil spirits. Cats were often pictured as witches' companions, and some people thought that, after seven years' service, the cat might even become a witch. Since black was the color of the devil, black cats inspired intense fear. **(5)** God-fearing people walking at night might see a black cat cross their path **like a bolt from the blue**. **(6)** Certain that they had seen a devil, they would break into a **veritable** panic. A cat that crossed from left to right was particularly frightening.

People often made ridiculous claims about cats. For example, in 1718 a man named William Montgomery claimed that two elderly women had been found dead in their beds on the morning after he had killed two noisy cats. **(7)** Montgomery **deluded** himself into thinking that the cats had been these women in disguise.

Such attitudes could lead to vicious persecution. **(8)** At times, any woman who owned a cat and who showed signs of **nonconformity** might be prosecuted as a witch. When people became excited they **left no stone unturned** in their quest to destroy what they believed was witchcraft. Cats might be massacred, or even burned at the stake. Even more horribly, hundreds of innocent people were killed because they were believed to be witches.

A less harmful, although no less silly, superstition revolves around mirrors, which many people believed had magical powers. Perhaps you remember Snow White's stepmother asking her magical mirror: "Mirror, mirror on the wall. Who's the fairest one of all?" The ancients believed that breaking a mirror would bring seven years of bad luck, avoidable only if the pieces were quickly buried. The seven-year figure was given by the Romans, who thought that the human body renewed itself every seven years. Others believed that a mirror broke because bad spirits appeared in it. Throughout history, people have feared that a mirror would steal the weak soul of a sick person or a newborn. **(9)** Of course, this idea had no **veracity,** yet some people would not allow infants to see a mirror until they reached one year of age.

(10) Most of us react with **incredulity** to these seemingly silly superstitions. Yet even some modern people believe in their **credibility**. Many high-rises do not have a thirteenth floor; the floor numbers sim-

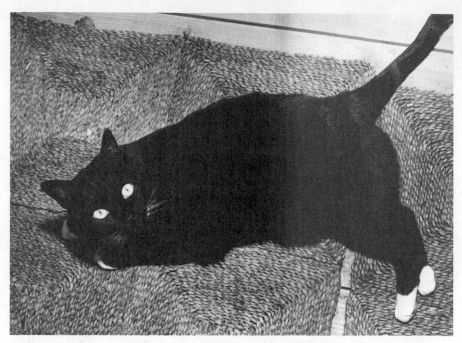

Cats have held a special place in our superstitions.

ply skip from twelve to fourteen. Perhaps you know somebody who shivers with fright when a black cat crosses a path at night and darts its fiery eyes. Whatever the origin of superstitions, it's clear that some haunt us, even today.

■ *Exercise*

Each numbered sentence below corresponds to a sentence in the Passage. Fill in the letter of the choice that makes this sentence mean the same thing as the corresponding sentence in the Passage.

1. Thirteen was believed to be a central number in the _____ of the witches.
   a. great charm   b. bad character   c. belief system   d. bad luck

2. A financial panic known as **Black Friday** left many people _____ .
   a. fearful   b. insane   c. poor   d. unhappy

3. In fact, dropping a salt container could make a _____ diner suddenly become frantic.
   a. calm   b. hungry   c. horrified   d. pleasant

4. Any _____ from this procedure would invite the invasion of the unlucky spirit.

   a. change b. benefit c. exist d. noise

5. God-fearing people walking at night might see a black cat cross their path _____ .

   a. darkly b. threateningly c. suddenly 4. unluckily

6. Certain that they had seen a devil, they would break into a _____ panic.

   a. dreadful b. sudden c. slight d. true

7. Montgomery _____ himself into thinking that the cats had been these women in disguise.

   a. helped b. fooled c. advised d. frightened

8. At times, any woman who owned a cat and who showed signs of

   _____ might be prosecuted as a witch.

   a. following the devil b. not doing as other do c. harming her neighbors d. not going to church

9. Of course, this idea had no _____ .

   a. support b. faith c. belief d. truth

10. Most of us react with _____ to these seemingly silly superstitions.

    a. sorrow b. disbelief c. scorn d. laughter

■ Discussion Questions

1. Why were infants not allowed to see mirrors?

2. Why did so many people think cats have supernatural powers?

3. Would you be comfortable living on a thirteenth floor? Why or why not?

CHAPTER

Word Elements: The Body and Health

In the past hundred years, medical scientists have learned much about how the human body works. As a result, they have developed new methods to prevent and treat health problems. Children can be immunized against once-dreaded diseases, including polio, measles, smallpox, and tetanus. Since 1900, life expectancy in the United States has risen from forty-seven years to seventy-four years. The word elements in this chapter deal with the human body and health. Part 1 presents four roots; Part 2 presents four prefixes. Although these word elements are commonly used in the sciences and health professions, they also form words that you will meet in your general reading.

Chapter Strategy: Word Elements: The Body and Health

Chapter Words

Part 1

audi	audit	*ped*	expedite
	auditory		impede
	inaudible		pedigree
patho, -pathy	empathy	*spec, spic*	conspicuous
	pathetic		introspection
	pathology		speculate

Part 2

a-, an-	anarchy	*bio-, bio*	biodegradable
	anonymous		biopsy
	apathy		symbiotic
bene-	benefactor	*mal-*	maladroit
	beneficial		malady
	benign		malevolent

306

Did You Know?

How Did Snacks Originate?

Health specialists constantly advise us to eat spinach, broccoli, and liver. Yet modern life is filled with food that may not be as healthy as spinach, but tastes good and is easily available in packaged form. Such snacks are sometimes called "junk foods." Despite this negative label, most of us are far more likely to snack on a package of potato chips or nachos than on a raw carrot. The popularity of junk food shows that it is likely to be with us for a long time, so let's see how some of the names originated.

The potato chip was invented in the 1860s. According to one story, one night, Chef George Crum had an annoying customer who kept complaining that the french fries were too thick. Finally, Mr. Crum cut the potatoes into very thin slices, and the potato chip was born. According to another account, the potato chip was invented by settlers of Spanish descent living in large haciendas in California. In any event, the first potato chip factory was founded in 1925.

In 1896 Leo Hirschfield, an Austrian immigrant, invented a chewy candy and gave it the nickname of his childhood sweetheart, Tootsie. This was the Tootsie Roll. In the 1940s, the daughter of a Mr. Lubin gave her name to Sara Lee cakes and desserts.

The ice cream cone was invented in 1904 at the St. Louis World's Fair. Ernest A. Hamwi, a Syrian immigrant, was selling *zalabias*, wafers that could be rolled up. When a person at the ice cream booth next to him ran out of plates, Hamwi substituted his rolled-up wafers, and the ice cream cone was born.

In the early 1900s eleven-year-old Frank Epperson accidently invented the popsicle by leaving a sweet drink out overnight in the cold. The liquid froze around the stick that had been used to stir it. Epperson originally called his invention the Epsicle, but the name was later changed to the more appealing popsicle.

M & M's got their name from the initial letters of the last names of Forrest Mars and Bruce Murrie. The candies first became popular during World War II among soldiers, who could eat them without making their trigger fingers sticky. Forty-five years later, M & M's remain a popular snack.

Learning Strategy

Word Elements: The Body and Health

With the many advances in medicine and the life sciences during this century, more and more scientific words have been made from the word elements in this chapter. Part 1 presents four common roots; Part 2 presents four common prefixes.

Element	Meaning	Origin	Function	Chapter Words
			Part 1	
audi	hear	Latin	root	audit, auditory, inaudible
patho, -pathy	feeling, suffering; disease	Greek	root; suffix	empathy, pathetic, pathology
ped	foot	Latin	root	expedite, impede, pedigree
spec, spic	look	Latin	root	conspicuous, introspection, speculate
			Part 2	
a-, an-	without	Greek	prefix	anarchy, anonymous apathy
bene-	good, well	Latin	prefix	benefactor, beneficial, benign
bio-, bio	life	Greek	prefix; root	biodegradable, biopsy, symbiotic
mal-	bad, harmful	Latin	prefix	maladroit, malady, malevolent

Word Roots

Part 1

The four roots in Part 1 are explained in more detail below.

audi (hear)

The word root *audi* is used in such words as *audience*, a group of people who hear a performance, and *auditorium*, a place where crowds gather to hear a performance.

patho,-pathy (feeling, suffering; disease)

The root *patho* has two meanings, and both stem from ancient Greek. First, *patho* can mean "feeling, suffering," as in the word *pathos*, meaning "a feeling of pity." A second meaning of *patho* is "disease," as in *pathologist*, a doctor who diagnoses disease, and *psychopath*, a person with a diseased mind. *Patho* can also be spelled *-pathy*, as in *sympathy*, suffering along with the sorrows of another.

ped (foot)

Ped is found in such words as *pedal*, a control operated by the foot, and *quadruped*, an animal with four feet. Some words made from *ped* reflect society's scorn for the lowly foot. *Pedestrian*, which refers to people who travel by foot, is also used to describe something that is dull or ordinary.

spec, spic (look)

The root *spec* is used in such words as *inspect*, "to look at carefully," and *despise*, to "look down on" or scorn someone. Glasses used to improve vision are called *spectacles*. Finally, the word *spy*, a person who secretly looks at the actions of others, may also derive from the root *spec*.

Words to Learn

Part 1

audi

1. **audit** (noun, verb)   ô′dĭt

   From Latin: *audit* (hear)

   examination of financial accounts by an outside agency (noun)

   > Companies registered on public stock exchanges must submit their accounts to a yearly **audit.**

   > The **audit** revealed that an employee had been stealing money.

   to examine accounts (verb)

   > Large accounting companies often **audit** major corporations.

   ▶ *Related Word*
   auditor (noun)   The *auditor's* report revealed that the company had made a large profit.

   NOTE: At one time, official examinations of financial accounts were held in public so all could hear. In modern times, however, such examinations are done in written form.

2. **auditory** (adjective)   ô′də-tôr′ē

From Latin: *audi* (hear)

referring to hearing

> A parakeet's **auditory** sense can easily identify another bird's individual call.

3. **inaudible** (adjective)   ĭn-ô′də-bəl

From Latin: *in-* (not) + *audi* (hear)

not able to be heard

> Dog whistles are **inaudible** to human ears.

NOTE: The opposite of *inaudible* is *audible*, meaning "capable of being heard."

patho, -pathy

4. **empathy** (noun)   ĕm′pə-thē

From Greek: *em-* (in) + *-pathy* (feeling, suffering)

understanding of or identification with another person's feelings

> The woman who had been crippled as a child had **empathy** for those with physical handicaps.

▶ *Common Phrase*
empathy for

▶ *Related Words*
empathic (adjective)   (ĕm-păth′ĭk)   Mr. Heishema's *empathic* comments helped us face the death of our grandfather.
empathize (verb)   We *empathize* with your problems.

NOTE: How does *empathy* differ from *sympathy?* Sympathy simply means to feel sorry for another person. However, if we have empathy, we can actually identify with or experience the feelings of another human being.

5. **pathetic** (adjective)   pə-thĕt′ĭk

From Greek: *patho* (feeling, suffering)

pitiful; arousing pity

> The injured dog made a **pathetic** attempt to climb the stairs.

6. **pathology** (noun)   pă-thŏl′ə-jē

From Greek: *patho* (disease) + *-logy* (study of)

the study of disease

The science of **pathology** was greatly enhanced when the microscope came into general use.

disease and its cause; symptoms of disease

The **pathology** of cystic fibrosis is being studied by scientists.

▶ *Related Words*
pathological (adjective) (păth′ə-lŏj′ĭ-kəl) He was a *pathological* liar. (*Pathological* can mean mentally ill.)

pathologist (noun) The *pathologist* diagnosed the disease.

A *pathologist* is a medical doctor who investigates body tissue samples (biopsies) for disease. Do you know what these medical doctors do?

1. dermatologist

2. opthamologist

3. cardiologist

(*Answers:* 1. doctor specializing in the skin 2. doctor specializing in the eye 3. doctor specializing in the heart)

---

ped

7. **expedite** (verb) ĕk′spə-dīt′

From Latin: *ex-* (out) + *ped* (foot) (*Expedīre* meant "to free a person's feet from fetters or chains.")

to speed up; to accomplish quickly

We **expedited** delivery of the package by sending it via express mail.

▶ *Related Word*
expedition (noun) (ĕk′spə-dĭsh′ən) Balboa made the first European *expedition* to the Pacific Coast. (*Expedition* means "journey.")

NOTE: Do not confuse *expedite* with *expedient* (which means "convenient").

8. **impede** (verb) ĭm-pēd′

From Latin: *im-* (in) + *ped* (foot) (*Impedīre* meant "to entangle.")

to hinder; to block

The ice on the road **impeded** our progress.

▶ *Related Word*
   impediment (noun)   (ĭm-pĕd′ə-mənt)   Laziness is an *impediment* to success.

9. **pedigree** (noun)   pĕd′ə-grē′

From Latin (*ped*) through Old French: *pie* (foot) + *de* (of) + *grue* (crane) (In a pedigree or family tree, an outline shaped like a crane's foot was used to show the different generations.)

ancestry; certificate of ancestry

   Because the horse's **pedigree** included many champion racers, it sold for a high price.

European nobles, concerned about their pedigrees, commonly ordered elaborate studies of their ancestries. Since members of the nobility often married each other, most were related. As a result, nobles of the French court of Versailles usually addressed each other as "cousin," rather than trying to remember exact family relationships.

---

spec,spic

10. **conspicuous** (adjective)   kən-spĭk′yoo-əs

From Latin: *con-* (closely) + *spec* (look)

easy to notice; attracting attention

   My aunt's bright red dress was **conspicuous** in the crowd of people wearing dark colors.

▶ *Related Word*
   conspicuousness (noun)   *Conspicuousness* may attract attention, but not admiration.

11. **introspection** (noun)   ĭn′trə-spĕk′shən

From Latin: *intro-* (within) + *spec* (look)

self-examination of one's thoughts and feelings

   Sandra did some **introspection** about her life goals before she decided to marry.

▶ *Related Words*
   introspect (verb)   Poets often *introspect* about their feelings.
   introspective (adjective)   Poets are *introspective* people.

12. **speculate** (verb)   spĕk′yə-lāt′

From Latin: *spec* (look)

to wonder about; to think about

> Economists **speculated** whether the U.S.S.R. could adapt quickly to a free-market economy.
>
> Archeologists **speculate** about the reasons why the ancient Peruvian plain of Naqca resembles an airport landing field.

to engage in a risky business

> Many people who **speculated** on junk bonds lost money.
>
> People who **speculate** on the stock market can become rich, or they can suddenly lose all their money.

▶ *Related Words*
> **speculation** (noun)   (spĕk′yə-lā′shən)   There has been much *speculation* about the causes of economic cycles.
>
> **speculative** (adjective)   (spĕk′yə-lə-tĭv)   The theory that large doses of Vitamin C can prevent illness is still highly *speculative*. (*Speculative* means uncertain or risky.)

Exercises

Part 1

■ Definitions

Match each word in the left-hand column with a definition from the right-hand column. Use each choice only once.

1. expedite _____

2. inaudible _____

3. pedigree _____

4. pathetic _____

5. pathology _____

6. empathy _____

7. impede _____

a. identification with another person

b. to hinder

c. noticeable

d. to wonder about

e. examination of financial accounts

f. not able to be heard

g. self-examination of one's thoughts

h. study of disease

i. record of ancestry

8. audit _____   j. referring to hearing

9. auditory _____   k. pitiful

10. introspection _____   l. to speed up

■ *Meanings*

Match each word element to its meaning. Use each choice only once.

1. patho _____   a. foot

2. spec _____   b. look

3. audi _____   c. feeling, suffering; illness

     d. hear

4. ped _____

■ *Words in Context*

Complete each sentence with the word that fits best. Use each choice only once.

a. audit   e. pathetic   i. pedigree
b. auditory   f. pathology   j. conspicuous
c. inaudible   g. expedite   k. introspection
d. empathy   h. impede   l. speculate

1. The _____ children gathered food from garbage pails.

2. The sound was so far away that it was _____ to us.

3. Carrying a heavy load will _____ your ability to run.

4. You will _____ matters if you telephone rather than mail this information.

5. Scientists have found that the _____ of mental illness often has a chemical basis.

6. The ear is part of the body's _____ system.

7. Susanne's loud voice and rapid movements made her _____ in the quiet room.

8. Taking some time for _____ helps us to understand our lives.

9. Mothers of older children often feel _____ for parents traveling with infants.

10. The count's _____ showed that his ancestors included many kings and queens.

■ Using Related Words

Complete each sentence using a word from the group of related words above it. You may need to capitalize a word when you put it into a sentence. Use each choice only one.

1. pathological, pathologist

Physicians are now able to freeze cancerous tumors that cannot be removed by surgery. After the _____ has determined that a tumor is malignant, its location is determined through ultrasound techniques. Then, liquid nitrogen is injected to freeze the tumor. This destroys the _____ tissue without harming healthy organs.

2. expedite, expedition

In 1911, two teams set out to be the first to reach the South Pole. Battling through the freezing, unknown land, each tried hard to

_____ its progress. Norwegian Roald Amundsen's _____ reached the pole first. British Robert Falcon Scott reached it a month later, but on the return journey, his team perished in the cold.

3. impede, impediments

The United States Food and Drug Administration (FDA) investigates all new drugs before they can be released for sale. Many people feel that this can _____ the use of experimental drugs that are needed immediately. Recently, the FDA has removed some _____ and allowed immediate use of drugs to treat diseases such as AIDS.

4. introspection, introspect

_____ can be an important tool of the science of psychology. The great psychiatrist, Sigmund Freud, was able to

form a theory of dreams by trying to _____ about his own dreams. From his self-analysis, Freud drew the conclusion that dreams were hidden wishes.

5. speculate, speculation

Scientists _____ that there is a natural limit of about eighty years to the average life. They are trying to confirm

this _____ with evidence.

■ *Reading the Headlines*

This exercise presents five headlines that might have been taken from newspapers. Read each one carefully and then answer the questions that follow. (Remember that small words, such as *a* and *the*, are often left out of newspaper headlines.)

PHYSICIANS SPECULATE THAT HEALTHY EATING IMPEDES DEVELOPMENT OF HARMFUL CHOLESTEROL

1. Are the physicians certain that eating has an effect?.

_____

2. Is it thought that healthy eating hinders cholesterol development? _____

INTROSPECTION IS A CONSPICUOUS ELEMENT IN ATHLETE'S BOOK

3. Does the athlete write about his thoughts? _____

4. Is introspection a small part of the books? _____

DAMAGED AUDITORY NERVE OFTEN CAUSES HIGH SOUNDS TO BE INAUDIBLE.

5. Is the nerve related to sight? _____

6. Can high sounds be heard? _____

GOVERNMENT ASKS ACCOUNTANT TO EXPEDITE AUDIT OF FIRM SUSPECTED OF ILLEGAL DEALINGS

7. Is the accountant asked to work slower? _____

8. Is the accountant looking at financial records? _____

MILLIONAIRE DEMONSTRATES EMPATHY FOR PATHETIC STARVING CHILDREN

9. Does the millionaire understand how the children feel?

_____

10. Are the children in a happy state? _____

Word Elements

Part 2

Part 2 concentrates on four prefixes that are often used in words about the body and in the health sciences.

a-, an- (without)
> The words *amoral* and *immoral* help us to understand the prefix *a-, an-* by contrasting it with *im-* (meaning "not"). An *immoral* person is *not* moral: this person has a sense of right and wrong, and yet chooses to do wrong. An *amoral* person is *without* morals: such a person has no sense of right or wrong. The prefix *a-* is used in many medical words, such as *aphasia* (loss of speech) and *anesthetic* ("without feeling," referring to chemicals that make patients unconscious during operations).

bene- (good, well; helpful)
> *Bene-* is used in such words as *benefit* (something that is helpful) and *beneficiary* (one who receives help or money from another).

bio-, bio (life)
> The prefix *bio-* is used in the word *biology*, "the study of living things." You may have taken a biology course in school. *Biochemistry* deals with the chemistry of living things. A word you have already studied in this book, *autobiography*, includes *bio* as a root.

mal- (bad, badly; harmful)
> The prefixes *mal-* and *bene-* are opposites. *Mal-* is seen in the word *malpractice*, or "bad practice." Doctors and lawyers may be sued for

malpractice. In 1775, the playwright Richard Sheridan coined the word *malaprop* as a name for his character, Mrs. Malaprop, who used words that were not appropriate (or "badly appropriate"). One of her malapropisms is, "He's the very pineapple of politeness." (She should have used the word *pinnacle*.)

Words to Learn

Part 2

a-, an-

13. **anarchy** (noun)   ăn′ər-kē

From Greek: *an-* (without) + *arkhos* (ruler)

political confusion; disorder; lack of government

> After the government collapsed, the small country was in a state of **anarchy.**

> **Anarchy** resulted when no one could control the rioting and looting.

▶ *Related Word*
Anarchist (noun, person)   The *anarchist* planted bombs in public places.

14. **anonymous** (adjective)   ə-nŏn′ə-məs

From Greek: *an-* (without) + *onoma* (name)

not revealing one's name; of unknown identity

> In the past, many women authors remained **anonymous** to protect the publication and sales of their books.

> An **anonymous** letter revealed where the treasure was hidden.

▶ *Related Word*
anonymity (noun)   The generous donor wished to preserve his *anonymity*.

15. **apathy** (noun)   ăp′ə-thē

   From Greek: *a-* (without) + *-pathy* (feeling)

   lack of emotion, feeling, or interest

   > Student **apathy** resulted in poor class attendance.
   >
   > Ms. Nguyen's **apathy** toward the contest changed to enthusiasm when she saw that her son was winning.

   ▶ *Related Word*
      apathetic (adjective) (ăp′ə-thĕt′ĭk) Bob was *apathetic* about life and displayed little interest in anything.

   NOTE: Apathy is a somewhat negative word.

bene-

16. **benefactor** (noun)   bĕn′ə-făk′tər

   From Latin: *bene-* (well) + *facere* (to do)

   a person who gives financial or other aid

   > The college named a hall in honor of the generous **benefactor.**

17. **beneficial** (adjective)   bĕn′ə-fĭsh′əl

   From Latin: *bene-* (well) + *facere* (to do)

   helpful; producing benefits

   > Regular exercise is **beneficial** to your health.
   >
   > My association with a major accounting firm was **beneficial** to my career.

18. **benign** (adjective)   bĭ-nīn′

   From Latin: *bene-* (well) + *genus* (birth) (*Benignus* meant "well-born, gentle.")

   kind; gentle

   > Santa Claus is a **benign,** fatherly figure.

   not containing cancer cells

   > Most skin growths are **benign.**

   NOTE: The antonym, or opposite, of *benign* is *malignant.*

bio-, bio

19. **biodegradable** (adjective)   bī'ō-dĭ-grā'də-bəl

From Greek: *bio-* (life) + Latin: *de-* (down) + *gradus* (step)

capable of being chemically broken down by natural biological processes.

> Sewage is **biodegradable** and can be transformed into fertilizer by the action of bacteria.

NOTE: Biodegradable substances break down into natural elements.

As our society becomes increasingly concerned about excessive waste, the word *biodegradable* has become more popular. Many companies now claim that their products are biodegradable. However, the word, strictly interpreted, should mean not harmful to the environment. Paper, for example, is biodegradable in small amounts, but if too much is discarded, the excess will not be broken down and may harm the environment. Food may be biodegradable, but if it is buried in landfill, it will often be preserved rather than being naturally reprocessed. Claims are made by companies that certain plastics are biodegradable. However, many of these plastics simply break down into smaller particles and cannot be transformed into naturally occurring elements. The best way to assure a healthy environment is to produce less garbage by recycling and reusing.

---

20. **biopsy** (noun)   bī'ŏp'sē

From Greek: *bio-* (life) + *opsis* (sight)

the study of living tissue to diagnose disease

> The **biopsy** showed that the mole was not cancerous.

NOTE: To diagnose disease with a *biopsy,* a doctor will cut away a small piece of living tissue and inspect it under a microscope.

The words *biopsy, benign,* and *pathology* are often used in the diagnosis of cancer. If cancer is suspected, a doctor will take a *biopsy* of cell tissue, which is then examined for *pathology* (by a *pathologist*). If the biopsy shows the tumor to be *benign,* it is harmless. If the tumor is *malignant* (note the *mal-* prefix), it is harmful and must be treated.

---

21. **symbiotic** (adjective)   sĭm′bĭ-ŏt′ĭk

From Greek: *sym-* (together) + *bio* (life)

living interdependently; referring to a relationship where two organisms live in a dependent state

> Peanut plants have a **symbiotic** relationship with the nitrogen-fixing bacteria that live on their roots.

> The **symbiotic** relationship between the mother and son was so strong that they could not live apart.

NOTE: Symbiotic relationships can be either biological or social. If they are social, *symbiotic* can be a negative word.

► *Related Word*
 symbiosis (noun)   (sĭm′bĭ-ō′sĭs)   The two types of microbes lived in *symbiosis*.

mal-

22. **maladroit** (adjective)   măl′ə-droit′

From Latin: *mal-* (badly) + French: *à droit* (to the right; proper)

clumsy

> **Maladroit** people do not make good dancers.

having no judgment; tactless

> The woman's **maladroit** remarks hurt her sister.

► *Related Word*
 maladroitness (noun)   Due to *maladroitness*, my friend often cut himself when preparing dinner.

23. **malady** (noun)   măl′ə-dē

From Latin: *mal-* (badly) + *habēre* (to keep) (*Mal habitus* meant "ill-kept, in bad condition.")

disease; bad condition

> The common cold is a **malady** that occasionally affects everyone.

NOTE: Malady can describe a nonphysical bad condition. One might say, for example, "The *malady* of discontent spread throughout the land."

24. **malevolent** (adjective)   mə-lĕv′ə-lənt

From Latin: *mal-* (bad) + *volens* (wishing)

ill-willed; evil; filled with hate

The **malevolent** master beat the slave.

▶ *Related Word*
   malevolence (noun)   The *malevolence* of the ruler was shown when he used poison gas against his own citizens.

Exercises

Part 2

■ Definitions

Match each word in the left-hand column with a definition from the right-hand column. Use each choice only once.

1. benefactor _____
2. biodegradable _____
3. benign _____
4. apathy _____
5. symbiotic _____
6. biopsy _____
7. anarchy _____
8. malady _____
9. malevolent _____
10. beneficial _____

a. illness
b. evil
c. living interdependently
d. lack of feeling
e. helpful
f. keeping an identity secret
g. donor
h. capable of being broken down by natural processes
i. political confusion
j. kind; not containing cancer cells
k. study of living tissue
l. clumsy

■ Meanings

Match each word element to its meaning. Use each choice only once.

1. bio- _____   a. bad

2. bene- _____   b. good

                       c. life

3. a- _____   d. without

4. mal- _____

■ Words in Context

Complete each sentence with the word that fits best. Use each choice only once.

a. anarchy   e. beneficial   i. symbiotic
b. anonymous   f. benign   j. maladroit
c. apathy   g. biodegradable   k. malady
d. benefactor   h. biopsy   l. malevolent

1. We were happy to learn that my father's tumor was

   _____ .

2. In past centuries, a wealthy _____ would often support an artist or musician.

3. Since the composer of the tune "Greensleeves" is

   _____ , no one knows who wrote it.

4. The doctor took a sample of my skin tissue for a

   _____ .

5. _____ about one's surroundings increases garbage on the street.

6. Researchers find that plants are _____ to the quality of indoor air.

7. The _____ criminal deliberately released oil into the ocean.

8. Most people try to use _____ containers that will not cause harm to rivers and streams.

9. He was a(n) _____ athlete, so he avoided all sports.

10. Anne's _____ kept her in bed for a week.

■ *Using Related Words*

Complete each sentence using a word from the group of related words above it. You may need to capitalize a word when you put it into a sentence. Use each choice only once.

1. anarchy, anarchists

   In the past, some political theorists felt that without an all-

   powerful government there would be _____ .
   They feared the power of citizens who, if given freedom, could

   become _____ . However, the successful governments of North America show that people in a democracy can run an effective government.

2. anonymous, anonymity

   In former years, mothers who gave up children for adoption of-

   ten preserved their _____ . In addition, parents who adopted children were unknown to the birth mother. Today,

   however, there is a trend away from _____ adoption.

3. apathy, apathetic

   Recent U.S. elections have shown that fewer citizens are voting.

   Failure to vote shows disturbing _____ toward government. Since government action affects all of us, we should

   not remain _____ . Learn about the candidates and vote!

4. symbiotic, symbiosis

Human beings live in _____ with the bacteria

that line their digestive tracts. In a _____
arrangement, humans supply a home for the bacteria, and the bacteria help to digest food. When people take antibiotics, they can destroy these bacteria and cause temporary indigestion.

5. maladroit, maladroitness

Certain medical conditions cause people to be

_____ . Parkinson's disease results in small

tremors, or shaking motions. _____ results when sufferers are not able to control their movements.

■ *Reading the Headlines*

This exercise presents five headlines that might have been taken from newspapers. Read each one carefully and then answer the questions that follow. (Remember that small words, such as *a* and *the*, are often left out of newspaper headlines.)

BENEFACTOR PREFERS TO MAINTAIN ANONYMITY

1. Did the person help others? _____
2. Does the person want the public to know who he is?

_____

APATHY OF CITY'S POLICE RESULTS IN ANARCHY IN STREETS

3. Do the police care about keeping order? _____
4. Are the streets orderly? _____

USE OF BIODEGRADABLE CARTONS SHOWN TO BE BENEFICIAL TO COMPANIES

5. Can the cartons be broken down by natural processes?

_____

6. Does the use of the cartons harm the companies?   _____

LIVER BIOPSY REVEALS EXISTENCE OF STRANGE NEW MALADY

7. Was tissue taken from a living person?   _____

8. Has a new illness been found?   _____

STUDIES SHOW THAT SYMBIOTIC RELATIONSHIPS BETWEEN PARENTS AND CHILDREN OFTEN RESULT IN MALEVOLENT FEELINGS

9. Are the parents and children independent?   _____

10. Do the parents and children have a good relationship?

_____

Chapter Exercises

■ *Practicing Strategies: New Words from Word Elements*

See how your knowledge of word elements can help you to understand new words. Complete each sentence with the word that fits best. Use each choice only once.

a. anemia   e. audiovisuals   i. malfunctioning
b. antipathy   f. benediction   j. malodorous
c. atonal   g. biohazard   k. pedicure
d. audiotape   h. malaria   l. spectator

1. A tape one listens to is a(n) _____ .

2. The _____ enabled students to both listen to and see the material they had to learn.

3. In a(n) _____ , one's feet and toenails receive cosmetic care.

4. At one time, it was thought that "bad air" caused the disease of

_____ .

5. A _____ may harm living things.

6. Something not working well is _____ .

7. The word _____ means "without tune or tone."

8. A _____ is a blessing, or "good words."

9. A _____ looks at a performance or display.

10. When you hate people, you have feeling against them, or

_____ .

©Copyright 1992 Houghton Mifflin Company

■ Practicing Strategies: Combining Context Clues and Word Elements

Combining the strategies of context clues and word elements is a good way to figure out unknown words. In the following sentences, each italicized word contains a word element that you have studied in this chapter. Using the meaning of the word element and the context of the sentence, make an intelligent guess at the meaning of the italicized word. Your instructor may ask you to check the meaning in your dictionary when you have finished.

1. No bacteria can infect a patient in an *aseptic* operating room.

   Aseptic means _____ .

2. The pathologist studied the cell closely under the microscope to determine if there was any *cytopathology*.

   Cytopathology means _____ .

3. The shape of the object was *pediform*.

   Pediform means _____ .

4. The blind person was *audile* and often listened to recordings of textbooks.

   Audile means _____ .

5. A person's *biorhythms* control the timing of urges to eat and sleep.

   Biorhythms mean _____ .

■ *Practicing Strategies: Using the Dictionary*

Read the following definition. Then answer the questions below it.

> **gap** (găp) *n.* **1.** An opening, as in a wall; cleft. **2.** A break or pass through mountains. **3.** A suspension of continuity; hiatus: *a gap in his report.* **4.** A conspicuous difference; disparity: *a gap between expenses and receipts.* **5.** *Elect.* A space traversed by an electric spark; spark gap. **6.** *Computer Sci.* An absence of information on a recording medium, often used to signal the end of a segment of information. **7.** *Electronics.* The distance between the head of a recording device and the surface of the recording medium. —*v.* **gapped, gap·ping, gaps.** —*tr.* To make an opening or gap in. —*intr.* To be or become open. [ME < ON, chasm.]

1. After *gap* was first recorded in Old Norse, in which language was

   it next used?   _____

2. Give the number and the part of speech of the definition of *gap* most

   used in computer science.   _____

3. What is the third person singular form of *gap* when used as a verb?

   _____

4. Give the number and the part of speech of the definition that best fits this sentence: "We entered the bombed building through a gap

   in the wall."   _____

5. Give the number and the part of speech of the definition that best fits this sentence: "There is a large gap between good and evil."

   _____

■ *Writing with Your Words.*

This exercise will give you practice in writing effective sentences using the vocabulary words. Each sentence is started for you. Complete it with an interesting phrase that also indicates the meaning of the italicized word.

1. Hard work is *beneficial* to _____

   _____ .

2. The *pathologist* _____

   _____ .

3. From my *auditory* sense, I could tell _____

   _____ .

4. One way to be *conspicuous* is to _____

   _____ .

5. The *pathetic* child _____

   _____ .

6. *Anarchy* resulted when _____

   _____ .

7. Traffic movement on the freeway was *impeded* because _____

   _____ .

8. He was so *maladroit* that _____

   _____ .

9. If your intentions are *benign,* _____

   _____ .

10. If you want to *expedite* progress, _____

   _____ .

Passage

Breakthroughs in Surgery

Have you ever stopped a cut from bleeding or removed a splinter? If so, you have performed minor surgery. Surgery ranges from treating cuts to removing a brain tumor. Because of many breakthroughs, modern surgery is safe and relatively painless.

The earliest surgery was performed in ancient India, China, Egypt, and Greece. **(1)** As early as 2000 B.C., **anonymous** surgeons made substantial advances. In both ancient times and the Middle Ages, surgeons were often priests. However, an order in the 1200s forbade European Christian clergy to practice medicine or law.

Surgery next came into the hands of barbers. Since training was not required, many barbers were totally unprepared for their work. **(2)** Their **maladroit** techniques caused pain and suffering. When a tooth was pulled, a band might be hired to play music so that the cries and **pathetic (3)** moans of the patient would be **inaudible** to others. Although surgery later became more respectable, patients still endured suffering and danger. In fact, the fastest surgeon was considered the best, for **(4)** if the surgeon **expedited** the procedure, the patient would suffer less.

In the middle of the 1800s, surgery was made safer and less painful by two great advances: anesthesia and asepsis.

As unbelievable as it seems today, patients were once conscious while they underwent operations. To ease the terrible pain, a person might be tied down or given alcohol while a leg was amputated. But in 1842, a U.S. physician from Georgia, Crawford W. Long, used the compound ether to make the patient unconscious during surgery. The process was named *anesthesia, a* for "without" and *aisthetos* for "feeling." A few years later, **(5)** public demonstrations of two tooth extractions using anesthesia made its use **conspicuous** throughout the world.

Surprisingly, some doctors disapproved of anesthetics. **(6)** Today it might seem that such people could only have **malevolent** motives, but in the 1800s, many physicians were afraid to interfere with "natural processes" such as pain. For this reason, some refused to use anesthetics in childbirth. However, Queen Victoria of England, mother of nine children, could **empathize** with women who gave birth, and she declared that anesthetics were a blessing.

Surgery had become less painful, but it was still dangerous. In Joseph Lister's Scottish surgical ward, forty-five percent of all patients died from a mysterious condition called "sepsis" or infection. **(7)** Lister **speculated** that, somehow, the "germs" described by Louis Pasteur were causing these deaths. He insisted that surgeons' hands, instruments, bandages, and operating rooms be cleaned with carbolic acid to kill germs. This procedure was called *asepsis, a* for "without" and *sepsis* for "rotten." **(8)** Thus, the germs that caused the **pathology** were prevented from entering the surgical opening. The results of asepsis were extremely **beneficial.** Soon after Lister started using it, an **audit** of hospital records showed that deaths after surgery dropped to fifteen percent.

(9) Strangely, Lister's results were greeted with some **apathy,** for many physicians did not believe in the germ theory that formed the basis of his treatment. **(10)** Such doubt **impeded** acceptance of asepsis, and for over ten years, many hospitals refused to change their unclean practices. In 1877, however, a spectacular operation proved that Lister was correct. He lived to see asepsis being used by every surgeon.

The modern world has seen many advances in surgery. In open heart surgery, clogged arteries leading to the heart can be rerouted and replaced by open passages. Malfunctioning kidneys and hearts can be replaced with healthy ones. At one time, any tumor would be cut out, in case it might be cancerous. Today, surgeons take a small sample, or **biopsy,** to determine if a tumor is malignant or **benign** before deciding if major surgery is needed.

The recent use of lasers, or light beams, for surgery eliminates much bleeding and pain. A gall bladder removed by ordinary surgery requires a cut of about twelve inches, a week-long stay in the hospital,

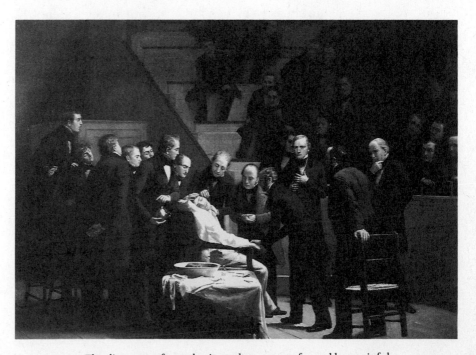

The discovery of anesthesia made surgery safer and less painful.

and months of pain. With lasers, the same surgery can be done with three small cuts, each the size of a quarter. The patient spends one night in the hospital and suffers little pain.

Laser rays can also painlessly eliminate many of the red "port wine" birthmarks on faces. Currently, eye surgeons are perfecting ways to cure nearsightedness.

Modern surgery is effective and relatively painless. Fortunately for us, it has come a long way from the techniques of the Middle Ages.

■ *Exercise*

Each of the following numbered sentences corresponds to a sentence in the Passage. Fill in the letter of the choice that makes this sentence mean the same thing as the corresponding sentence in the Passage.

1. Many _____ surgeons made substantial advances.
   a. skillful b. unknown c. ancient d. intelligent

2. Their _____ techniques caused pain and suffering.
   a. harmful b. old-fashioned c. stupid d. clumsy

3. Moans of the patient would be _____ to others.
   a. not heard b. not loud c. not many d. not pleasant

4. If the surgeon _____ the procedure, the patient would suffer less.
   a. finished b. reversed c. tried d. hurried

5. Demonstrations using anesthesia made it _____ throughout the world.
   a. successful b. noticed c. travel d. used

6. Today it might seem that such people could only have _____ motives.
   a. evil b. real c. stingy d. no

7. Lister _____ that germs were causing these deaths.
   a. thought b. knew c. said d. dreamed

8. The germs that caused the _____ were prevented from entering.
   a. wound b. cut c. disease d. reaction

9. Lister's results were greeted with some _____ .
   a. lack of belief b. lack of friendliness c. lack of interest
   d. lack of helpfulness

10. This doubt _____ acceptance of asepsis.
    a. slowed   b. helped   c. assured   d. defeated

■ *Discussion Questions*

1. What great medical advance was made by Joseph Lister?

2. Describe the major steps that helped to lessen surgical pain.

3. Laser surgery is still developing. Describe one problem that might be treated with lasers in the future. Explain how.

CHAPTER

12

Word Elements: Speech and Writing

This chapter presents word elements about speech and writing, the two major forms of human communication. The first part of the chapter contains three elements related to speech; the second part gives two elements related to writing. Part 2 also presents three pairs of words that people often confuse in speech and writing and helps you to use these confusable words correctly.

Chapter Strategy: Word Elements: Speech and Writing

Chapter Words:

Part 1

dict	contradict	voc, vok	advocate
	dictator		provoke
	edict		revoke
log, -logy, loq	colloquial		vociferate
	ecology		
	loquacious		
	monologue		
	prologue		

Part 2

-gram, -graph,	demographic	Confusable Words	affect
-graphy,	epigram		effect
graph	graphic		conscience
scrib, script	inscription		conscious
	manuscript		imply
	nondescript		infer

Did You Know?

What Are Slang Expressions?

Slang refers to words that are used in informal speech, but are not acceptable in formal English. Most of us use slang at one time or another, in its many different varieties. Sports such as baseball, football, and hockey have their own words. Hundreds of slang expressions exist to describe wealth, physical attractiveness, or intelligence—and the opposites of these qualities. A well-developed slang vocabulary is also used in lunch counters and fast-food places. Finally, as any parent knows, each generation of teenagers creates a new version of slang. Although vocabulary books don't usually teach slang, it is fun to consider the histories of a few vivid phrases. Many have been in our language for well over a hundred years. In fact, such common words as *joke* and *fad* originated as slang and slowly became respectable.

old man, as in the sentence "I left my old man at home." "Old man" has referred to a father since the 1840s. In the 1890s, it was also used for a husband. Today it is used in both ways and has come also to mean steady boyfriend. In contrast, the expression "old woman" has referred to a wife since 1775.

smooth or *slick,* as in "He thinks he's smooth" or "He thinks he's slick." Since 1893, *smooth* has described someone who acts in a sophisticated manner. The slang word *slick,* which has a similar meaning to *smooth,* has been used in England since 1594. *Slick* has gone through several meaning changes. In 1818, it meant "skillful." Shortly afterward it was used to describe trickiness or cleverness. In the 1840s, people used it to mean "well-groomed." *Slick* presently has many slang meanings, but the original sense of *sophisticated* is still used from time to time.

blab, as in "He blabbed my secrets all over town." As a noun, *blab* occurred in England as early as 1374, when it meant a gossip or a person who informed on the crimes of others. *Blabber* has meant "to talk too much, to let out secrets" since the 1300s. Americans coined the expression "a blabbermouth" in the 1920s.

The lunch counters, take-out restaurants, and truck stops that dot the United States and Canada have a well-developed slang of their own. Do you know what these terms mean?

1. red lead
2. CB with
3. let it walk
4. stack

(*Answers:* 1. ketchup 2. cheeseburger with fries 3. to go outside the store 4. pile of pancakes)

Learning Strategy

Word Elements: Speech and Writing

Human beings are skilled communicators. Not surprisingly, we have many word elements that deal with communication in oral and written form. Part 1 of this chapter concentrates on speech, and Part 2 deals with writing. Part 2 also discusses three pairs of words that people often confuse when they speak and write.

Element	Meaning	Origin	Function	Chapter Words
		Part 1		
dict	speak	Latin	root	contradict, dictator, edict
log,	word;	Greek;	root;	colloquial, ecology,
-logy,	study of;	Latin	suffix	loquacious,
loq	speak			monologue, prologue
voc, vok	voice; call	Latin	root	advocate, provoke, revoke, vociferate
		Part 2		
-gram, -graph,	write	Latin;	suffix;	demographic, epigram,
-graphy, graph		Greek	root	graphic
scrib, script	write	Latin	root	inscription, manuscript, nondescript

Word Roots

Part 1

The word roots for Part 1 are explained below in more detail.

dict (speak)
  This root appears in several common words. *Dictation* is something spoken by one person and copied down by another. *Diction* is either one's choice of words or the clearness of one's speech.

Speech is now a key element of popular music. *Rap,* which replaces singing with speaking, is one of the most creative and important developments in current music. Its roots come from African chanting, spoken blues, the performances of James Brown, and the *toasts* of Jamaican disk jockeys. In rap, rhythm and beat are more important than melody. Lyrics often deal with current social issues, and some rap groups are extremely controversial. Popular performers include M.C. Hammer and Vanilla Ice.

log, -logy, loq (word; study of; speak)

To be *eloquent* is to speak well. A *dialogue* is speech, or a conversation, between two or more people. The suffix *-logy* means "study of." You may have taken courses in *biology* (the study of living things), in *psychology* (the study of the mind), or *anthropology* (the study of human beings).

voc, vok (voice; call)

A record that contains the human voice speaking or singing is called a *vocal* recording. *Vocabulary,* meaning "things spoken by the voice," or "words," also comes from *voc.* You will not confuse this root with the other word roots in this chapter if you remember to associate it with the word *voice.*

Words to Learn

Part 1

dict

1. **contradict** (verb)   kŏn'trə-dĭkt'

   From Latin: *contra-* (against) + *dict* (speak)

   to say or put forth the opposite of something

   > It is not polite to **contradict** the statements of others in public.
   >
   > Unfortunately, the evidence gathered from the experiment **contradicted** the scientist's theory.

   ▶ *Related Words*
   contradiction (noun)   The testimony of the witness contained many *contradictions.*

contradictory (adjective)   There is *contradictory* evidence about the benefits of removing asbestos from buildings.

2. **dictator** (noun)   dĭk'tā-tər

From Latin: *dict* (speak) (A dictator is a ruler who speaks with power; whatever the ruler says, is done.)

a ruler with total authority

> The **dictator** announced that the price of flour and rice would be increased by thirty percent.

▶ *Related Word*
  dictatorial (adjective)   (dĭk'tə-tôr'ē-əl)   The club leader acted in a *dictatorial* manner.

3. **edict** (noun)   ē'dĭkt'

From Latin: *e-* (out) + *dict* (speak)

an order or decree

> The king issued an **edict** requiring all men to join the army.
> There was a city **edict** prohibiting pets in high-rise buildings.

log, -logy, loq

4. **colloquial** (adjective)   kə-lō'kwē-əl

From Latin: *com-* (together) + *loq* (speak) (When we "speak together" with friends, our speech is colloquial.)

informal conversation or expression

> The word "yeah" is a **colloquial** way of saying "yes."

▶ *Related Word*
  colloquialism (noun)   The word *buddy* is a *colloquialism*.

5. **ecology** (noun)   ĭ-kŏl'ə-jē

From Greek: *oikos* (house) + *-logy* (study of) (Ecology is concerned with the environment, the "home" or "house" in which we all live.)

the study of the relationship of living things and their environment

> Specialists in **ecology** find that the growth of an animal population depends upon its food supply.

▶ *Related Words*
  ecological (adjective)   (ĕk'ə-lŏj'ĭ-kəl)   Acid rain has ruined the *ecological* balance of many lakes and ponds.

ecologist (noun) The *ecologist* investigated the effects of air pollution on tree growth.

As human beings change their environment through industrial and technological advances, the science of ecology is increasingly needed to protect plant and animal life.

The rain forests of South America, Africa, and Asia are being cleared to obtain lumber and to provide farm land. Ecologists have demonstrated how this may lead to the extinction of forest animals. Even human life may be endangered, as the roots of forest trees help to hold water. When these trees are cut, water evaporates, causing dryness that kills plants, and eventually leads to human starvation.

In 1987, scientists confirmed that there was a dangerous hole in the protective ozone layer that surrounds our atmosphere. This hole, centered over Antarctica, may indirectly cause skin cancer in humans and animals as well as have a dangerous warming effect on the earth's temperature. Researchers feel that the ozone hole may be due to the use of industrial chlorofluorocarbons, which are found in aerosol cans, refrigerators, and some styrofoam fast-food containers.

---

6. **loquacious** (adjective) lō-kwā'shəs

From Greek: *loq-* (speak)

Very talkative

My **loquacious** sister kept me on the telephone for over an hour.

► *Related Words*
loquaciousness (noun) Judy's *loquaciousness* became very annoying.
loquacity (noun) Because of his *loquacity*, Raymond enjoyed appearing on the talk show.

7. **monologue** (noun) mŏn'ə-lôg'

From Greek: *monos* (one) + *log* (speak)

a speech or performance by one person

The comedian Richard Pryor is noted for his **monologues.**

8. **prologue** (noun) prō'lôg'

From Greek: *pro-* (before) + *log* (speak)

the introduction to a play or book

The author described the historical background of the book in the **prologue.**

an introductory event

> The Japanese bombing of Pearl Harbor was the **prologue** to United States involvement in World War II.

voc, vok

9. **advocate** (verb) ăd'və-kāt'; (noun) ăd'və-kĭt

From Latin: *ad-* (toward) + *voc* (to voice, call)

to urge publicly; to recommend (verb)

> Members of Amnesty International are **advocates** for human rights and the prevention of torture.

a person who publicly urges a cause (noun)

> In the nineteenth century, there were many **advocates** of free public education.

▶ *Common Phrase*
advocate of

10. **provoke** (verb) prə-vōk'

From Latin: *prō-* (forward) + *voc* (to voice, call) (*Prōvocāre* meant "to challenge.")

to cause anger or action

> By insulting the police, Dwight **provoked** them into arresting him.

> Changes in graduation requirements **provoked** comments from angry students.

> The student's intelligent question **provoked** a thoughtful response from the professor.

▶ *Related Words*
provocation (noun) (prŏv'ə-kā'shən) The insult was a *provocation.*

provocative (adjective) (prə-vōk'ə-tĭv) Her *provocative* comment made me reexamine my position. (*Provocative* can sometimes mean "sexy," as in "provocative clothing.")

11. **revoke** (verb) rĭ-vōk'

From Latin: *re-* (back) + *vok* (to call)

to cancel or withdraw

> Judges often **revoke** the licenses of drunk drivers.

► *Related Word*
    revocation (noun) (rĕv′ə-kā′shən) The *revocation* of civil
    rights caused many people to flee the country.

12. **vociferate** (verb) vō-sĭf′ə-rāt′

From Latin: *voc* (voice) + *ferre* (to carry)

to speak loudly; to cry out

> The politician **vociferated** the need for reform in government.
> The people **vociferated** "Long live the king!"

► *Related Word*
    vociferous (adjective) The *vociferous* crowd cheered the team.

Exercises

Part 1

■ *Definitions*

Match each word in the left-hand column with a definition from the
right-hand column. Use each choice only once.

1. contradict _____	a. introduction to book or play
2. prologue _____	b. to recommend
	c. to say loudly
3. edict _____	d. to say something opposite
4. colloquial _____	e. person with sole power
5. loquacious _____	f. informal
	g. very talkative
6. dictator _____	h. order
7. advocate _____	i. study of the relationship of life and environment
8. ecology _____	j. helpless
9. provoke _____	k. to arouse to anger
10. monologue _____	l. speech by one person

■ *Meanings*

Match each word element to its definition. Use each choice only once.

1. dict _____   a. speak; study of; word

2. log, -logy, loq _____   b. speak

                              c. voice; call
3. voc, vok _____

■ *Words in Context*

Complete each sentence with the word that fits best. Use each choice only once.

a. contradict   e. ecology   i. advocate
b. dictator   f. loquacious   j. provoke
c. edict   g. monologue   k. revoke
d. colloquial   h. prologue   l. vociferate

1. The professor delivered a fascinating one-hour

   _____ on the French Revolution.

2. The _____ woman talked throughout our card game.

3. I am a(n) _____ of more money for education.

4. Insulting people will often _____ an argument.

5. When a mother and father _____ each other, a child may not know whose directions to follow.

6. Students should use formal rather than _____ English when they write term papers.

7. The _____ of the area was disturbed when a flood destroyed much of the food supply of the animals.

8. October's drop in stock prices was a(n) _____ to the economic problems of November.

9. In his speeches, the union leader would _____ the slogan "Higher wages now!" over and over.

10. The government issued a(n) _____ declaring that all citizens must be off the streets by 10 P.M.

■ *Using Related Words*

Complete each sentence using a word from the group of related words above it. You may need to capitalize a word when you put it into a sentence. Use each choice only once.

1. revoked, revocation

    At one time, plastic tubing for plumbing, or PVC was banned from use in many cities. Recently, the ban has been

    _____ in various areas. However, this

    _____ often does not cover high-rise buildings. Copper tubing for plumbing must still be used in many of these taller structures.

2. ecology, ecological

    Global warming has a major effect on world

    _____ . Melting ice causes higher sea levels, and the wildlife that occupies shorelines and shallow water has difficulty surviving. Areas that once supported crops turn into deserts.

    As the earth warms, the _____ balance is upset.

3. provoke, provocation

    Dueling, or settling differences with guns or swords, was popular for many years. A small insult could _____ one man into challenging another. A gentleman was considered

    a coward if he ignored a _____ . This romantic, but dangerous, practice killed many people, including Alexander Hamilton, the first Secretary of the Treasury of the United States.

4. dictator, dictatorial

In *The Caine Mutiny*, a novel of World War II, a ship's captain

acts like a _____·_____ . His _____
and senseless policies frighten his crew, who finally refuse to follow his orders.

5. contradicted, contradictory

Animals may sometimes confuse us by using _____
body language. For example, a dog may wag its tail while growling. The tail-wagging, a friendly action, is _____
by the threatening growl. At such times, one should approach a dog with caution.

■ True or False?

Each of the following statements contains at least one word from this section. Read each statement and then indicate whether you think it is probably true or probably false.

____   1. It is easy to provoke a person who has a quick temper.

____   2 Ecological balance refers only to human life.

____   3. A government edict would probably use colloquial language.

____   4. You would be pleased if someone contradicted you in public.

____   5. Dictators commonly rule in a democracy.

____   6. Most law enforcement officials advocate crime.

____   7. People are usually loquacious when they vociferate.

____   8. A prologue is given after a book ends.

____   9. A monologue involves one person.

____   10. A child who broke his mother's rules might have privileges revoked.

Word Roots

Part 2

The second part of this chapter presents two word elements that deal with the concept of writing. Then, three pairs of confusable words, which college students often have trouble distinguishing, are introduced.

-gram, -graph, graph, -graphy (write)
> This suffix has three spellings. It is spelled *-gram*, as in *telegram*, a written message sent by wires (*tele-* means "far"). The spelling *-graph* is used in *autograph*, a person's signature, or "self-writing" (*autos* means "self"). Finally, the suffix can be spelled *-graphy*, as in *photography* (literally, "writing in light"). *Graph* can also function as a root.

scrib, script (write)
> This root is found in many common words. A *script* is the written form of a television program, movie, or play. When small children make written marks, they often *scribble*. A *scribe* writes down the words of other people.

Words to Learn

Part 2

-gram, -graph, -graphy, graph

13. **demographic** (adjective)   dĕm′ə-grăf′ĭk

From Greek: *demos* (people) + *-graph* (write)

referring to the study of population characteristics

> The largest **demographic** study done in the United States is the national census.

> ▶ *Related Word*
> **demography** (noun)   (dĭ-mŏg′rə-fē)   *Demography* reveals that an increasing number of people work in the field of high technology.

14. **epigram** (noun)   ĕp′ĭ-grăm′

From Greek: *epi-* (on) + *-gram* (write)

a short, clever saying, often in rhyme

Benjamin Franklin's **epigram** on the value of consistent work was "Little strokes fell great oaks."

15. **graphic** (adjective)   grăf′ĭk

From Greek: *graph* (write) (*Graphe* meant "drawing, writing.")

referring to drawings or artistic writing

My computer software can create charts, drawings, and other **graphic** displays.

described vividly or clearly

The author's description of the Civil War battle was so **graphic** that we could imagine the sound of guns and the sight of blood.

▶ *Related Word*
graphics (noun)   The Hyatt hotel chain had its *graphics* professionally designed.

scrib, script

16. **inscription** (noun)   ĭn-skrĭp′shən

From Latin: *in-* (in) + *script* (write)

carving on a surface

Many U.S. coins bear the **inscription** *E pluribus unum*, meaning "one from many."

a signed message on a picture or in a book

People often write **inscriptions** inside the covers of books that they give as gifts.

▶ *Related Word*
inscribe (verb)   (ĭn-skrīb′)   The engraver *inscribed* the date of my college graduation on the ring.
The year of U.S. independence, 1776, is *inscribed* in the nation's memory. (In this sentence, *inscribe* is used in a non-physical manner.)

17. **manuscript** (noun, adjective)   măn′yə-skrĭpt′

From Latin: *manu* (by hand) + *script* (write)

the original text of a book or article before publication (noun)

The author submitted his **manuscript** to several publishers.

referring to writing done by hand (adjective)

> It took many years to master the beautiful **manuscript** lettering used to produce books by hand.

Before printing was invented, scribes laboriously copied whole books by hand. The manuscripts they created were often beautiful works of art, and they were quite expensive.

Johann Gutenberg invented modern printing in about 1450. The famous Gutenberg Bible was his first printed production. The printing process brought about a social revolution because it made books, and therefore knowledge, less expensive and more widely available.

NOTE: Manuscript writing (done with disconnected letters) is often distinguished from cursive writing (done with connected letters).

18. **nondescript** (adjective)   nŏn'dĭ-skrĭpt'

From Latin: *non-* (not) + *de-* (down) + *script* (write) (Something nondescript can't be written down because it is hard to describe.)

not distinct, difficult to describe because it lacks individuality

> The criminal's **nondescript** appearance allowed him to escape.

Confusable Words

19. **affect** (verb)   ə-fĕkt'

to have an influence on; to change

> Sunlight often **affects** people's moods in a positive way.

20. **effect** (noun)   ĭ-fĕkt'

a result

> Sunlight often has a positive **effect** on people's moods.

NOTE ON POSSIBLE CONFUSION: Try to remember that *affect* is usually a verb and *effect* is usually a noun, as in the following two sentences.

> Seymour *affected* my life.
>
> Seymour had an *effect* on my life.

21. **conscience** (noun)   kŏn'shəns

sense of right and wrong; moral sense

Conscience dictates that we do not steal from others.

▶ *Related Word*
 conscientious (adjective) (kŏn'shē-ĕn'shəs) A *conscientious* student will often receive good grades. (*Conscientious* means "hard-working, thorough.")

22. **conscious** (adjective) kŏn'shəs

aware; awake

 Because a local anesthetic was used, Nathan was **conscious** throughout the operation.

NOTE ON POSSIBLE CONFUSION: Remember that *conscience* is a noun and *conscious* is an adjective, as in the following two sentences.

 My *conscience* was bothering me.
 I am *conscious* of my shortcomings.

23. **imply** (verb) ĭm-plī'

to suggest; to say something indirectly

 Jean **implied** that she was angry with us by speaking harshly.

▶ *Related Word*
 implication (noun) (ĭm'plĭ-kā'shən) His *implication* was clear to us.

24. **infer** (verb) ĭn-fûr'

to conclude; to guess

 I **infer** from your comments that you are angry.

▶ *Related Words*
 inference (noun) (ĭn'fər-əns) The chemistry student drew an *inference* from the results of her experiment.
 inferential (adjective) (ĭn'fə-rĕn'shəl) This requires *inferential* thinking.

NOTE ON POSSIBLE CONFUSION: It may help you to remember that someone who *implies* gives hints; someone who *infers* draws conclusions from hints.

Exercises

Part 2

■ Definitions

Match each word in the left-hand column with a definition from the right-hand column. Use each choice only once.

1. conscience _____   a. to hint

2. imply _____   b. short, witty saying

3. demographic _____   c. carving on a surface

4. infer _____   d. original text of a book

5. epigram _____   e. to draw a conclusion

6. affect _____   f. result

7. inscription _____   g. referring to population statistics

8. manuscript _____   h. referring to drawings or artistic writings

9. graphic _____   i. aware

10. nondescript _____   j. a sense of right and wrong

                              k. not distinct

                              l. to influence

■ Words in Context

Complete each sentence with the word that fits best. Use each choice only once, and capitalize when necessary.

a. demographic   e. manuscript   i. conscience
b. epigram   f. nondescript   j. conscious
c. graphic   g. affect   k. imply
d. inscription   h. effect   l. infer

1. The author's _____ was 473 pages in length.

2. _____ surveys reveal that many people in the Canadian province of Quebec speak both English and French.

3. The description of food was so _____ that it made us hungry.

4. I try not to let my busy social life _____ my ability to study.

5. I was not _____ of the fact that I had broken any rules.

6. The governor of Florida was concerned about the

_____ of high-rise building on the ocean front.

7. The people of Florida will probably _____ from the governor's comments that high-rise building would not improve the ocean front.

8. The private detective wore _____ clothes so that no one would notice him.

9. "Man proposes, God disposes" is an example of a(n)

_____ .

10. My _____ prevents me from doing wrong.

■ *Using Related Words*

Complete each sentence using a word from the group of related words above it. You may need to capitalize a word when you put it into a sentence. Use each choice only once.

1. demography, demographic

_____ shows that an increasing number of

mothers of young children are working. This _____ trend points to a need for high-quality and widely available child-care facilities.

2. inscriptions, inscribed

Designed by Yale architectural student Maya Lin, the memorial for the Vietnamese war is a long slab of black granite.

_____ in the surface are the names of all American soldiers who died in battle. People throughout the United

States come to see the _____ honoring those who have fallen in battle. Many visitors are moved to tears.

3. affect, effect

Which has a greater _____ on a person, heredity or environment? For many years, scientists believed that heredity had a far greater influence. However, more recently, environment

has been shown to _____ people strongly. For example, in a study done by Skeels in the 1930s, when children were removed from an orphanage and given loving attention, their IQs increased dramatically.

4. consciences, conscientious

Early Protestant settlers in America were said to have had the "Protestant work ethic." According to this, their

_____ would bother them if they did not work

hard enough. Thus, these people were often _____ workers.

5. implied, inferred

In his speech, the president _____ that more money had to be raised to support the club's new programs. The

people in attendance _____ that a money-raising event was needed, and a member of the crowd proposed a bake sale.

■ *True or False?*

Each of the following statements contains one or more words from this section. Read each sentence carefully and then indicate whether you think it is probably true or probably false.

____   1. Studying usually has a positive effect on grades.

____   2. We are conscious when we sleep.

____   3. Epigrams are usually clever.

____   4. Authors write manuscripts.

—   5. A conscience tells you to commit murder.

—   6. If a book had graphic descriptions of the explorer's adventures, we would infer that it had some vivid action.

—   7. If you wanted an inscription put on a watch you were buying, it would probably affect the price.

—   8. A demographic study might serve as the basis of taxation.

—   9. It is easy to remember what a nondescript person looks like.

—   10. If you imply that others are stupid, you will make friends.

Chapter Exercises

■ *Practicing Strategies: New Words from Word Elements*

See how your knowledge of word elements can help you to understand new words. Complete each sentence with the word that seems to fit best. Use each choice only once.

a. biography   e. graphology   i. postscript
b. describe   f. hologram   j. prescription
c. dictate   g. interlocution   k. revocalize
d. graph   h. phonograph   l. travelogue

1. The study of handwriting is _____ .

2. A(n) _____ is a three-dimensional written picture in which a whole object seems to appear.

3. A _____ often displays numerical information as a drawing, or in written visual form.

4. When we voice something again, we _____ it.

5. A _____ is something that must be written out before you can get medicine. (*Pre-* means "before.")

6. A _____ record is writing made from sound. (*Phono-* means "sound.")

7. When we speak and others copy down our words, we

_____ .

8. A spoken account of a trip might be called a

_____ .

9. Something written at the end of a letter is a

_____ . (*Post-* means "after.")

10. A book written about someone's life is a(n) _____ .

■ *Practicing Strategies: Combining Context Clues and Word Elements*

Combining the strategies of context clues and word elements is a good way to figure out unknown words. In the following sentences, each italicized word contains a word element that you have studied in this chapter. Using the meaning of the word element and the context of the sentence, make an intelligent guess at the meaning of the italicized word. Your instructor may ask you to check the meaning in your dictionary when you have finished.

1. The word "t-o-y" has three *graphemes*.

   Grapheme means _____ .

2. In her *elocution* lessons Randy learned to pronounce words clearly and present arguments effectively.

   Elocution means _____ .

3. Many people gave talks about the economy at the *colloquium*.

   Colloquium means _____ .

4. The *entomologist* specialized in ants, bees, and spiders.

   Entomologist means _____ .

5. The *seismograph* made a record of the strength of the earthquake.

   Seismograph means _____ .

■ *Companion Words*

Complete each sentence with the word that fits best. Choose your answers from the words below. You may use each word more than once.

Choices: draw, of, into, on

1. Mothers are often conscious _____ their babies' every movement.

2. Don't provoke me _____ starting a fight.

3. I am an advocate _____ equal pay for equal work.

4. Weather often has an effect _____ people's moods.

5. The crowd will _____ an inference from the speaker's implications.

■ *Writing with Your Words*

This exercise will give you practice in writing effective sentences using the vocabulary words. Each sentence is started for you. Complete it with an interesting phrase that also indicates the meaning of the italicized word.

1. The *nondescript* person _____

   _____ .

2. I have *contradictory* feelings about _____

   _____ .

3. According to the *edict*, _____

   _____ .

4. The *dictator* _____

   _____ .

5. If you want to *provoke* a negative response, _____

   _____ .

6. The speaker *implied* _____

_____ .

7. We *inferred* from the speech that _____

_____ .

8. I am *affected* by _____

_____ .

9. A *conscientious* worker _____

_____ .

10. I *advocate* _____

_____ .

Passage

The Man Who Did Not Cry Wolf

Centuries of folklore and tradition have expressed distrust and fear of wolves. We speak of starvation as "having the wolf at the door." It is the wolf who tricks the folktale figure, Little Red Riding Hood. Finally, an evil person is called a "wolf in sheep's clothing."

Only a few brave people have ever tested these legends by observing wolves at close range. Farley Mowat was one such person. **(1)** The Canadian government was concerned that wolves were damaging the **ecology** of the Arctic by eating so many caribou that the animal was disappearing. It therefore sent Mowat to see what **effect** hungry northern wolves were having on the caribou herds. **(2)** In his book, *Never Cry Wolf,* Mowat's description of a year living close to wolves **contradicts** the traditional image of the "big, bad wolf."

From the beginning, Mowat's encounters with wolves surprised him. Weaponless, he found himself at their mercy three times; although they could have killed him, they simply walked away. Even when he **provoked** them by walking into their territory, the wolves did not attack.

(3) The **implication** was clear: the senseless viciousness of the wolf was largely in the human imagination.

Fascinated, Mowat was determined to observe the wolves at close range. He defined his own territory, lived in a tent, and watched them through a telescope. **(4)** To keep his presence undisturbing, Mowat tried to dress and act in a **nondescript** manner.

Mowat's wolf family consisted of a couple, "George" and "Angeline," their wolf pups, and "Uncle Albert," a single male. Mowat saw great care and affection between the couple and toward their children. The entire wolf den was organized around feeding the pups. Each afternoon, George and Uncle Albert went off to hunt, returning the next morning. **(5)** However, Angeline, apparently **conscious** of her responsibilities as a mother, stayed home watching her youngsters.

In fact, wolves seemed to love their young. During family play, sometimes a pup's lively nipping and licking wore Angeline out, but the good-natured Uncle Albert was always ready to take her place. **(6)** Mowat gives a **graphic** description of wolf games of "tag," with Uncle Albert playing "it." Uncle Albert was also an effective, if unwilling, babysitter. All three adults carefully instructed the puppies in hunting.

At first, the wolf calls disturbed Mowat. **(7)** The animals would come together and **vociferate** in high-pitched howls for several minutes, sending chills of fear down his spine. Gradually, he began to realize that they could communicate different messages. After listening to wolf howls one day, Ooteck, Mowat's Eskimo companion, became greatly excited and rushed off. A few hours later, he returned with a host of visitors. How had Ooteck known where to find them? Ooteck said he had gotten the information from the wolves' howls. Another time, Ooteck claimed that two wolf packs, separated by many miles, announced the presence of caribou herds to each other.

As he continued to watch the wolves, Mowat began to wonder what they ate. For most of the year, the caribou were far away. How did the den support itself during this time?

One day he watched Angeline trap twenty-three mice in one afternoon. Could it be that the great beast of the north could support itself on the lowly mouse?

To test the ability of a large animal to live on mice, Mowat used himself as a subject. For several months, he ate only mice, developing several recipes! He reported that this diet did not **affect** his health, and he remained as vigorous as ever. **(8)** He drew the **inference** that wolves could also live on a diet of mice.

Did wolves hunt caribou? Mowat found that the wolves hunted a few, mainly weak or old, caribou. By removing the animals who would find it hard to survive, the wolves actually strengthened the caribou herd. If wolves were not killing the caribou, who was? Mowat decided that most were hunted by human beings.

Wolves vociferate together in high-pitched howls.

(9) Mowat's experience with arctic wolves was the **prologue** to efforts to make people more aware of wolves. His book played an important role in saving the northern wolf, which, he estimated, now numbered less than 3,000. Mowat urged the government to **revoke edicts** that gave rewards for dead wolves. (10) In response to the pleas of Mowat and other **advocates** of wildlife preservation, people are now taking steps to protect this awesome animal.

■ Exercise

Each numbered sentence below corresponds to a sentence in the Passage. Fill in the letter of the choice that makes this sentence mean the same thing as the corresponding sentence in the Passage.

1. The Canadian government was concerned that wolves were damaging the _____ of the Arctic.
   a. weather balance   b. environmental balance   c. balance of power   d. balance of fur trapping

2. Mowat's description of a year living close to the wolves _____ the traditional image of the "big, bad wolf."
   a. draws on   b. denies   c. shows   d. supports

3. The _____ was clear.
   a. talk   b. moral   c. suggestion   d. singing

4. Mowat tried to dress and act in a(n) _____ manner.
   a. unnoticeable   b. soft   c. lovely   d. wild

5. However, Angeline, apparently _____ of her responsibilities as a mother, stayed home watching her youngsters.
   a. aware   b. because   c. forgetful   d. resentful

6. Mowat gives a(n) _____ description of wolf games of "tag."
   a. long   b. accurate   c. scientific   d. vivid

7. The animals would come together and _____ in high-pitched howls for several minutes.
   a. cry out   b. sing beautifully   c. ask for help   d. disturb others

8. He drew the _____ that wolves could also live on a diet of mice.
   a. conclusion   b. note   c. picture   d. explanation

9. Mowat's experience with arctic wolves was the _____ to efforts to make people more aware of wolves.
   a. climax   b. introduction   c. resistance   d. answer

10. In response to the pleas of Mowat and other _____ of wildlife preservation, people are now taking steps to protect this animal.
    a. models   b. supporters   c. donors   d. leaders

■ Discussion Questions

1. What events first made Mowat suspect that wolves were not as vicious as people believed?

2. How do the wolves compare with human parents?

3. Killing wolves and selling their skins is one way for people who live in the Arctic to support themselves. Do you think the Canadian government should allow this? Why or why not?

REVIEW

Chapters 9–12

■ Reviewing Words in Context

a. annals	f. expedite	k. speculate
b. anonymous	g. impede	l. trivial
c. conscience	h. magnitude	m. unilateral
d. defiant	i. nonchalant	n. veracity
e. destitute	j. nonsectarian	o. behind the eight ball

1. The author remained _____ by publishing under another name.

2. The committee members were angry when the chairperson made

   a(n) _____ decision without consulting them.

3. The Red Cross, a _____ organization, is not connected with any religious group.

4. Ralph was surprisingly _____ and did not seem disturbed when his teacher told him he would flunk the course.

5. The _____ of the scientific society contain records of all its meetings.

6. Because of his good character, nobody ever doubted the

   _____ of Mr. Berry's reports.

7. Brenda felt as if she were _____ because she could never keep up with the course requirements.

8. Not doing assigned homework may _____ your progress in school.

9. If I stole some money, my _____ would probably bother me.

10. The sun is a star of great _____ .

11. Gossiping is a _____ and time-wasting pursuit.

12. It is interesting to _____ about what the world will be like in the year 3000.

13. The _____ person had to receive help from welfare.

14. The _____ child refused to obey his parents or teachers.

15. If I concentrate on a task, I can usually _____ my progress and finish it early.

■ *Passage for Word Review*

Complete each blank in the Passage with the word that makes the best sense. The choices include words from the vocabulary lists and related words. Use each choice only once.

a. beneficial   e. expedition   i. monotony
b. bipartisan   f. inaudible   j. prologue
c. conscious   g. inscription   k. veritable
d. deluded   h. loquacious   l. a bolt from the blue

The City Mouse and the Country Mouse
(A Modern Version of an Aesop Fable)

Once a sociable city mouse who liked to drop in on relatives paid a visit to his cousin, who lived in the country. The city mouse did not like the

(1) _____ of eating grain for every meal, as his country cousin did. He invited the cousin to come back with him to the city, where the food was more varied and better. The

(2) _____ city mouse talked for hours about this wonderful food, and he convinced his country cousin to try it.

The next day the two mice set off on a(n) **(3)** _____ to the city. The food proved to be as good as the city mouse had promised. For his first meal, the country mouse ate three chocolate cupcakes, two strawberry tarts, and seven types of imported cheese. And this was

just a(n) **(4)** _____ of the things to come. Cakes, cookies, candy, and fancy cheese replaced the grain of the country diet.

Every night was a **(5)** _____ banquet.

But one night, as they were happily eating, the two mice were not

(6) _____ of the fact that they had attracted the attention of a cat. The cat's movements were so quiet that they were

(7) _____ to the mice. Suddenly the cat pounced on them like (8) _____ . They fled in terror back to their mousehole. When they were safe inside, the country mouse said to his city cousin, "The food is good, but cats are dangerous. Living in fear

is not (9) _____ to my health. You shouldn't have

(10) _____ me into thinking that city life is better than country life." The country mouse packed his bags and went back to the safe, dull countryside.

■ Reviewing Learning Strategies

New words from word elements   Below are some words you have not studied that are formed from classical word elements. Using your knowledge of these elements, write in the letter of the word that best completes each sentence. Use each choice only once.

a. accredited   e. biometrics   i. pedometer
b. aerophobia   f. dictaphone   j. sociology
c. auding   g. galvanometer   k. telepathy
d. binary   h. malcontent   l. verdict

1. _____ is the branch of science that measures statistical data on living things.

2. We can believe in the skill of a doctor or dentist who is

   _____ .

3. A jury is said to "speak the truth" when it gives a

   _____ .

4. Something _____ consists of two parts.

5. A machine that measures how far you have walked is a(n)

   _____ .

6. The study of social behavior is called _____ .

7. Named after Luigi Galvani, a pioneer in electricity, a

   _____ measures electrical current.

8. Sensing or feeling from far away is _____ , since
   tele means "far."

9. If you are not content, you are _____ .

10. Listening is sometimes called _____ .

Index of Words and Word Elements

Word elements are printed in italics

Index of Key Terms